Barrio Democracy in Latin America

Barrio Democracy in Latin America

PARTICIPATORY DECENTRALIZATION AND COMMUNITY ACTIVISM IN MONTEVIDEO

Eduardo Canel

THE PENNSYLVANIA STATE UNIVERSITY PRESS
UNIVERSITY PARK, PENNSYLVANIA

Library of Congress Cataloging-in-Publication Data

Canel, Eduardo, 1953–
Barrio democracy in Latin America : participatory
decentralization and community activism in Montevideo /
Eduardo Canel.
p.   cm.
Includes bibliographical references and index.
Summary: "Reconstructs the experience of participatory
urban governance in three impoverished communities in
Montevideo, Uruguay. Offers an account of various
experiences and explains successes and failures in
reference to the distinct traditions and resources found in
each community"—Provided by publisher.
ISBN 978-0-271-03732-5 (cloth : alk. paper)
ISBN 978-0-271-03733-2 (pbk. : alk. paper)
1. Political participation—Uruguay—Montevideo.
2. Decentralization in government—Uruguay—Montevideo.
3. Montevideo (Uruguay)—Politics and government.
I. Title.

JS2720.M6C36 2010
323'.0420989513—dc22
2010018242

It is the policy of The Pennsylvania State University Press to use
acid-free paper. Publications on uncoated stock satisfy the minimum
requirements of American National Standard for Information
Sciences—Permanence of Paper for Printed
Library Material, ANSI Z39.48–1992.

FOR *Ana*

CONTENTS

MAPS

TABLES

PREFACE

This book is the result of studying urban social movements for nearly two decades. In the mid-1980s, following Uruguay's return to democratic rule, I visited the country to study the multiple social movements that had emerged toward the end of the military regime. It was a personally gratifying moment because it marked my return to the country I was forced to flee at a young age in 1973, a place I could not return to for a long twelve years. A contagiously cheerful mood could be felt across the barrios of Montevideo, as poor and rich citizens alike celebrated the beginning of a new era, leaving behind the darkest chapter in the country's history, during which torture, fear, and intimidation had extinguished the relative social peace and open political life of the past.

My research project then was very timely given the growing academic and political interest in social movements. It was widely believed at the time that the movements' presumed democratic practices and values would contribute to the renewal of political institutions and to the democratization of social relations in fundamental ways. Unfortunately, the sense of optimism that people felt after the first national elections since the military coup was short-lived. The vibrant movements that had proliferated in the fight against the dictatorship during the much-celebrated "insurrection of civil society" had vanished or were barely managing to survive when I returned in 1987 to start my doctoral fieldwork on urban social movements in the barrios of Montevideo.[1] Confronted with weakening social activism and growing disillusionment with democratic institutions, I felt compelled to redirect my research project toward explaining why urban social movements had dwindled in post-dictatorial Uruguay.

I returned to Montevideo in the late 1990s to examine the state of community activism within the new political and institutional context created by the election of the Frente Amplio coalition to the city government. Soon

---

1. For a description, see Canel 1992.

after the 1990 inauguration of this first leftist municipal government in the city's history, the charismatic mayor Tabaré Vázquez announced a far-reaching program to decentralize the municipal system and invited city residents to join his administration in a common project to democratize city politics. The initial response was overwhelming, as thousands of enthusiastic community activists joined forces to build a new model of urban governance that promised to empower communities and to redistribute resources in favor of the urban poor.

Although the initial enthusiasm had subsided by 1998, as I conducted my research I found that decentralization had changed city politics in fundamental ways, creating new opportunities for communities to practice a new kind of democratic citizenship and to have a say in the design of urban development programs. I found barrios that were thriving under the new decentralized municipal system. In one community I was welcomed by many of the local activists I had met back in 1987, who were now local government leaders. They proudly gave me a tour of the neighborhood to show off their accomplishments since my last visit eleven years earlier. I was thrilled to confirm that many of the projects that were on the drawing board when I had first visited the community had since been realized: the neighborhood had a brand-new high school and a community-run health center, the project to connect the area to the city's sewer system was well underway, a new park had been built, and construction of an impressive social and cultural center was almost complete. What was most striking to me was the strong sense of ownership that activists felt regarding these accomplishments; they were convinced that these projects had come to fruition thanks to their own efforts, particularly their ability to navigate the changing waters of municipal politics since the introduction of decentralization in the early 1990s.

In contrast, in other neighborhoods I found many community activists who were struggling to adapt to the requirements of the new institutions created by decentralization. Many of them were disappointed with the experience, blaming city officials for failing to deliver "real" local democracy. Ongoing bickering and conflict had become permanent fixtures of their meetings, and they loudly expressed their unequivocal anger toward municipal authorities or toward one another. When I asked them what they had gained under the new system, they had very few things to include on their list of accomplishments. They seemed at a loss when it came to adapting to the exigencies of a new participatory local system that called on them to switch from taking a more familiar, contentious stance, toward comanaging the city in partnership with municipal officials.[2]

In 2004, I returned with a simple research question: why were some communities better able than others to seize the opportunities offered by participatory decentralization? Most prior analysis of the experience in Montevideo had focused primarily on the general strengths and flaws of the model of institutional reform adopted by the city government, but had paid scant attention to local variation across districts. For ten months I studied decentralization from the vantage point of three communities to understand how centrally planned institutional reforms were experienced at the local level and to learn more about how local idiosyncrasies and conditions may have shaped the operation of local institutions. I chose to examine the workings of local government in three districts that had adapted to the new political reality with different levels of success. I focused on the new bodies created by city officials to facilitate resident participation—the neighborhood councils—where community activists met one another and engaged with municipal authorities. I found that explaining variation in local experiences with participatory democracy required a more historical and ethnographic approach than those employed by other authors, a point to which I will return in the introduction.

The organization of the book is straightforward. In the introduction I outline the main argument and identify the primary features of the model of participatory decentralization introduced in Montevideo, all of which is set against the backdrop of changes in the city's urban fabric over the past twenty years. I also link the emergence and subsequent evolution of decentralization to changes in the region's political landscape and recent shifts in development discourse. In the following three chapters I provide an account of the histories and idiosyncrasies of each of the communities studied and discuss the unique ways in which they experienced participatory decentralization. In the final chapter I summarize the empirical findings and outline the theoretical conclusions of this study.

2. Canel 2001b.

ACKNOWLEDGMENTS

In writing this book I benefited from the insights and support of many individuals to whom I feel deeply indebted. I start by thanking the community activists who shared with me their impressions about their participatory experiences. They kindly invited me into their homes and to their meetings, allowing me to get a glimpse into their lives and a better sense of the challenges and opportunities they faced in their efforts to build local democratic practices. I hope that the accounts presented in these pages accurately reflect their experiences and contribute, however modestly, to a better understanding of the rich and often challenging journey that they embarked on when engaged with participatory decentralization in their communities. I also wish to acknowledge the generous support given to me by the staff of the three districts covered in this study, especially Cristina Oholeguy, Cecile Regent, and Emma Menoni, and by Susana Regent, a longtime activist and a former coordinator/secretary in district 13. They were always eager to share their intricate knowledge of the communities, steering me through the complex maze of local politics and helping me get a sense of both the history of decentralization at the grassroot level and the idiosyncrasies and traditions of each barrio. At city hall, I express my gratitude to Willan Masdeu from the Participation and Coordination Unit of the Department of Decentralization for facilitating access to very useful documentation not easily found in the districts.

Many colleagues, directly or indirectly, helped shape my thinking on participatory decentralization. In Montevideo, I acknowledge the help of Alicia Veneziano, whose analysis of participatory decentralization constituted a reference point to formulate my own ideas. My sincere gratitude is also extended to Danilo Veiga for his friendship and ongoing support. Danilo's work on demographic trends in Montevideo helped me contextualize many of the local processes analyzed in the book. I also thank Alvaro Portillo, Arles Caruso, and Eduardo de León, three prominent analysts and participants in the process of decentralization who helped me understand many of the broader challenges facing the participatory project in the city. My appreciation also goes to Guillermo Font for publishing the award-winning electronic bulletin VECINET, which provides the opportunity to access at a distance valuable information and analysis about participatory decentralization in the barrios of Montevideo.

At York University, a special thanks goes to my colleagues at the Centre for Research on Latin America and the Caribbean (CERLAC), the International Development Studies program, and the Department of Social Science for enriching the academic community that nurtures my intellectual work on a day-to-day basis. In particular, my deeply felt appreciation goes to my dear friend and colleague Judith Hellman, who supported me in countless ways through the various stages of preparing the manuscript. I cannot overstate how much her early enthusiasm for my preliminary research findings encouraged me to write this book. Subsequently, her careful reading of each draft and her insightful feedback vastly improved the original manuscript, both in content and form.

At Penn State University Press, I extend my gratitude to senior editor Sandy Thatcher for his enthusiastic support and encouragement, for believing that the lesser-known story of participatory decentralization in Montevideo should be told, and for publishing a book on a country that most English-language publishers hesitate to cover for fear of not attracting a large enough audience. I also want to thank Nicholas Taylor for his impeccable copyediting work and for his patience while working with me during the book editing stage. Nicholas's careful reading of the manuscript allowed him to identify several ideas that needed to be clarified and to make countless editing suggestions that vastly improved the original text.

I acknowledge the support of the Faculty of Arts of York University for providing some of the funding that made this project possible. I also acknowledge the assistance of the following people whose help was crucial to allowing me to complete the manuscript: the two anonymous reviewers provided very useful feedback on how to improve the original text; Marshall Beck, who skillfully translated all Spanish-language quotes found in this book; Lorena Alesina, who carefully transcribed countless of hours of interview tapes; Leandro Vergara and Paula Hevia-Pacheco, who helped with the transcription of earlier interviews I had conducted with community activists in one of the neighborhoods; and Alicia Abayian from Uruguay's National Institute of Statistics, who promptly and professionally prepared the maps included in the book.

I conclude by thanking my family—my mother, Milka; my late father,

Eduardo; and my sisters, Teresita and Cristina—for their love and support. I thank my children, Diego and Maia, for enriching my experience in countless ways and for constantly reminding me that life is a precious gift worth living. My gratitude also extends to Gonzalo for his good nature and understanding. Last but not least, my heartfelt gratitude goes to my wife, Ana Franco, for her ongoing support, unlimited patience, and endless love. Our story as a couple intertwines in a surprising way with my research for this book. It was thanks to a fieldtrip to Montevideo in the 1990s that our paths crossed once again, as I had the good fortune of reconnecting with her thirty years after our brief but wonderful adolescent romance in the late 1960s. For the past ten years we have shared our lives in Canada, enjoying the privilege of being together every day of the year. It is to Ana that I dedicate this book as a token of appreciation for everything that she gives me and for what she sacrificed to come to Toronto.

Introduction

In 2004 I attended a ceremony at Montevideo city hall to celebrate the inauguration of the fourth cycle of neighborhood councils since participatory decentralization was established in the city in the early 1990s. The grand Salón Azul—which is normally used to host receptions for foreign notables and prestigious guests—was packed with an unusual crowd, as more than six hundred newly elected councilors had descended on city hall with relatives and friends to celebrate their involvement in this exciting chapter in the administration of their city. Although visibly swollen with pride to be the mayor's personal guests, these grassroot leaders looked out of place in such elegant surroundings. Waiters in black pants, white jackets, and bow ties moved through the crowd serving cocktails and canapés under crystal chandeliers suspended from twenty-foot ceilings. Councilors joked with one another about their new official roles—as if trying to downplay the status attached to these new positions—and chatted informally about politics and local issues, as family members snapped pictures to capture this remarkable moment. The excitement and the sense of accomplishment were quite understandable. For most councilors this was their very first visit to city hall in an official capacity; nearly 70 percent were newcomers to the position, this being the largest councilor renewal since the first elections were held in 1993.

Key officials from city hall, including the mayor, the directors of the city administration, and members of the municipal assembly, joined the celebrations. Underscoring the importance of the event, members of the press interviewed the guests, hoping to catch a sound bite for the late evening news, while the lights of television cameras followed the mayor as he moved through the crowd. Formal greetings came first from Ana Olivera, the director of decentralization at city hall and a former *compañera* I knew from our days of radical student activism in the early seventies. A seasoned leader of the Communist Party today, she offered a warm welcome to the new councilors and, with an aura of cheerful self-confidence, she briefly outlined the main accomplishments of decentralization and the challenges and opportunities that lay ahead. Her enthusiastic speech contrasted with the more subdued address by Mayor Mariano Arana, a restrained urban planner and former professor at the school of architecture. Nevertheless, his presentation was followed by a long and loud standing ovation, an indication of the popularity of a mayor who still commanded an impressive approval rating of more than 60 percent after nearly ten years in office. Once the formal speeches were over, city officials mingled with councilors and their guests in an atmosphere of informality and openness that revealed how much city politics had changed since the Left came to power in 1990, determined to build a new relationship between municipal officials and city residents.

The new system of participatory decentralization introduced by the leftist Broad Front administration created a more favorable institutional framework for citizen participation, expanding opportunities for residents to have a say in the operation of their city and making the government more accountable.[1] A sympathetic city government responded positively to community initiatives and needs, and demonstrated an unequivocal political will to effectively redistribute resources in favor of the poor. While the reforms opened new possibilities to democratize relations between residents and the municipal state, not all communities benefited equally from these changes. Surprisingly, I found that among the communities covered in this book, the ones with the most militant traditions had the hardest time adjusting to participatory democracy, while the least radical responded most positively and benefited the most. Indeed, participatory decentralization was experienced quite differently across the city, as the new model of urban governance was not transferred mechanically and in the same manner to each barrio.[2]

1. The Frente Amplio (Broad Front) coalition was set up in 1971 by a rainbow of leftist and left-of-center parties (Socialists, Communists, and Christian Democrats), splinter groups from the country's traditional parties, and smaller groups from the far Left. Although it is a coalition—granting each member organization political and organizational autonomy—the Broad Front operates like a single political party, maintaining its own structures and congresses and presenting a single presidential candidate. Since it was set up, the coalition has expanded its support base and added a number of political organizations, as we will see below.

2. Participatory experiences produced widely different outcomes across Latin America, where for the past two decades Left-leaning mayors introduced participatory models of urban governance into hundreds of cities. In some cases, participatory schemes truly revolutionized urban politics, effectively empowering the urban poor and redistributing resources, but in other cases these initiatives encountered formidable obstacles and failed to bring about the desired change. In attempting to explain such diverse outcomes and to identify the conditions that may enable participatory democratic practices to flourish, researchers highlight various factors,

My approach differs from most studies of participatory decentralization in Montevideo, which explain the outcome of participatory processes in reference to the strengths and weaknesses of the institutional model that brought them about. The features of the model are indeed relevant. By setting the "rules of the game," institutional frameworks define the authority and responsibilities to be delegated as well as the incentives for citizen participation.[3] Yet institutional approaches cannot fully explain situations, such as the one covered in this book, where the same set of rules is applied uniformly across a single city but produces drastically different local outcomes. Explaining local variation within the same city, I argue, requires holding the features of the institutional model as a constant and focusing instead on the *lived* experience of participation in each barrio. Exploring participation from this standpoint reveals how much the distinct traditions of each community became embedded in the day-to-day workings of local institutions, thereby shaping the widely different outcomes I found across the city. Thus I argue that the outcomes of citywide participatory reforms were largely context-specific.[4] Whether participatory decentralization produced cooperation or conflict, synergy or misunderstanding, success or failure at the district level was as much related to the features of the institutional model of participation adopted by the city government as it was to the interplay of a variety of local contingencies.

I argue that the ability of neighborhood activists to seize (or to miss) the opportunities offered by participatory decentralization depended on three distinct sets of local factors. The first factor was the adaptability of a barrio's associational culture to the framework of participatory decentralization. Associational cultures—understood as "patterns of interactions between organizations and the state"—emerge historically under particular sociopolitical environments and create the political-cultural context in

---

such as the incentives for participation embedded in the model of institutional design, the strength of local civil society, the nature of the political forces that introduce participatory reforms, and the influence of parties opposed to participation.

3. The impact of "rule structures" on citizen participation is persuasively highlighted by Wampler's (2007) painstaking comparative study of eight Brazilian municipalities.

4. Many researchers have shown that models of decentralization produce different outcomes when applied to diverse contexts, but their case studies seldom consider differences within a single country or within the same city, as I do in this book. Three exceptions are Wampler's (2007) study mentioned above, Baiocchi's (2003) edited collection on participatory budgeting in several Brazilian cities, and Goldfrank's (2007) comparative assessment of participatory experiences in Montevideo, Porto Alegre, and Caracas.

which social movements and civil society organizations operate.[5] I argue that when these national associational cultures intersect with the specific traditions of each barrio, they generate distinct *local* associational cultures that frame the attitudes and outlook of activists in each community. These local associational cultures consist of the overall traditions of collective mobilization, attitudes toward political authority and the state, leadership capacities, organizational resources, and levels and kinds of social capital produced historically by each barrio. I found that the capacities produced by these local cultures varied widely across the city, and that some of them were more adaptable than others to the requirements of participatory decentralization.

The second local factor shaping the experience of participation was the impact of the socioeconomic conditions found in each district on the ability and disposition of community activists to work together within the bodies of local government. Poverty certainly constrained people's general disposition to participate, a complaint often made by activists as they explained their neighbors' reluctance to join participatory initiatives in their communities. In some districts, however, deep cleavages and widespread poverty actually divided residents and undermined community cooperation and solidarity. The third local contingency was the ability of individual local officials to nurture trusting and cooperative relations with community activists. The accounts narrated in subsequent chapters will illustrate how much the capacities and personalities of particular officials influenced how participation was experienced in each district. In some cases, local officials brought capacities that blended with local associational cultures and established constructive working relations with local activists. In other cases, however, they clashed with grassroot leaders, producing conflict and animosity.

Establishing Participatory Decentralization in Montevideo

Montevideo has a population of 1.3 million people, and although it is not large by Latin American standards, this capital city is home to more than 40 percent of the country's population and is the definite center of economic, political, and cultural power. Before 1990, the city government was

---

5. For a discussion of the concept of associational cultures, see Pearce 1997. See also Hilhorst's (2003) discussion of the distinct "associational patterns" found in the Cordillera region of the Philippines.

controlled by the country's traditional political parties and relied on a centralized, bureaucratic, paternalistic, and clientelistic system of government.
City politics rested on a large bureaucracy that administered municipal
services inefficiently and was inaccessible for most city residents. A clientelistic network linked the city administration to residents through traditional neighborhood associations headed by strong political bosses who
used their connections with traditional parties to grant favors in exchange
for political support. This system discouraged citizen participation and
autonomous community organizing because it favored personal connections, creating dependency relations between communities and individual
political bosses associated with the party in power. Not surprisingly, Montevideo did not have a strong tradition of territorially based urban movements.

Following democratization, the incoming Colorado municipal administration worked hard to reestablish this clientelistic system.[6] Soon after
assuming power in 1985, the city government created the Special Projects
Advisory Unit (Unidad Asesora de Proyectos Especiales, UAPE) to support
social assistance and local development programs. Claiming that most
city residents were not represented by existing organizations in civil society—organizations that they argued were ideologically further to the Left
than the average Montevideano—UAPE declared many legitimate grassroot organizations ineligible to receive municipal funds and began to establish direct links with city residents.[7] The city's Emergency Food Relief
Program, for example, bypassed existing food community networks—
comprising forty-three soup kitchens that fed more than ten thousand
people, and sixty community-based organizations that purchased and distributed food in the barrios—instead distributing food tickets directly to
poor residents through newly set up "ghost" neighborhood associations
linked to the ruling Colorado party.[8]

The city government strategy helped marginalize many legitimate grassroot organizations, but it failed to restore either the Colorados' political

6. The Colorado and the Blanco parties are the two traditional parties that ruled Uruguay
for most of the nineteenth and twentieth centuries. As the dominant political party, the Colorados are credited with modernizing Uruguayan political life and establishing the country's
welfare system and democratic traditions. A discussion of the party system is provided later
in this chapter.

7. The position of the city government was outlined in two documents produced by UAPE
in 1985 (see IMM 1985a, 1985b). Horacio Martorelli, a well-known sociologist who headed the
local development unit of the city government, also articulated them in a May 1988 personal
interview. See also Martorelli 1986.

8. Canel 1992, 1993.

strength or the clientelistic networks in Montevideo. While the party regained its national political dominance—capturing the presidency in the two national elections (1984, 1989) following the end of the military regime—it steadily lost political support in Montevideo. By the end of the Colorado municipal administration (1985–89) only 10 percent of Montevideanos believed that the city government had done a good job, and only 9 percent thought that it had outperformed the military administration.[9]

Breaking with political tradition in the 1989 municipal race, Montevideanos elected the Broad Front leftist coalition, and for the first time in the country's history the Left seized what effectively was the second most powerful government in Uruguay.[10] The newly elected Socialist mayor Tabaré Vázquez, a charismatic oncologist and newcomer to party politics, promised to establish a new mode of urban governance to improve the quality of both government and service delivery. Drawing from the Broad Front's long-standing commitment to social equity and its uncompromising opposition to neoliberalism, he pledged to redistribute urban resources in favor of the less privileged in order to address the negative impact of free-market policies that had been implemented by the military and by successive Colorado governments since the return to democratic rule five years earlier. To this end, as promised during the electoral campaign, the Broad Front administration introduced a program of sweeping institutional reforms to promote political and administrative decentralization and to encourage citizen participation in the running of the city.[11] The mayor's vision included the creation of neighborhood councils invested with wide-ranging decision-making powers.[12] Vázquez's plan met with fierce opposition from traditional city politicians from the Colorado and Blanco parties who feared that it would reduce their local political power and eliminate what remained of their clientelistic networks.

Required to secure legislative approval for the reforms, Vázquez appointed a multiparty commission to deliberate over a new model of participatory

9. Rubino 1991; and Bergamino et al. 2001.

10. The Broad Front received 35 percent of the vote. Although this ensured control of the city government, it failed to secure a majority in the Municipal Assembly, the city's legislative body, a factor that would seriously limit the party's capacity to implement participatory decentralization, as we will see below.

11. The coalition ran on a detailed, thirty-page platform that prioritized social equality, citizen participation, and decentralization. See Frente Amplio 1989.

12. For a description of the internal debates within the Broad Front about what kind of decentralization should be adopted, see Veneziano 2005; and Chávez 2004. Both Veneziano and Chávez report that within the parties that made up the Broad Front coalition, support for Vázquez's participatory model ranged from enthusiastic to lukewarm.

decentralization. After intense negotiations, the commission reached a compromise and the city's legislative assembly approved the new model of decentralization in 1993. To the disappointment of many activists in the barrios, key features of the original plan—such as the transfer of decision-making powers to neighborhood councils—were drastically altered, as the new model only conferred consultative and monitoring authority on the local bodies. The new arrangements also added a new, unelected organ of political representation—the local junta—as the highest political authority in each district. The main features of this model are outlined below.

Most analysts of participatory decentralization in Montevideo link the subsequent decline in resident participation to design flaws of the model that seriously curtailed the more novel participatory features of the original project.[13] These researchers argue that the outcome of the political compromise illustrates the strength of the country's political parties and the relative weakness of the city's urban social movements. Benjamin Goldfrank, for instance, compared the initial phases of the participatory experiences in the cities of Porto Alegre and Montevideo; while in both cities the initial impetus for the reforms came from leftist administrations with similar goals, they each produced different results. In the southern Brazilian city, vibrant urban social movements pushed city officials to deepen the participatory aspects of the model. In contrast, in Montevideo, a city with weaker urban movements, the political establishment successfully constrained the most radical participatory features of decentralization.[14] I will examine the impact of these changes to the original model in subsequent chapters when I discuss the experience of each community. For now, I only suggest that in spite of these important limitations, the political compromise brokered in the corridors of power permitted the implementation of a project of participatory decentralization that opened new opportunities for citizen involvement in municipal affairs.

The new model called for a number of institutional and administrative reforms, beginning with the creation of the Department of Decentralization at the level of the central administration.[15] This new unit was charged

13. For a review of the process leading to the adoption of the new compromise model, see Winn and Ferro-Clerico 1997; Goldfrank 2002; Veneziano 2005; Chávez 2004; and Moreira 1993.

14. Goldfrank 2003. Given the relative weakness of civil society and the low levels of territorially based organization in the city, Montevideo may be better compared with the experiences of the Brazilian cities of Alvorada and Gravatai. See Silva 2003.

15. Until 2010, when a new municipal level of government was introduced, Uruguay had an unusual political system, comprising only two levels of government: a national government

with promoting and coordinating municipal restructuring through the Divisions of Local Administration and Deconcentrated Services and for implementing social policies through the Divisions of Social Promotion and Health. The reforms divided Montevideo into eighteen new districts. Map 1 shows their borders and highlights the three districts covered in this study.[16]

The reforms clustered the city's sixty-two neighborhoods into these larger political-administrative units. Each district was internally diverse, as it was made up of several neighborhoods with different histories, needs, and socioeconomic backgrounds. Recognizing this diversity, each of the eighteen zones was further divided into subzones corresponding to the boundaries of established neighborhoods, and representation by subzone within each district was promoted as an important element of the new structures.

The success of the reform project rested, in part, on the ability of the new city government to build the capacity of communities to participate, to promote harmonious relations within each zone, and to foster a new territorial identity based on the new boundaries. The decentralization project aimed to improve service delivery by deconcentrating municipal services and to enhance the quality of municipal governance by facilitating citizen participation. To this end, it called for the creation of three new local bodies within each of the eighteen districts—the district communal centers (*centros comunales zonales*), the local juntas (*juntas locales*), and the neighborhood councils (*consejos vecinales*). These three local pillars of the new institutionality became the vehicles to facilitate, respectively, administrative, political, and social decentralization.[17]

The local juntas are organs of political representation and constitute a form of local municipal government with limited authority. These organs were added to the decentralized model during the political negotiations that led to the approval of the decentralization plan, giving the political establishment automatic representation and control over decision making in local government. The new institutional arrangements grant local juntas the status of supreme authority at the local level. Local juntas make final

---

and nineteen provincial or departmental governments led by mayors or *intendentes*. The Department of Montevideo is made up of Montevideo city and some semirural areas. For the sake of simplicity, however, I will refer to the departmental government as the city government. The 2010 reform created eight municipal governments in Montevideo, with five elected members each, that replaced the unelected local juntas, described below.

16. The average population size in the districts is 75,000 people, ranging from a high of 134,000 to a low of 34,000.

17. Winn and Ferro-Clerico 1997.

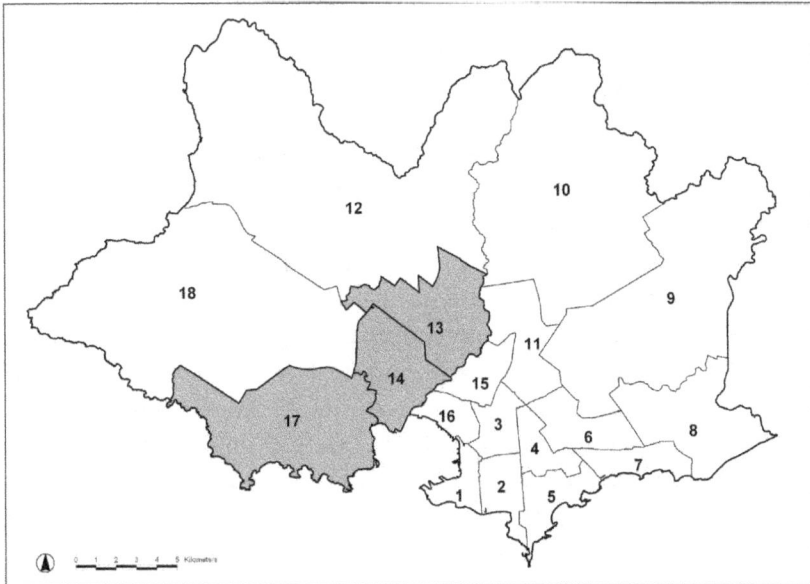

MAP 1. Decentralized political-administrative districts in Montevideo (2004). Courtesy of Alicia Abayian, National Institute of Statistics, Uruguay.

decisions about local issues, determine priorities over resource allocation, and supervise the overall administration of the communal centers. They have limited powers, however, as they may only make decisions within the parameters established by the central municipal government. These nonelected bodies have five honorary members appointed by the mayor from a list submitted by each political party that runs in the municipal elections.[18] Members of the local juntas serve for a period of five years, which overlaps with the mayor's term in office. The formula employed to allocate the five council seats in each local junta gives the winning party three seats, and the other two seats are allocated among the other parties based on the number of votes they receive.[19] Local juntas meet twice per month in closed sessions.

Each local junta's one full-time secretary has become the de facto central political figure in the local decentralized structures and the most visible individual at the district level. The local secretary is a political appointee

18. Parties are not bound to hold elections to prepare these lists. In fact, the Broad Front coalition is the only political force that runs primary elections in each area to select its candidates.

19. This criterion follows the same proportional representation system that guides the allocation of seats in the city government's legislative body.

who acts as the mayor's representative at the district level and is charged with overseeing the overall operation of local government in each district. Although formally a full-time functionary of the local junta, technically the highest authority, the influence of the secretary often overshadows the authority of the part-time, honorary members. A paid official with direct access to the mayor, the local secretary acts as the central node of the whole system of local government, liaising with the three bodies of local government and linking them with one another and with the central city administration. Alicia Veneziano has argued that the extensive powers of the local secretary constitute one of the primary weaknesses of the decentralization model, an argument I will return to when I review the operation of local government in each of the three districts covered in this book.[20]

The district communal centers act as local branches of the municipal administration and were designed to promote administrative decentralization and service deconcentration. Each communal center is managed by a locally based director drawn from the city bureaucracy, who is supported by a team of administrators, local crews, two social workers, and an urban planner. Each center offers a range of services, and has units dealing with social development, administration, and public works. These services include a variety of women's and youth programs, day care centers, senior centers, and community development works. Communal centers are also responsible for the maintenance of public lighting and green areas (i.e., parks and plazas) and for sweeping local streets. Residents can also make administrative demands through the communal center, including requests for emergency services in green areas, repairs of public lighting or removal of garbage, and a variety of social services, such as requests for sex education workshops or milk donations to schools or social institutions. They may also use the communal center to report industrial pollution or a lack of running water.

The neighborhood councils are designed to act as consultative organs of social representation for the participation of civil society in municipal affairs. The number of council members varies from zone to zone, ranging from twenty to forty people. In contrast to the members of the local juntas who are appointed by the mayor, local councilors are elected locally every thirty months by direct popular vote in elections organized by the district communal center and community organizations. Candidates can run for councilor as representatives of a local organization or they can

20. Veneziano 2005.

nominate themselves by securing ten signatures from other neighbors who endorse their nomination. To be eligible to vote or to run for councilor an individual must live or work in the area and be at least eighteen years old. Each council has a steering committee that meets weekly in addition to monthly plenary sessions that bring together all councilors. Plenary sessions are usually open to other residents who wish to attend. Decisions are made by simple majority vote among elected councilors. In addition, each council has a number of commissions focusing on specific themes relevant to the district—such as roads and public works, the environment, recreation and culture, and so forth—that are open to any interested resident.

Neighborhood councils are the bodies where representatives from the various neighborhoods are expected to negotiate the plurality of interests found within the district, to articulate demands, and to put together local development projects to be presented to local officials. As I will show, not all councils are successful in this regard, and some suffer ongoing conflicts and misunderstandings. The councils are the institutional spaces where community activists—equipped with their own histories, traditions, and expectations—construct collective practices that express their political outlook and their own understandings (or misunderstandings) of the principles of participatory democracy. Subsequent chapters will illustrate the different practices that emerge within these councils—as local traditions shape relations among activists and local government officials—and how much the boundaries separating state and civil society tend to dissolve in day-to-day operation. On the one hand, neighborhood councils are constituted as the organs for the autonomous participation of civil society and are even encouraged to define their own operational traditions and to establish relations and partnerships with nonmunicipal agencies. On the other hand, they constitute an integral component of the new institutional makeup of participatory decentralization that structures and regulates their activities in multiple ways. Oftentimes councilors feel frustrated as they try to perform their roles under these conditions. Many end up wondering whether they act as true representatives of civil society vis-à-vis the municipal state or whether they have become spokespersons of local institutions within their communities, a tension that is exacerbated when the city government fails to meet community needs and expectations.

The municipal reforms also initiated a series of participatory processes to open more fluid channels of communication between the city government and communities, with the hope that this would make public management more efficient and also ensure a more equitable redistribution of resources.

One of these participatory processes was the institutionalization of consultation in the allocation of resources through the municipal budget. Participatory budgeting—as this process is called, borrowing from the successful experience in the city of Porto Alegre—involves a three-stage process of dialogue and consultation among the city government, local authorities, and community organizations. This consultation produces a management plan (*compromiso de gestión*) that commits the municipal government to a specific allocation of resources in each of the city's eighteen zones, the implementation of which is supposed to be monitored by local organizations.[21]

In addition, the city government has involved residents in a number of participatory experiences, including two city forums called Montevideo en Foro, where hundreds of community activists met to discuss the shape of decentralization and to propose ways of deepening local democracy. Another participatory experience engaged residents and other stakeholders to draft strategic development plans for each district. Called PLAEDEZ (Plan Estratégico de Desarrollo Zonal, or Strategic Plans for District-Level Development), the process involved several months of discussion within districts to identify community needs and aspirations and to agree on a common five-year local development plan. The success of this process to attract resident participation varied widely across districts, and in most cases people tended to delegate the task to the secretary of the local junta and the technical personnel working at the district level.

In spite of the many shortcomings of the project of participatory decentralization, which I will discuss in this book, it marked a significant departure from the paternalistic, top-down styles used under the old system

21. Participatory budgeting in Montevideo gave residents limited say until it was modified in 2005 to allow residents to vote through secret ballot on specific projects concurrently with elections for neighborhood council. The process worked as follows: The initial allocation for each district was defined centrally, and unelected local juntas made the final recommendations to the city administration, which in turn made the final decision. In the first stage, neighborhood councils were convened to evaluate the implementation of the management plan from the previous fiscal year and to establish budget priorities for the following year. The council's recommendations were forwarded to the local junta, which had the authority to modify or reject the council's proposals before final approval. In the second stage, the mayor and the heads of various units of the municipal government visited each district to consult in open neighborhood assemblies where local representatives presented their report. Their presentations were followed by a brief speech by the mayor, and then the floor was opened for comments and questions from residents. The last stage started when city officials studied the proposals to try to fit them within the government's priorities and available resources. Although the final say rested with city officials, further discussions usually occurred with local government representatives to fine-tune requests or to explain why certain measures had not been approved. The process concluded with the drafting of a management plan for each zone and for the city as a whole. The final budget was then presented to the city's legislative body for approval.

of city politics. The new participatory spaces have offered Montevideanos opportunities to help define public policies, to shape the city budget, and to determine priorities in the allocation of municipal resources. With this program, the Broad Front administration invited residents to engage in the management of the city, participate in elections for neighborhood councils (as candidates or voters), present demands directly to local government via the district's council, comanage projects with municipal authorities, and attend open forums at the district level. As a result, decentralization helped narrow the distance between residents and city government officials and facilitated access to municipal authorities.[22] Nevertheless, as I point out above, not all communities were able to seize the opportunities offered by decentralization, and many in fact had significant trouble dealing with the growing challenges raised by the rapidly changing city that I describe in the next section.

Changes in the Urban Fabric: Social Fragmentation and Spatial Polarization

Every time I arrive in Montevideo I am struck by the beauty of this city, one of the southernmost capitals in the world. To get to town from the airport I always take the scenic route alongside the traditional *rambla*, lined with tall palm trees next to the white sandy beaches stretching for more than ten kilometers through the entire southeastern part of the city. Along the muddy-brown waters of the River Plate estuary that Uruguayans call "the sea," luxuriant green foliage grows in the humid climate and flowers blossom even in the winter. The rambla is always thronged with Montevideanos from all sectors of society, people who come to the coast to enjoy themselves at any time of year. As I travel along the shore on my way toward

22. Veneziano (2005) points out that the experience of running the city created a new "governing culture" in a political coalition that only knew the role of political opposition. She cites as an example the fact that the Broad Front resolved without much tension the typical dilemma that leftist governments face when they come to power: governing in the interests of the social class that supported them or becoming a government of all the residents, albeit with a clear orientation to redistribute resources and empower marginalized citizens. The Left in Montevideo resolved this dilemma in favor of the second option, especially under the administration of Mayor Arana, producing a more pragmatic culture among Frente Amplio leaders that acknowledged the political imperative of building consensus through negotiations with other political parties and social actors. Veneziano's analysis of electoral trends in the city also shows that participation may be shifting from a logic centered on political identity to one in which social and territorial interests take precedence.

Pocitos, the neighborhood where I will settle during my research stay, I see people calmly resting on benches, sipping the traditional herbal mate, joggers trotting alongside the rambla, and the occasional professional dog walker skillfully managing some twenty purebred dogs belonging to the well-to-do families that live in this part of the city. I first pass through the upper-class neighborhood of Carrasco, home to some strikingly beautiful century-old houses—the lone survivors of earlier days when the area was a beach resort for the city's aristocracy—and some of the most stunning new residences in Montevideo. When I enter the middle-class neighborhoods of Punta Gorda and Malvín, the houses become smaller but the scenery remains gorgeous. At a distance, I can finally recognize the skyline dotted with high-rise condominiums overlooking the River Plate that announces I am close to Pocitos. So many condos have sprung up in Pocitos that they form a thick wall separating the rest of the city from its coastline and mak-ing this upper-middle-class neighborhood—with nearly ten times the aver-age population density of the city—feel packed and overcrowded.[23]

The city's architecture in the neighborhoods along the southeastern coast, the marvelous art deco buildings in the traditional downtown area, the many monuments in public spaces, and the wide boulevards spread across the city speak volumes about the former period of splendor in the mid-twentieth century, when Uruguay was renowned for its high standard of living, advanced social policies, and democratic traditions. These accom-plishments made Uruguayans feel proud to be different in a region marked by profound social inequalities and political instability, a feeling that was reinforced by their overwhelming European parentage that set them apart from other Latin American countries. Nor was this pride based entirely on a problematic racial/ethnic snobbery. The smallest country in the region had produced the highest levels of social development, a rich tradition of artistic and intellectual creation, and some remarkable international soccer victories that made it a mecca for soccer aficionados. Understandably, there was no shortage of adjectives to name this "urban" or "middle-class" society that saw itself as meritocratic and highly integrated, or "hyper-integrated," to borrow a term coined by Germán Rama. Outside its borders, the country became known as the "Switzerland of America," reinforcing Uruguayans' feelings that this country constituted an island of modernity and equality that had more in common with Europe than with Latin America.

---

23. Pocitos has 22,000 residents per square kilometer, while the average population density in the city is 2,500.

Montevideo is indeed a beautiful city, and not surprisingly it is ranked as the best place to live in South America, ahead of better-known urban centers like Buenos Aires, Santiago, or Rio de Janeiro.[24] Apart from the coastline, Montevideanos enjoy much cleaner air than residents of any other capital city in Latin America and have proportionally more urban green space and trees than residents of any other city in the region.[25] As I approach the neighborhood of Pocitos, however, I am confronted with numerous signs that tell me that much has changed, even since my last trip in 1998, and that in many respects this is no longer the Montevideo where I grew up. At each major intersection I come across groups of children darting among stopped cars, hoping to receive a few coins from drivers in exchange for cleaning windshields, selling an assortment of cheap goods, or entertaining by juggling balls. I also see garbage pickers slowly moving through the city pulling homemade carts—a few lucky ones with the assistance of visibly underfed horses—as they sift through the leftovers of middle-class families to uncover something to eat or to trade for cash. These are the faces of another Montevideo that has emerged. Montevideanos increasingly recognize that they live in a more fragmented society where people are more aggressive, and with reports of rising crime they feel increasingly insecure. The noticeably heightened security—iron bars on every window, multiple reinforced locks on every door, private security guards, and enclosed balconies even on the top floors of apartment buildings—tells me that on this side of town, residents feel themselves to be under threat.

Indeed, over the past few decades the city's social fabric has steadily been torn apart, forcing upper- and middle-class city residents to come face-to-face with the social ills typical of urban social exclusion—rising violence, crime rate, drug addiction, street begging, homelessness—found across Latin America. An indication that the social integration that allowed Montevideanos to live in relative social harmony is over may be found in the

---

24. The Quality of Living Survey conducted annually by Mercer Human Resource Consulting compares 350 cities worldwide, taking into account thirty-nine indicators, including political, social, economic, and environmental conditions; access to health care, education, entertainment, transportation, and other public services; crime rate and availability of personal security services; and so forth. The survey is designed to help transnational companies determine compensation packages for personnel assigned overseas. See http://www.montevideo.gub.uy/ciudad/espacios-publicos/espacios-publicos.

25. The city hall Web site reports that Montevideo has more green space than any other city in all of Latin America: half the urban area is covered with green space, and its 410,000 trees give it the highest ratio of trees to residents (1:3). See Mercer's 2009 Quality of Living survey highlights, the Americas, at http://www.mercer.com/referencecontent.htm?idContent=1340665.

alarming rise in poverty. Uruguay plunged into poverty during the military regime but had steadily improved following the return to democracy. By 2003, however, poverty had reached unprecedented levels in a country that had enjoyed a relatively high standard of living. According to official statistics, poverty doubled after 1993, and the number of indigent people increased by more than 300 percent during the same period. In 2004, close to one-third of the 3.3 million Uruguayans lived in poverty, 100,000 were indigent, and nearly 50 percent of children were born in poor homes.[26] As the country fell into poverty and increasingly resembled its neighbors, clearly the comforting notion of Uruguayan "exceptionalism" no longer made sense. The feeling of uniqueness that had made Uruguayans so proud gave way to the realization that the country had become "Latin American-ized," as Uruguayans often say in despair.[27] Corroborating these trends, the country plummeted fifteen places on the United Nations Development Programme Human Development Reports world ranking, from a comfort-able twenty-ninth place in 1975 to forty-sixth two decades later.[28]

This decline left permanent scars on the urban landscape, changing the lives of city residents in multiple ways. Indeed, for the past twenty years Montevideanos have increasingly lived de facto in two separate cities, both in social and spatial terms. Map 2 shows how poor people were segregated within the city space. The map also shows poverty levels in the three districts covered in this study.

Census results show that the city core has been losing population at an alarming rate, as thousands of impoverished residents were forced to migrate to the urban periphery due to rising rents following the liberalization of the rental market and the general increase in the cost of living. In fact, while 70 percent of the city's sixty-two neighborhoods lost populaion between 1995 and 2004, the few areas that experienced growth were all located in the urban periphery, experiencing disproportionately higher

26. Following democratization in 1984, the number of households living in poverty de-clined sharply, from 36.2 percent in 1986 to only 8.6 percent eight years later—giving Uruguayans hope that they would recover the relative equality of the past. Unfortunately, poverty levels started to climb once again in the mid-1990s, and by 2002 one-fifth of all households were poor (Kaztman and Retamoso 2005). Data for the country as a whole show that the number of people living in poverty doubled between 2000 and 2003 (rising from 16.7 percent to 33.6 percent), bringing poverty back to mid-1980s levels; between 2003 and 2004, indigence rose from 2.8 percent to 4.0 percent (Armas 2005).

27. The idea of the country's Latin Americanization was also adopted by academics. See Veiga 1989; and Canzani 1989.

28. But it still ranks among the top cities in Latin America, the continent with the greatest social inequalities.

MAP 2. People living in poverty in Montevideo (2004, percentages). Courtesy of
Alicia Abayian, National Institute of Statistics, Uruguay.

social problems and fewer urban services.[29] Map 3 shows the areas of the
city affected by overcrowded housing.[30] It also shows that one of the districts
covered in this study (district 17) was the area most affected by this condition, a point I will return to in chapter 3 and in the concluding chapter.

Some of the "new poor" who moved toward the periphery settled in public housing projects or built their own houses on cheap, legally acquired
land, while thousands of others settled in irregular squatter settlements
called *asentamientos*.[31] By 2004, 10 percent of Montevideanos had found
shelter in one of the 364 asentamientos that sprang up across the city,
where they were crammed in high-density areas lacking basic urban services.[32] The capital city, with slightly over 40 percent of the country's population, became the home of three-quarters of all people living in irregular
squatter settlements.[33]

29. Instituto Nacional de Estadística 2004, 6.
30. Overcrowded housing is defined as a condition where there are more than three people per bedroom within a household.
31. Veiga and Rivoir 2005.
32. Asentamientos had come to occupy 6.2 percent of total urban space. See IMM 2004a.
33. Quoting Cecilio, Kaztman and Retamoso (2005) report that even as early as 1984, 93.5
percent of marginal settlement residents had been born in cities, and three-quarters of them
in Montevideo.

MAP 3. Percentage of Montevideo households that are overcrowded (2004, percentages). Courtesy of Alicia Abayian, National Institute of Statistics, Uruguay.

This growing spatial and social distance between social classes produced by deteriorating social conditions increasingly segregated Montevideanos as residents started to interact more with social equals than with people from other social groups, a change that undermined the relatively high levels of social integration found in better times.[34] These trends segregated the poor in neighborhoods with strikingly higher levels of poverty, unemployment, and hunger and substantially less access to services, making it harder for them to cope with or to move out of poverty.[35] Table 1 shows the degree to which social and spatial marginality overlap in today's Montevideo, where neighborhoods located in the urban periphery have much

34. Kaztman and Retamoso 2005; and Veiga and Rivoir 2005. As the poor clustered along the periphery of the city, better-off city residents congregated in the southeastern and central areas. In contrast to other cities in Latin America, however, these upper-class populations did not enclose themselves in gated communities. There are only ten gated communities (housing 315 families) in Montevideo, compared to 434 in Buenos Aires (13,500 families). See Svampa, quoted in Kaztman and Retamoso (130).

35. The "social emergency" that hit thousands of residents in the city periphery generated a flood of demands for basic services, which placed additional strains on city coffers at a time when the municipal budget was already overstretched. All this despite the fact that Uruguay ranks second in terms of social spending (23.5 percent of GNP), while the average in Latin America and the Caribbean is only 13.8 percent.

Table 1   Social exclusion in Montevideo by region (2004, percentages)

	Eastern coast	Central	Urban periphery
Unemployment	8.7	11.9	16.0
Low education	15.0	22.2	39.7
No sewage	2.7	1.1	20.0
Poverty	8.6	19.3	51.6
Indigence	0.8	1.3	9.0

Source: Veiga and Rivoir 2005.

higher rates of social exclusion than the upper- and middle-class neighborhoods situated in the eastern costal areas.

Increased social exclusion and poverty greatly altered life in poor neighborhoods. Throughout most of the twentieth century, the traditional working-class neighborhoods that had sprung up around industries enjoyed access to basic urban services and were relatively homogeneous in social terms. The worlds of work and neighborhood overlapped so that the solidarity produced on the factory floor spilled over into the barrio, fostering strong fraternal ties, community solidarity, and social organization. When the country's industries collapsed and unemployment skyrocketed, as we will see in the chapters that follow, this balance was permanently upset, undermining social integration and producing all manner of social problems.

To make matters worse, some of these communities were overwhelmed by the arrival and settlement of the newly impoverished, who came with different traditions and outlooks. While earlier urban growth had been driven by European immigrants and people from the country's interior who came to seize the expanding opportunities offered by industrial jobs, the newcomers who settled within or in the outskirts of established working-class communities were driven by growing poverty and despair. Rather than being "pulled" into the city by the prospect of improving their lives, these people were "pushed" toward the urban periphery by forces beyond their control. The fracturing of the social fabric of working-class communities—produced by the disappearance of the material basis of their existence (the jobs created by industries) and exacerbated by the influx of the new poor—made these poor neighborhoods increasingly similar to the new urban ghettos that mushroomed in other Latin American cities, where groups with contrasting traditions and cultures came together in areas with relatively high levels of social disorganization and need.[36] These conditions

36. Pereira (2003, 2) argues that "the traditional 'worker neighborhood' or the ones that were the result of migration from the countryside to the city are no longer the paradigm for poor areas in Latin American cities."

undermined community organization and solidarity, as I discovered in the communities discussed in this book, and affected the operation of local government in each of the districts.

These problems were created by the country's economic decline, caused by the collapse of the model of import substitution industrialization (ISI) and state interventionism.[37] Uruguay's atypical economic prosperity had been due to a fortuitous combination of ISI policies and rising prices for Uruguay's beef exports. But those good times ended in the 1960s when the country's economy started to show signs of stagnation. If the exhaustion of the ISI model brought industrial development to a halt, the subsequent free-market and trade liberalization policies adopted by governments since the 1980s completed the destruction of the country's waning industrial base. The shift from state-led to market-led development policies reduced by half the relatively high share of employment that industry and the public sector enjoyed in the country's job structure.[38] The decline of industry accelerated in recent years, as its share of GNP fell from 29 percent in

37. Since the early twentieth century, Uruguay established an unusually high number of state enterprises, a trend that continued after World War II, making the public sector the single largest employer in the country and granting the state significant influence in economic matters. In the 1920s, several state enterprises secured state monopolies in key areas of production, public utilities, and transportation, including telephone and electricity services (Usinas Eléctricas y Teléfonos del Estado, UTE, in 1912), the administration of Montevideo harbor (Administración Nacional de Puertos, ANP, in 1912), and fishing activity (Servicio Oceanográfico y de Pesca, SOYP, in 1916). Further, a variety of financial monopolies were set up, such as the Bank of the Republic of Eastern Uruguay (Banco de la Republica Oriental del Uruguay, in 1911), acting simultaneously as the country's central bank and a commercial institution; the Mortgage Bank of Uruguay (Banco Hipotecario del Uruguay, in 1912); the State Insurance Bank (Banco de Seguros del Estado, in 1911), offering public insurance; and the Caja Nacional de Ahorro Postal (1919). More state enterprises were instituted ten years later, including the Frigorífico Nacional (1928); and the Administración Nacional de Combustibles, Alcoholes, y Portland (ANCAP, 1931), to administer the monopoly of alcohol, the import, refining, and distribution of all oil products, and the production of Portland cement. In 1932, the government extended to ANP a monopoly over all port activity in the country. Another wave of nationalizations occurred in the postwar period (1948–1952) when several British utility companies passed to state control, including the Administración de Ferrocarriles del Estado (AFE), to manage the railway industry; the Administración Municipal de Transporte (AMDET), providing bus service in Montevideo; and the Obras Sanitarias del Estado (OSE), administering the nation's supply of running water and sewage. In the 1950s the state intervened in or nationalized the various meatpacking industries in response to the crisis in this sector (more on this in the El Cerro chapter). All state enterprises were legally constituted as autonomous entities (*entes autónomos*) enjoying their own *personería jurídica* as well as significant freedom to make decisions, though they were ultimately accountable to the government. For a full analysis of state enterprises in Uruguay, see Solari and Franco 1983.

38. The share of industrial employment fell from 32 percent in 1970 to 16 percent in 2002, and that of state jobs declined from 28 percent to 16 percent between 1970 and 1999 (Kaztman and Retamoso 2005).

1985 to 19 percent in 2003.[39] The disappearance of industrial and state jobs was deeply felt across Montevideo, but it especially brought disaster to working-class neighborhoods, as I discovered through my regular visits to these communities.[40]

The negative effects of these structural trends were exacerbated by factors beyond anyone's control. Uruguayans have the blessing and the curse to be sandwiched between the two largest economies in South America, and they are keenly aware that their fortunes are tied to their neighbors' ups and downs. Popular wisdom expresses this with the saying "When Argentina or Brazil catches a cold, the Uruguayan economy gets pneumonia!" Indeed the Brazilian devaluation of 1999 and the Argentinean debacle of 2002 brought havoc to Uruguay's economy. In the first seven months of 2002 alone, the country lost nearly 80 percent of its foreign reserves, as Argentineans rushed to withdraw their deposits from Uruguayan banks, fearing that they no longer offered their usual financial security. The country's exports collapsed (since most of them were destined for these struggling countries), GDP per capita shrank by 19 percent,[41] inflation hit 24 percent, and unemployment skyrocketed to a historic high of 19 percent. All of this triggered a recession that would last until 2003, precisely the year I returned to the country to study community participation in poor neighborhoods.[42]

The economic collapse also forced many to search for better opportunities abroad. As I drove by the gates of the Spanish embassy each day, I saw endless lines of people with chairs and sleeping bags determined to spend the night on the street hoping to obtain one of the few appointments handed out each morning by overworked consular staff. Sadly, the country that had previously opened its doors to thousands of immigrants was now effectively expelling their grandchildren back to Europe at a time when European governments were not keen to receive them. Some Uruguayans managed to find the birth certificates of their grandparents and

39. Bertola and Bittencourt 2005.

40. The city of Montevideo not only shared in this general decline of industry, but it also experienced a proportionally steeper decline in industrial output, losing its traditional supremacy as the country's manufacturing center. Montevideo produced 78 percent of the country's GDP in 1960, while in the early 1990s its share had fallen to 60 percent (Kaztman and Retamoso 2005).

41. Armas 2005.

42. Not surprisingly, the percentage of people who believed the country's economy was bad increased from 35 percent in 1994 to 50 percent in 1999 to 62 percent in 2004 (Canzani 2005).

reclaimed their ancestral European citizenship, thereby allowing them to return to the "old" world armed with a precious EU passport (placing them a notch above thousands of others trying to survive as undocumented immigrants). Between 1985 and 2004, nearly two hundred thousand people left the country—half of them during the 1999–2003 economic debacle—joining a diaspora of over half a million people, a figure that represents 15 percent of those still living within the country.[43]

The Evolution of Decentralization in Montevideo

Remarkably, despite coming to power amid the worst crisis Montevideanos had ever experienced, the Broad Front administration steadily expanded its base of support fifteen years after it came to power. While Tabaré Vázquez won the city government with nearly 35 percent of the vote in 1989, five years later Broad Front candidate Mariano Arana was elected with an impressive 44 percent, an increase of almost ten percentage points, and was reelected to a second term in May 2000 (the first elections separate from presidential elections) with 58 percent of the vote. The Left appeared to have consolidated its power in the city when Ricardo Ehrlich, the new Broad Front candidate, received an impressive 61 percent of the vote in 2004 (almost double the support that had originally brought Vázquez to power fifteen years earlier), in what constituted the largest majority for any political party in the city's history.[44]

The rise in support was not surprising. Indeed, the record of three successive leftist administrations demonstrated that the Broad Front could be an effective manager in a city facing increasingly greater challenges, and also served as an indication that the coalition had the political will to redistribute urban resources to benefit the urban poor.[45] After more than a

43. Caetano 2005. In 1989, a few years after the return to democracy, nearly one-third of youth were considering international migration as an option (Calvo and Pellegrino 2005).

44. Data from opinion polls show similar approval rates for the city administration (Ibarra 2001). Electoral results for the municipal elections held in May 2005 gave the Broad Front candidate Ricardo Ehrlich 60.9 percent of the vote, while the Blanco candidate Javier Garcia received 10.4 percent and the Colorado candidate Pedro Bordaberry received 26.9 percent. In the Municipal Assembly the Broad Front earned twenty representatives, compared to only three for the Blancos and eight for the Colorados.

45. Montevideo's city government raises its own revenues through taxation to fund the many services it offers, and it also receives transfer payments from the national government. Since the return to democracy in the mid-1980s, *intendencias* significantly increased their revenues and spending. Montevideo's municipal budget, for example, more than doubled between

decade in power, the Broad Front had an impressive record of accomplishments to its credit, including significant improvements to public works[46]
and a number of impressive social policies for low-income residents, as
well as specific programs targeting women, youth, senior citizens, and the
disabled.[47] These programs became increasingly more important in light
of the social emergency that hit Montevideo toward the end of the 1990s.
The lack of response to this crisis from the national government prompted
the municipality to direct resources to deal with issues that typically fall
under the jurisdiction of national ministries (such as health and housing),
demonstrating the Broad Front's political commitment to prioritize poor
city residents.[48] Dividing the city into four areas according to different poverty levels, table 2 shows how much the areas contributed in city taxes and
how much they received in the form of municipal spending, documenting

---

1990 and 1994, as did the per capita budget of other departmental governments across the
country. See Filgueira et al. 1999.

46. Since 1990, public lighting increased by 62 percent and the percentage of working
bulbs rose from 55 percent to 90 percent. Garbage collection per person more than doubled
(from 169 kilos in 1992 to 430 kilos in 1997) and the number of illegal garbage dumps went
down from 1,700 to 150 between 1990 and 1994. While in 1992 only 76 percent of city residents lived in homes connected to municipal sewage, by 2005 nearly all households were connected. By 1997, the city government was paving twice as many square meters of road per year
as the previous Colorado administration (IMM 1998b, 2002; and Chávez 2004).

47. In the area of housing, the city government distributed 220 hectares of land to cooperatives for eight thousand families, granted legal land titles to five thousand squatter families,
built more than one thousand new housing units for poor families, and set up a municipal
housing fund. In terms of public health, it tripled the number of municipal health-care clinics,
opening new clinics in poor districts to facilitate access to primary care. The Broad Front government developed various programs to attend to women and children. It opened eighteen
municipal day care centers, distributed more than 1.5 million liters of powdered milk, and created public spaces with games for young children. Specific job creation programs for youth
were created in partnership with NGOs (e.g., Tacurú, El Abrojo, Gurises Unidos, San Vicente).
The Girasoles program hired young people to clean up green spaces across the city, while
Puerto Joven provided assistance to microenterprises set up by young entrepreneurs. The city
also set up a health-care program for women (Programa de Atención Integral a la Mujer), a
twenty-four-hour hotline for victims of domestic violence, a program called Comuna Mujer
designed to both encourage women to come together at the district level and offer legal services and specific support for victims of domestic violence, and training programs for women
councilors. It also set up a number on initiatives to support disabled people, including training programs, preferential allocation of spaces in street fairs, and affirmative action policies
setting aside 4 percent of all vacancies in the municipality for such residents. The city government also invested heavily in multiple programs to promote cultural activities, and established
public transport subsidies for students, young people, and seniors (Habitat 2000; IMM 1998a,
1998b, 2002; and Chávez 2004).

48. The $340 million, five-year budget for the 2000–2005 period, for example, allocated
50 percent for public works and services, 30 percent for social programs, and only 20 percent
for administration. These figures include salaries.

Table 2   Resource redistribution in Montevideo (1993–2003)

Poverty area	Inhabitants	Taxes paid (percentages)	Investment received (percentages)	Per capita expenditure (pesos)
< 20%	568,000	74	35	1,241
20–30%	151,000	10	9	1,130
30–40%	179,000	6	10	1,125
> 40%	447,000	11	46	2,083

Source: Masdeu 2003.

that the city government did in fact redirect significant urban resources toward poorer neighborhoods. The areas with poverty levels greater than 40 percent, for instance, contributed only 11 percent of total tax revenues but received nearly half of municipal expenditures, the highest per capita expenditure in the city.

The table also shows that per capita investment was very similar in the other three areas, indicating that the commitment to redistribution did not preclude investing in richer areas of the city. The Broad Front also invested in urban infrastructure and programs that benefited middle- and upper-class residents, especially during the second and third administrations under Mayor Arana. During these periods, the city government made significant improvements to the quality of the city's beach areas (in part helped by the removal of sewage disposal from city beaches), upgraded different parts of the valued rambla, and started several urban renewal projects, including the successful restoration of the colonial Ciudad Vieja. Through these initiatives the Broad Front demonstrated that it could effectively avoid the zero-sum dilemma of taking from the rich to give to the poor, showing that it was willing to govern for the entire city.[49]

Most analysts identify three periods in the evolution of participation. The initial period (1990–93) generated the most spontaneous and widespread participation as thousands of residents came out to countless community

49. Not surprisingly, an opinion poll commissioned by the city government in 2001 confirmed that Montevideanos had an overwhelmingly positive view of the performance of the city government, especially in terms of managing urban services such as public transportation, street maintenance, garbage collection, and sewers. When asked whether they would like to return to the pre-1990 municipal system, an overwhelming 64 percent said no. But the poll also revealed a marked skepticism toward the workings of participatory democracy, as only 36 percent of respondents believed that decentralization had effectively transferred power to residents. Thus the results showed that support of the city government was based primarily on its success in improving service delivery rather than its opening of city politics through participatory local democracy. See Bergamino et al. 2001.

forums hoping to shape the character of decentralization and to identify the needs of their communities. The second period (1993–98) started with the inauguration of the new structures of local government forced on Vázquez by the political establishment, all of which effectively disempowered the organs for the participation of civil society, but resident participation in elections for neighborhood councils continued to grow. The third phase (1998–2004) was marked by a fall in participation, high desertion rates among councilors, and declining voter turnout.

Resident participation in the elections for neighborhood councils reflects these trends, as shown in table 3. The evolution of electoral participation shows an expansive phase that peaked in 1998, followed by slightly lower levels of voter turnout in 2001 and a decline of nearly 25 percent in the 2004 elections. After a normal period of growth, electoral participation stabilized at around 8 percent of eligible voters, a level of participation that continued until 2008, the last election for which data is available.

Most analysts attribute the decline in participation and in voter turnout to the changes in the model of decentralization that severely restricted the responsibilities and powers of neighborhood councils after 1993. While this was an important factor, the concrete experiences of participation discussed in this book will show that the decline in participation was also related to the local contingencies identified earlier in this chapter and to the deepening economic crisis affecting the country after 1999. For instance, city authorities responded to the crisis by shifting spending toward social emergency programs to address the immediate and urgent needs of thousands of Montevideanos, effectively taking resources away from the public works that had earned the government so much support. The crisis strained city coffers in more serious ways as many Montevideanos simply stopped paying municipal taxes, prompting a reluctant Mayor Arana to warn that they could

Table 3   Voter turnout for neighborhood council elections in Montevideo (1993–2004)

Year	Percentage of eligible voters	Number of voters
1993	7.28	68,558
1995	8.77	82,496
1998	11.20	106,909
2001	10.70	100,552
2004	8.11	76,643

Source: IMM 2004c.

not "respond to all the needs and demands of the population."[50] To make matters worse, a series of unprecedented decisions by national governments reduced transfer payments while demanding increased contributions from the municipality to the national treasury. These financial problems meant that the city government could not meet the avalanche of demands arising in the poorer districts, angering councilors and demoralizing community activists, and ultimately producing a decline in participation.[51]

Models of Urban Governance and the Rise of the Left in Latin America

The introduction of participatory decentralization in Montevideo illustrates broader changes in the politics of Latin America. This experience is part of an emerging trend of participatory urban governance sweeping through Latin America that includes not only the high-profile case of participatory budgeting in Porto Alegre but also hundreds of participatory experiments in other major cities in the region. Such experiments—supported by a wide range of social movements, popular organizations, NGOs, and progressive municipal governments—turned local spaces into real-life laboratories of social transformation and democratization, with different degrees of success. In so doing, they helped shape a new paradigm of urban governance based on the principles of democratic participatory citizenship and redistributive justice, aiming to democratize social and political life and to improve public delivery of services.

50. Quoted in Chávez 2004, 135. This came in spite of the significant savings from the reduction of municipal payroll as the number of municipal employees fell from slightly over 12,000 when the Broad Front first got elected to 9,800 in 2000. By the start of the millennium the employees of Montevideo city hall represented 1.77 percent of the employed labor force in the city, the lowest in the country. Other municipalities had much higher percentages: Durazno (8.83 percent), Rocha (7.45 percent), Tacuarembo (6.95 percent), Treinta y Tres (6.80 percent). See IMM 2002.

51. For instance, the national government arbitrarily cut transfer payments to Montevideo city by 50 percent between 1990 and 1994 before eliminating them altogether. Moreover, in 1993 it started to demand that the municipality pay value added tax on all expenditures, plus an additional 3 percent in social security contributions to the national government for each employee on its payroll. Since none of these new measures was extended to other municipalities in the country, the Broad Front coalition complained that they were the targets of political discrimination. These new exigencies meant that the city had to transfer 20 percent of its budget to the national coffers precisely at a time when city residents needed more municipal programs to help them cope with the serious social and economic problems they faced. See Filgueira et al. 1999. When the Broad Front won the national elections in 2004, it reversed these decisions and transfer payments were resumed, giving the city a healthy budget surplus of $7.8 million (La República, 7/25/2006).

Over the past ten years we have witnessed an undeniable shift in the region's political landscape, as close to 80 percent of Latin Americans opened the millennium in countries with left-of-center governments, a striking contrast with decades past when all but a few were ruled by military dictators. As the "pink tide" swept across Latin America, earlier academic and political interest in the experiences of "the Left in the city" (to cite the name of an influential book on participatory urban governance[52]) gave way to passionate debates about the significance of the broader changes that had finally brought the Left into the presidential palace of so many countries in the region. In focusing on these wider transformations, however, we risk overlooking the value of more localized democratic participatory experiences, such as the one discussed in this book, initiatives where some of the most exciting practical alternatives to neoliberalism have been forged.

The rise of the Left as a credible political force to lead national governments in Latin America is associated with growing disenchantment with free-market policies and liberal democracy, and with the shift toward moderation and the acceptance of electoral politics on the part of the leftist parties. Yet the growing fortunes of the Left have also resulted from years of experience in running city governments and from the innovative experiences in democratic participation that leftist city governments have introduced at the municipal level. These experiences demonstrated that the Left not only could efficiently administer some of Latin America's largest cities (in itself not an easy task), but also that it had the political will and imagination to introduce innovative forms of governance that helped redistribute resources to the urban poor while revitalizing democratic practices at the local level. As a result, political parties of the Left, like the Broad Front coalition in Uruguay, gained political support beyond their traditional constituencies as followers of more conservative political parties cast their votes for them, either because they were inspired by the reform policies or because they no longer viewed voting for these parties as a gamble.

Changing Development Discourse and the Rise of Civil Society as an Agent of Development

The experience of participatory decentralization in Montevideo offers an alternative to the model of decentralization advocated by the "Washington

52. Chávez and Goldfrank 2004

consensus." Proponents of neoliberalism conceive participation as an instrument to transfer responsibilities to civil society and the market, while reducing state involvement in production and redistribution. They view civil society as an arena of self-regulation where rational individuals pursue their own interests through a plurality of interest groups and voluntary associations.[53] They no longer envision the state as a provider of goods and services, as in the model of the developmentalist state, but rather as an enabling force to facilitate the conditions for citizens and markets to generate well-being without direct state assistance or interference.[54] This perspective advocates a consumerist form of "market citizenship," which conceives citizenship as the expression of self-interested individual behavior and upholds civil and political rights while dismissing social rights as a disposable luxury.[55] Based on the premise that the individual constitutes the basic unit of political life, the citizen becomes primarily a consumer of goods and services, who is empowered to the extent that his or her ability to make choices in a competitive market is enlarged. By turning citizenship into an individual affair, the neoliberal view hides the political character of citizenship and does away with the notion of public responsibility.

Alternative participatory experiences, such as the ones discussed in this book, promote participation as one component of a broader process to empower citizens to become protagonists in more radical processes to deepen democracy, redistribute resources, and expand social citizenship. They advocate a democratic-participatory view of citizenship, which links democratic participation, equitable justice, and public responsibility. Arguing that choices about budgetary expenditures and service delivery are ultimately political choices about resource allocation and redistribution, these experiments encourage more bottom-up democratic input, public debate, and negotiation to produce consensus on the kinds of service to be offered as well as how and where those services should be delivered. Since citizenship entails making political rather than market choices, participation becomes a vehicle to deepen democratic citizenship by facilitating the process through which citizens engage in processes to promote equitable development. This emerging view emphasizes the social responsibilities of citizenship by challenging citizens to transcend their narrow

53. Howell and Pearce 2001, 65.

54. Not surprisingly, advocates of this position argue that privatization and decentralization have a symbiotic relationship and that the former is the "ultimate form of decentralization" (Litvack et al. 1998, 20).

55. Yashar 2005, 47.

individual interests by becoming involved in shaping agendas of equitable social transformation, even when these agendas may clash with their immediate interests as consumers.[56]

The emerging language of the "post-Washington consensus," however, made the differences between neoliberal advocates and their opponents less obvious. Concerned with responding to growing criticisms of the failures of structural adjustment policies and the widespread social and political problems caused by the unleashing of unrestrained free-market capitalism in the context of extreme inequalities typical of Latin America, major international development institutions backed down from their aggressive neoliberal agendas, embracing notions of sustainable, egalitarian, participatory, and democratic development and advocating targeted policies to address the needs of the poor, even if this meant increased social spending. Many skeptics rightly point out that these policies constitute a repackaged form of neoliberalism (i.e., neoliberalism with a human face) and that the pro-poor policies represent compensatory measures to control market failures, rather than a serious rethinking of the role of unrestrained free markets in development. Notwithstanding these valid criticisms, the post-Washington consensus produced an agenda that is more sensitive to the poor and more responsive to demands arising from civil society than earlier and more aggressive versions of neoliberalism, encouraging mainstream international development institutions to promote institutional reforms to integrate citizens in the formulation and implementation of development programs. These mainstream institutions went so far as praising leftist municipal administrations for their efficient delivery of services to the most needy and for their innovative approaches to institutional reform. The Workers' Party (Partido dos Trabalhadores, PT) experiment of participatory budgeting in Porto Alegre, for example, became a high-profile case and was presented quite favorably on the World Bank's Web page as an effective model worthy of being emulated by other developing countries.[57]

The apparent political convergence between mainstream development institutions and their opponents is explained by the emergence of a new

56. Dagnino (2003) argues that this emerging view produced a new language of citizenship used by diverse social actors to frame their demands as rights and entitlements. Many of these movements, she argues, do not simply ask for an extension of existing rights to marginalized citizens or demand the "right to equality." They also assert the right to invent new rights, including the "right to difference," as in the case of differential rights advocated by native groups and minorities across the region.

57. The PT administration was awarded the prize for "best practice" in city governance by the UN Habitat Conference in 1996 (Goldfrank 2003).

consensus about what constitutes development and how to achieve it, as earlier debates about priorities (growth versus equity) and models (state-led versus market-led development) gave way to more nuanced and balanced approaches.[58] The old state-versus-market debates were replaced by a new common sense that accepted some level of state intervention and regulation and some degree of market competition as necessary to promote development. As debates about the role of the state switched from whether it *should* intervene to *how* it should intervene, researchers and policy makers shifted attention toward the ability of state institutions and state capacities to build effective governance.[59] The shift to good governance rested on a growing consensus among all sectors of the political spectrum about the need to make the state more democratic and transparent, more responsive to societal demands, and more efficient.[60] Important differences remained, however, especially in relation to what should be the primary aim of good government: should it be to create the conditions to make markets more efficient or to expand democracy and empower citizens?[61]

The emerging emphasis on empowerment and capacity building to enable individuals to change their circumstances—coupled with the abandonment of models that privileged either states or markets as the exclusive engines of development—gave rise to the "third" route to welfare provision and development. Indeed, civil society, which had been overlooked in the market-versus-state debates, was "discovered" as an agent of development. In a short period of time, civil society took center stage in the development field when it was revealed that it was a rich reservoir of untapped resources—knowledge, values, bonds of trust, and capacities—that were essential to advancing the goals of development. It was argued that these resources constituted an alternative form of capital available to the poor—social capital—that was solemnly declared as the "missing link" in development. Arguing that a vibrant civil society was key to fostering democracy and economic growth, it was also proposed that civil society could help relieve states from financial burdens, avoid the kind of dependencies produced

58. For a review, see Gwynne and Kay 1999.

59. Howell and Pearce 2001, 65.

60. Some authors will argue that state reform is a precondition for the emergence of a new model of development. See Vellinga 1998, 17.

61. Debates also shifted from technical concerns about the *means* of development to more holistic and morally informed understandings of the *goals* of development (Elliot 2008). These goals came to be understood as the expansion of entitlements, capabilities, choices, and freedoms. As a result, policy makers were challenged to find ways to allow individuals to become full participants in society and develop the capabilities to influence the world around them (Sen 1999).

by welfare programs, and remove the profit motive that drives privatized service provision.[62]

The discovery of civil society as a central agent of development gave rise to a new triadic model of development in which civil society was said to be an equal partner alongside the state and the market.[63] But this "third way" model conceives civil society as complementary to the state and the market, as long as civil society organizations accepted the basic organizing principles of market societies and worked in partnerships with the state and the private sector to make capitalism more ethical. This shift in development discourse toward cooperation, partnership, and synergy between civil society, states, and markets called for citizen input in the design, implementation, and monitoring of community development projects. Further, it produced a new language to refer to the development process: community-driven, bottom-up, or grassroot development; participation, social capital, good governance; and so forth. The use of these terms reflected a shift in how the roles of states and civil societies were understood in mainstream development discourse; the former would become an enabling force of markets or community participation, while later would surrender its supposedly former role as a passive recipient of state goods and services and provide for itself. Inviting civil society organizations to abandon oppositional stances and to join state agencies as partners to foster development, this new discourse posed a true dilemma for grassroot organizations, as they had to choose between risking co-optation if they engaged in partnerships or irrelevance if they decided to refuse the invitation.[64]

High hopes were attached to the potential of civil society actors—often referred to in the singular to underscore their unitary character—to provide the badly needed civic energy to revitalize political life, produce democratic-egalitarian practices, and promote economic development.[65]

---

62. Howell and Pearce 2001, 67.

63. The rise to prominence of civil society is also explained by powerful political developments that occurred toward the end of the twentieth century (some of which are external to Latin America), including the "revival" of civil society that led the struggles against authoritarianism in eastern Europe and Latin America, global trend toward democratization that offered new opportunities for civil actors to organize, growing public dissatisfaction with formal party politics, the growing importance of NGOs and grassroot organizations in filling the "policy void" produced by a neoliberal state retreating from welfare provision, and the global opportunities for coordinated collective action across borders, creating what some have called a global civil society. See Carothers 1999–2000.

64. Howell and Pearce 2001.

65. Van Roy (1998) argues that the widespread and often uncritical adoption of the term "civil society" turned it into an "analytical hat-stand" used by people with opposing political agendas.

These optimistic views about the potential contribution of civil society to development offered a healthy alternative to the state-market debate, but they were not without problems, as I will show in this book. They tended to romanticize civil society—as the place where citizens engaged with one another to transcend their narrow interests to work for the common good through deliberative democratic practices—failing to recognize that not everything that occurs within civil society leads to civility or the public good (itself a highly contested notion).[66] My research on the workings of neighborhood councils will show that it is not uncommon for groups of citizens to refuse to put aside their corporate interests in the name of collective needs, and that even when community activists wish to cooperate to work for the public good, they may be unable to do so because they lack the capacity to work together effectively in particular institutional and socioeconomic contexts.

Another problem with some views of civil society that underpin current analysis is that they fail to recognize that civil society is "as much a creature of the state as it is of society."[67] Indeed, a flourishing civil society requires guarantees of both citizenship rights and democratic normative frameworks to regulate civic practices, conditions that can only be ensured by robust and legitimate state institutions.[68] If powerful authoritarian regimes do not provide a hospitable environment for the emergence of

66. These views drew from early liberal traditions that established a sharp dividing line between civil society and state, and that considered civil society the site where civility and the common good were produced. This liberal view of civil society was radically different from that of the ancient Romans, who saw the state as an instrument of civil society rather than its antithesis. Adam Ferguson viewed civil society as synonymous with "polite" behavior, arguing that to guard against authoritarianism societies had to create independent communities within civil society. For Thomas Paine, the state itself, regardless of performance, constituted a block for society's hopes for equality and freedom. For Tocqueville, even democratic governments could suffocate civil society in the absence of strong community spirit, associationalism, and voluntarism. Political life outside the realm of the state, he argued, is not only possible but also necessary because a strong and vibrant civil society is the best antidote against tyranny. Even Gramsci, who is credited for resurrecting the concept, drew a similar distinction, arguing that since the state was an instrument of class rule rather than an expression of societal interests, civil society provided the trenches in a war of positions to foster counter-hegemonic struggles against capitalism. See Van Roy 1998. Earlier analyses in the Latin American context, especially during the times when civil society organizations constituted a powerful oppositional force against authoritarian rule, stressed that civil society was separate from—and stood in opposition to—the state, acting like Paine's "antidote" to the authoritarian tendencies inherent in all states. But following democratization in the 1980s, and in part due to the shifts in development discourse outlined above, many social movement organizations assumed less contentious roles, entering into partnerships with states. See Foweraker 2003.

67. Van Roy 1998, 21.

68. See Oxhorn 2006; Van Roy 1998; and Evans 1996b.

vibrant civil societies, a claim contradicted in part by the experiences of Latin America and eastern Europe, weak states can also cripple civil society by failing to create the necessary institutional guarantees for its successful operation. Turning the face-to-face trust and cooperation that may emerge within communities into generalized trust is not straightforward, and is also contingent on the existence of strong legal guarantees provided by state institutions.[69]

My research on participatory decentralization shows that states and civil societies constitute interdependent entities that develop "in tandem, not at each other's expense," as efforts to strengthen civil society are often integral components of parallel projects of state building.[70] In the case of Montevideo, for example, the impulse to strengthen civil society and to open new avenues for citizen participation came primarily from the state, not from civil society. Elected to city hall in a municipality with frail urban movements and a disenchanted citizenry, the Broad Front charted a reform path to renew municipal politics, hoping to reinspire citizens who had become disillusioned with the "low-intensity" democracy that followed military rule. The governing coalition also hoped to reactivate its own support base. The goal of strengthening civil society and fostering citizen participation, therefore, entailed a broader process of renewing municipal state institutions and party structures. Further, my research also shows that in each barrio the lines of separation between state and civil society were significantly blurred when activists joined the bodies of local government set up by the city administration, a point I will discuss in subsequent chapters.

The construction of mutually supportive partnerships between state and civil society is central to the work of the Berkeley sociologist Peter Evans.[71] His focus on the synergy of civil society and the state seeks to avoid the pitfalls of the romantic views of civil society while acknowledging the potential contribution of civil society and the state to processes of development and democracy. Evans argues that every actor operating at the local level—including community organizations, state officials, and NGOs—needs allies to compensate for its own weaknesses, as each party acting alone lacks all the resources necessary to pursue its goals effectively. Community

---

69. See Harriss 2001.

70. Carothers 1999–2000, 27. In fact, as Carothers also points out, the actions of successful civil groups typically ended up strengthening rather than weakening state institutions, as their victories often led to the enactment of laws extending new rights or protecting the environment, leading to greater state regulation and the establishment of new government agencies.

71. Evans 1996a, 1996b, 2002.

organizations, for example, are often short of material resources and social capital, and may also be constrained by a preoccupation with narrow, local concerns. NGOs, in contrast, may possess resources and know-how but can only use them effectively when embedded in communities and linked up with state agencies. State agencies may possess greater power and resources, but they badly need cooperation from communities or partnerships with NGOs to implement effective programs. Thus community organizations wishing to realize their potential as effective political actors must complement internal solidarity with partnerships and alliances with other actors, such as grassroot organizations, NGOs, and state agencies. To use the language of social capital, communities must complement their internal bonds of trust ("bonding" social capital) by allying with other communities of similar socioeconomic status ("bridging" social capital) and individuals or institutions in positions of power and authority in the state ("linking" social capital).[72] While internal community cohesion is vital to foster bridges or links with other actors, it is not necessarily a sufficient condition to nurture the capacities to do so.[73]

In the case of Montevideo, neighborhood activists wishing to seize the opportunities offered by decentralization were challenged to forge internal bonds of trust, build bridges at the council level with other communities in their district, and establish constructive relations with municipal officials at the local and city level. The concepts of bonding, linking, and bridging social capital are closely connected to the three local contingencies identified at the beginning of this chapter as the key factors that explain the outcomes of participatory decentralization in Montevideo. As I will show, some communities possessed the necessary conditions, resources, and capacities to succeed in building these partnerships and navigating the new institutional networks created by decentralization, while others did not.

The emphasis on bridges and linkages suggests that community organizations or social movements operate within what Evans calls an "ecology of actors" and that their actions must be examined through their interactions within broad networks of interdependent agents—community organizations, social movements, NGOs, religious groups, state institutions/ officials, and political parties—rather than as isolated and autonomous actors.[74] Operating in these networks, state and non-state actors mutually

---

72. For a discussion of these three kinds of social capital, see Woolcock and Narayan 2000.
73. See O'Rourke's (2002) discussion of Vietnam.
74. Evans 1996a, 1996b, 2002.

influence one another in countless ways. At times, they may clash over the allocation of resources or over the definition of the values that should govern relations between citizens and states; at other times, local organizations and state officials may cooperate on specific projects.[75] My discussion of the three districts will illustrate both tendencies and show that when cooperation among communities and between communities and state officials occurs, these actors develop synergy, increasing "their respective capacities to provide collective goods"[76] and producing outcomes with greater effects than they may have had if each had operated individually. The ideal conditions for synergy, according to Evans, include the existence of robust state institutions that guarantee both citizenship rights and democratic frameworks, and relatively egalitarian social structures. While the first condition was met in Montevideo, the second was certainly lacking. Nevertheless, synergy was constructed in some districts, as I will show in subsequent chapters.

State and Civil Society Relations in Latin America

The election of the Broad Front and other leftist city governments across Latin America increased opportunities for synergy between civil society and the state. The prospects for that synergy, however, were conditioned by the historical patterns found across the region. Latin American civil societies emerged in the twentieth century under the shadow of powerful, authoritarian, corporatist states and operated under an overarching "state-centered matrix" that structured economic, political, and social relations.[77] In Uruguay, as in other countries in the region, the subordination of civil society was reinforced by import substitution policies that made the state a central actor in economic, social, political, and even cultural affairs.

75. Research on recent experiences of participatory decentralization in Latin America has focused precisely on the construction of synergistic relations between state and civil society actors. See Baiocchi 2002; Avritzer 2002; Santos 1998; Nylen 2003; and Fung and Wright 2003.

76. Evans 2002, 21.

77. See Cavarozzi 1993. In western Europe, civil society had emerged one hundred years earlier based on a clear demarcation between society and the liberal democratic state. In contrast, civil society did not emerge in nineteenth-century Latin America due to the weakness of state structures and the overwhelming influence of the private sphere, expressed in the existence of semiautonomous rural haciendas and the close links between private citizens and the state (Avritzer 2006, 36). In countries with strong corporatist systems, the state allocated resources selectively to specific corporate groups that it defined as legitimate recipients of entitlements and as representatives of larger societal interests, thereby setting guidelines for appropriate political behavior and forms of collective action.

These conditions changed with the emergence of more vibrant civil societies during the democratic transitions of the 1980s, especially in the Southern Cone of Latin America. Nevertheless, the Brazilian sociologist Leonardo Avritzer warns us that sweeping generalizations about a Latin American state–civil society matrix are only partially useful because they tend to render invisible important differences in the patterns found across the region, especially in the post-authoritarian period. Like most researchers, Avritzer acknowledges that the region lived through similar cycles of mobilization—a surge of civil society activity in the struggles against authoritarian governments followed by a general decline in the post-authoritarian period. But he argues that these cycles produced different outcomes in the kinds of state–civil society interactions that followed democratization. These variations, he suggests, can only be explained in reference to the unique histories, traditions, and institutional developments of each country.[78]

Avritzer identifies three distinct models of civil society that emerged toward the end of authoritarian rule. The "pre-liberal" model, which is the least relevant for this study, emerged in Andean countries like Peru and Colombia where state institutions were weak and fragmented and could not guarantee the basic normative frameworks and rights necessary for the operation of civil society. Civil society in these cases took some of the state's responsibilities in an effort to establish peace, security, and welfare in a context marked by the absence of state capacities. The "liberal-democratic" model is typical of countries of the Southern Cone that had developed more robust institutions before the demise of democracy, where political parties had effectively mediated between society and the state.[79] In these countries the military banned democratic institutions and political parties from all sides of the political spectrum, hoping to eliminate the "hazards" of formal democratic politics, though following democratization the political party system was essentially restored.[80] Civil organizations in the Southern

---

78. According to Avritzer (2006), the emergence of each kind of interaction between the state and civil society was contingent on the nature of authoritarian regimes (including their targets and economic policies); the historical strength of state institutions, democratic traditions, and party systems; the character of civil society prior to authoritarian rule; the nature of social movements during military regimes; and the social actors' level of renewal following democratization.

79. Avritzer (2006) only includes Argentina and Chile in this model, but with some qualifications it also describes aspects of the civil society that developed in Uruguay.

80. Still, the overall plan to shrink the political sphere backfired as political activity shifted toward communities and areas of social life outside the scope of formal institutions; eventually the field of politics was enlarged as private social roles and activities such as motherhood and food preparation turned into public spaces to condemn the regimes' repressive and exclusionary

Cone, argues Avritzer, seemed content to accept the legitimacy of the traditional political system and the narrow confines of liberal democracy instead of pressing for a new kind of political democracy.

The "civic-participatory" model emerged in Brazil, where democratic
institutions and political parties were less established and where civil society was weak and fragmented prior to the emergence of the military regime.[81] Avritzer argues that the relative weakness of Brazilian political
institutions provided ideal opportunities for the surge of more vibrant civil
society organizations during and after the transition to democracy. In this
context, Avritzer goes on, civil society embraced a new discourse of rights
and fought to extend the scope of citizenship, to challenge traditional forms
of political mediation, and to assert alternative social practices. It was in
Brazil where civil society organizations pressed hardest for institutional
reforms and for new forms of citizen participation; not surprisingly, the
country produced countless innovative grassroot experiences, including
participatory budgeting.

Curiously, Avritzer's discussion of the Southern Cone does not include
any references to the Uruguayan case, which I suggest shares most of
the features of the liberal-democratic model that emerged in Chile and
Argentina but also includes a few of the characteristics of Brazil's civic-
participatory model. Like Chile, Uruguay had strong democratic traditions
and effective party systems that were restored following democratization.
Similar to the other Southern Cone countries, Uruguay gave birth to a
vibrant civil society during the authoritarian period that was demobilized
following the restoration of liberal democracy. Civil society in these countries was unwilling or too weak to effectively redefine the matrix that framed
the relationship between the state and society or to challenge the political
parties' monopoly over political mediation. In particular, several studies
of the transition in Uruguay stress that the logic of political restoration tri-
umphed over political renewal, and explain this outcome in reference to
the historical centrality of the state and party system in Uruguayan political and social life.

The prominence of political institutions in Uruguay dates back to the
early twentieth century, when the modern state was constructed largely in

---

policies. Thus, paradoxically, the military attempt to privatize society by eliminating political
life produced the opposite effect of politicizing aspects of the private realm.

81. Avritzer (2006) also argues that to a lesser extent this model also emerged in Mexico.
I think that in this case he may be downplaying the capacity of the Mexican state to restore its
authority and overemphasizing the capacity of civil society to produce a new kind of politics.

the absence of a rigid class structure and in a context of "social stale-mate,"[82] in which no single social group was strong enough to impose its own project on the rest of society. The power vacuum that resulted provided a unique opportunity to a forward-looking urban political class under the leadership of José Batlle y Ordóñez to capture a relatively autonomous state and to implement a program of social reform that was highly advanced for Latin America.[83] The Batllista reformist project sought to create a merito-cratic society based on political democracy and welfare politics.[84] Working on the premise that the state was the central engine for societal transfor-mation, Batllismo created a civil society that was subordinate and often mobilized but never consulted except through electoral contests.[85] The Uru-guayan state became a force of social integration and a mediator between social groups, effectively guaranteeing basic welfare and upward mobility for Uruguayan citizens and the thousands of immigrants arriving from Europe. The effectiveness of these distributive programs gave the state and the political class unusually high levels of legitimacy that ensured social and political stability until the 1960s.[86]

Such peace was also secured through the early institutionalization of political democracy, the integration of all citizens into the political system, and the institutionalization of consensus and compromise between the country's traditional Blanco and Colorado parties through a Swiss-style collegiate executive system and proportional co-participation in the adminis-tration of state enterprises.[87] The effective operation of the country's political

82. See Rial 1989.

83. On the question of the relative autonomy of the Uruguayan state, see Barrán and Nahum 1982.

84. Rama 1987, 42. Batllismo is the political movement that carried out these reforms, rep-resenting the interests of the political class, the middle sectors, and the urban working classes. Batlle y Ordóñez, president during most of the first three decades of the twentieth century, is considered the father of the modern Uruguayan state. He initiated sweeping reforms, such as restricting the president's powers by creating a Council of Government (which later gave rise to the collegiate system of government), transforming the state into an active force in the country's development, separating church and state, introducing free universal education, and granting union rights, the eight-hour workday, the right to divorce, and the right to vote for women. See also Rama 1972.

85. Perelli and Rial 1983, 151.

86. Constanza Moreira describes the hegemonic Batllista culture that emerged as forward-looking, urban, secular, egalitarian, statist, and centered on modern political parties. See Chávez 2004, 93.

87. The collegiate executive system replaced the president with a council of nine elected members (three of them from the opposition party) who took turns serving as president of the body. In 1931, the Colorado and Blanco parties signed a deal to divide executive positions in state enterprises and ministries among them on a three-to-two basis in favor of the winning

system, coupled with high levels of social mobility, generated a political culture that cherished democratic values, accepted the central role of political parties to articulate citizen's demands, and in general rejected extra-institutional forms of collective action.[88] Such was the influence of the country's traditional parties that it is often argued that in Uruguay political identity took precedence over social identity, as party traditions and loyalties became more important than class belonging in defining an individual's identity.[89]

The symbolic weight of political parties in national culture was also due to their proven flexibility and adaptability, their multi-class, catchall nature, and a complex set of electoral laws that created a de facto "fragmented" two-party system.[90] Curiously, each of the two traditional parties comprised radically different ideological tendencies thanks to the country's electoral laws, which allowed each party to put forward numerous slates of presidential candidates under a single party banner, or *lema*. Each slate represented the multiple political factions—ranging from the extreme Right to the left-of-center—that coexisted within each of the two traditional parties. As a result, candidates with radically different political programs ended up running under the same party banner. The *lema* that won the most votes would claim the presidency in a single electoral round. Then, within the winning party, the candidate with the most votes would take the presidency.[91] This complex system allowed traditional parties to appeal to multiple social groups, to incorporate diverse interests into the political process, and, conveniently, to make it hard for other political contenders to emerge.[92]

---

party. The deal granted both parties access to state resources, thus encouraging clientelism and the growth of state employment, but it also secured political stability since losing an election did not mean being completely out of power.

88. So strong was the parties' role in the country's political life that even the military seldom challenged their centrality in a democratic system, retaining a figurehead civilian president (with limited powers and appointed directly by the military) during eight of the eleven years of military rule. In fact, when President Bordaberry proposed the abolition of the party system and its restructuring along corporatist lines, the military quickly removed him from power. Unlike other military regimes—which relied on a strongman—the Uruguayan military high command adopted a collegiate structure where decision making was achieved through consensus and compromise among the various factions within the three branches.

89. Beisso and Castagnola (1987, 10) defined Uruguayan society as "politico-centric" to underscore the fact that political loyalties constituted the political axis in the country's process of identity formation.

90. Aguiar 1985.

91. González 1985.

92. According to Aguiar (1985, 16–17) this worked as a "fragmented" two-party system, giving the Blanco and Colorado parties 90 percent of the votes until 1971.

The political monopoly of the Colorado and Blanco parties changed in 1971 when a rainbow of leftist and left-of-center parties came together to form a coalition called the Broad Front, which presented a single presidential candidate—a retired army officer well known for his progressive democratic politics—in the elections that year. The coalition, equipped with a program that blended the progressive aspects of the Batllista project with moderate socialist ideas, appealed to the urban middle sectors, workers, and intellectuals, and received 21 percent of the vote. Members of the Broad Front became the primary targets of repression under the military regime (1973–84), suffering imprisonment, torture, disappearances, and exile. Nevertheless, following democratization the Broad Front coalition became a serious contender to win the presidency, steadily expanding its base of support through electoral alliances with splinter groups from the Blanco and Colorado parties.[93] In a desperate attempt to prevent a Broad Front victory, the traditional parties pushed through a reform to the country's electoral laws, which was approved by razor-thin margin in a December 1996 plebiscite vote. The new electoral law required the election of the president by absolute majority vote, if necessary through a second runoff race between the candidates who received the most votes in the first round.[94] While this reform kept the leftist coalition out of power in 1989 when the Colorado and Blanco parties united in the second runoff vote to narrowly defeat the Broad Front, it proved ineffective to prevent the rise of the leftist coalition to power five years later.

In 2004—one hundred years after the Batlle y Ordóñez elections that marked the start of modern politics in the country—Uruguayan voters in a second ballot vote gave the Broad Front the majority it had been pursuing since its founding in 1971, effectively ending the political monopoly that traditional political parties had enjoyed since independence in the early nineteenth century.[95] Shortly after the elections, a stunned José Mujica— a former Tupamaro guerrilla leader who had been jailed and tortured by

93. The incorporation of new groups into the coalition was reflected in the adoption of new names alongside the original Broad Front (Frente Amplio): in the 1989 elections it ran as Frente Amplio–Nuevo Espacio, and in 2004 it adopted the awkwardly long name Frente Amplio–Nuevo Espacio–Nueva Mayoría. For the sake of simplicity I will refer to it as the Broad Front throughout the book.

94. In a radical departure from the previous system, the new law required contending parties to present a single presidential candidate and up to three for the mayoral race.

95. Indeed, Uruguay and Colombia are the only Latin American nations where traditional parties dating from the early nineteenth century continued to exist and to govern well into the twenty-first century. See Mainwaring 1988; and Gillespie 1985.

the dictatorship and who emerged as one of the most popular and charismatic politicians of the post-authoritarian period—remarked in his typical style, "Not even García Márquez would have imagined this!"[96] The changing political landscape clearly showed that contrary to the thesis of continuity and restoration, much had changed in Uruguay following the return to democratic rule. Indeed, the left-of-center coalition had remarkably increased its electoral support from 21 percent to 51 percent between 1984 and 2004, while the combined electoral vote of the Blanco and Colorado parties dropped from 76 percent to an abysmal low of 46 percent during the same period.[97]

While the convincing leftist victory marked a break with political tradition, it also testified to the endurance of the country's democratic institutions.[98] Similar to the Chileans on the other side of the Andes, Uruguayan citizens remained committed to the ballot box and used existing political party structures to change political course, a stance that in part set them apart from their neighbors in nearby Argentina. For example, in reaction to the 2002 economic debacle, furious Argentinean citizens took to the streets chanting "Que se vayan todos!" (Let them all go!) to condemn the entire political class and to show how little esteem they had for political institutions. In contrast, Uruguayans did not respond to the economic crisis with angry demonstrations, showing instead a remarkable adherence to the institutions of representative democracy and remaining very much at the center of the political spectrum.[99]

The Uruguayan experience differs from that of Chile or Argentina in two fundamental aspects. One difference is the frequent use by Uruguayan citizens of mechanisms of direct democracy, such as plebiscites and referenda, to voice their opinion on a wide range of issues in the period after

96. Quoted in Caetano 2005, 16. Mujica would have been even more surprised if he had known that he would be elected to succeed Vázquez as the country's president five years later.

97. The Colorado Party was the most badly wounded, dropping to a historic low of only 10 percent of the vote. This is the most remarkable given that the Colorados had ruled Uruguay for most of the twentieth century, with the few exceptions of Blanco or military rule.

98. The 2008 UNDP Human Development Report shows that Uruguayans' support of democratic institutions is much stronger than that of the rest of the region. For example, while 79 percent of Uruguayans agree with the statement that democracy cannot exist without a parliament, only 59 percent of Latin Americans support this view. Likewise, while 77 percent of Uruguayan citizens believe that democracy cannot exist without political parties, only 55 percent hold this position in the rest of Latin America. See Couriel 2008.

99. While the vote for the Broad Front marked an important political rupture, it did not necessarily represent a radical departure from political tradition. In fact, people voted for the coalition because the Left presented an increasingly more moderate program that showed significant continuity with the Batllista legacy.

democratization. For decades, Uruguayans had the constitutional right to call binding referenda to change the constitution or to repeal legislation—all they had to do was to collect signatures from 25 percent of registered voters—but the few referenda that were held before the military takeover were always sponsored by the Blanco and Colorado parties to approve limited constitutional amendments. In contrast, since the return to formal democracy, grassroot coalitions of social movements and parties from outside the political establishment started to use referenda to change government laws and to curb neoliberal reforms. Between 1989 and 2004, for example, citizens called eleven referenda or plebiscites.[100] The first referendum campaign was organized in 1989 to repeal the amnesty law passed by Parliament granting immunity from prosecution to military officers implicated in human rights abuses, unleashing passionate debates about democracy and human rights in the post-authoritarian period. Although only 35 percent of Uruguayans voted to repeal the law, the experience set the foundations for more successful referendum campaigns later on. In 1992, 79 percent of Uruguayans annulled a law that had given the government carte blanche to privatize public enterprises, and in 2003 they voted to repeal legislation that that would have effectively privatized the country's only oil refinery. In 2004, a rainbow coalition of grassroot organizations and political parties set up the National Commission in Defense of Water and Life (Comisión Nacional en Defensa del Agua y de la Vida, CNDAV), which organized a historic referendum through which Uruguayans overwhelmingly declared water a public good, and therefore off-limits to private companies. It was the first referendum of its kind anywhere in the world.

The second difference setting Uruguay apart from Chile and to a lesser extent Argentina is the implementation of participatory democracy covering nearly half the country's population in the capital city. In this regard, Uruguay shares some of the features of the Brazilian participatory experience highlighted by Avritzer and studied by many researchers. In his study of participatory budgeting in the Brazilian city of Porto Alegre, for example, Baiocchi argues that the Workers' Party government successfully installed a new mode of urban governance and fashioned an innovative "empowered-participatory" state–civil society regime.[101] The notion of regime used by

100. They also attempted unsuccessfully another four times to collect the required signatures to call a referendum; in one case in which they collected the signatures, the government rescinded the law before the referendum even took place. See Moreira 2005.

101. Baiocchi (2005, 18–20) distinguishes two possible types of regimes: tutelage and democratic affirmative. In tutelage regimes, the state may be open to societal demands but it places

Baiocchi underscores the idea that differences in the state's openness to societal demands and in the existing institutional mechanisms to process them may produce different patterns of relations between the state and civil society.[102] Baiocchi suggests that the new regime in Porto Alegre included a city government that was not only sympathetic to popular demands, but also one that was willing to give up its role as the ultimate decision maker and that seriously encouraged residents to determine spending priorities among themselves.[103] Participatory budgeting, he argues, succeeded in attracting participation because resident decisions were respected by city authorities, and also because the model tied the allocation of municipal resources to the level of participation of each community in the early stages of drafting the municipal budget.

Interestingly, Baiocchi also found that the new state–civil society regime established by the Workers' Party did not operate uniformly across the city of Porto Alegre. In fact, he offers a rich account of the unique and diverse experiences that community activists had as they engaged with participatory budgeting in each of the three communities covered by his study. By looking at participation from the vantage point of local communities and using extensive qualitative fieldwork, Baiocchi shows how local factors generated distinct "civic practices" in each district, even though they operated within the same set of rules established by the macro-institutional framework of participatory budgeting. As a result, he documents quite convincingly the existence of strikingly different sets of informal rules among districts about appropriate forms of behavior that guided relations both among community activists and between them and municipal officials.

Through my own research I also came across considerable variation in

---

strong constraints on civil society, selectively recognizing demands in exchange for political acquiescence and delivering goods through clientelistic or corporatist mechanisms. In contrast, democratic regimes are more open to societal demands and place fewer obstacles to civil society input. These democratic regimes may be further distinguished into two subtypes, which he calls representative and empowered participatory regimes. While the former is based on representation, the later relies on bottom-up participation to process societal demands (19).

102. State–civil society regimes shape the character of both civil society and the state and are clearly connected to the associative cultures discussed above. By defining the range of legitimate repertoires of civic action that can be accommodated by institutions, they establish the terms for citizen participation and the kinds of action that can legitimately be undertaken by collective actors. They also set the range of acceptable postures that institutions can assume in their relations with civil society (Baiocchi 2005). See also the useful discussion of citizenship regimes provided by Yashar (2005) in her discussion of indigenous movements in Latin America.

103. Baiocchi's work draws on Avritzer's (2002) discussion of the civic-participatory model and the work of Fung and Wright (2003) on deliberative democracy.

the lived experiences of participatory decentralization in each barrio. In the following chapters I will document these differences and explain them in reference to the particular interplay of the three kinds of local contingencies identified above—namely, the nature of local associational cultures, socioeconomic conditions, and the attributes of local government officials. I will focus on specific barrios to learn how each community experienced participatory decentralization and generated its own participatory practices in light of their unique conditions. I selected three working-class neighborhoods for in-depth analysis—Peñarol, El Cerro, and La Teja—with similar socioeconomic backgrounds and levels of social capital, but with seemingly different levels of success in building participatory local government. Each of these barrios possessed a rich history of collective organizing as well as large stocks of social capital that shaped how local activists related to participatory decentralization and to the other communities they met in the structures of local government.[104] I examine how the local associative traditions forged in these barrios played out at the district level, especially in the neighborhood councils, where activists interacted with the bodies of local government.

My reconstruction of the history of these communities reveals that they are a microcosm of the country's development and are integrally subject to shifts in economic and social policies and to the ups and downs of the economy. The lives of people from these communities, as I will show, were affected in fundamental ways by the rise and fall of large industries—meatpacking in El Cerro and the railways in Peñarol—or by the vicissitudes of a whole range of smaller, nationally owned industries—in La Teja—that had prospered under the country's import substitution policies but collapsed with trade liberalization after the 1980s. In each of the three areas, I met deeply committed activists who fought against difficult odds to improve the quality of life in their communities. Embedded in neighborhoods with a strong sense of identity and a rich history of collective struggle, these activists responded eagerly to the call to become protagonists in building participatory democracy in their barrios. Their remarkable stories, including their successes and failures, are narrated in the following chapters.

---

104. Since the decentralization reforms clustered the city's sixty-two neighborhoods into eighteen administrative districts, all communities found themselves sharing a district with neighborhoods with different traditions and needs. In some cases they managed to build district-wide bridges of solidarity, while in others this proved more difficult.

CHAPTER 1

Peñarol: Participatory Decentralization in an "Easygoing" Former Railway Town

> We're not like the folks in neighboring Sayago or Colón, who are more dynamic, more urban. We are more like people from a small town or a village; we're not moving at top speed; we're more easygoing.
>
> —Cristina

> The strength of Peñarol was its railway. But when the government shut it down, lots of people were left stranded; some moved elsewhere and some retired. The railway was the heart of Peñarol, and the neighborhood was just left there, like so many country folk living where the train never arrived: forgotten, abandoned to the pages of oblivion.
>
> —Alberto

Community Profile

When I first visited Peñarol in 1987 to conduct fieldwork for my doctoral dissertation, I was struck by the deep sense of history and the tranquil lifestyle that characterized this former railway town of thirty-five thousand people. To reach Peñarol from the southern part of the city, where sandy beaches stretch for miles all the way to the Brazilian border, I drive for about twenty minutes until I reach Avenida Garzón, a street shadowed by leafy *platano* trees that takes me to the center of the community. I first pass by Centro Comunal 13, a well-kept but painfully inadequate white house that serves as the office of local government, and then the former car-assembly plant turned into a scooter factory after the American giant General Motors shut down operations in the early 1980s. A few minutes later, the street curves and suddenly the remnants of the British presence are visible everywhere, imprinted in the architecture of aging buildings and on the street signs: Calle Newton, Calle Fulton, Calle Watt.[1] I come face-to-face with the set of nineteenth-century English-style row houses that announce the start of the *casco histórico*. The houses, built for the skilled workers of the British railway, sit across from *La Casona*, a larger house that served as the living quarters of British upper managers. At the end of Garzón, I see the train tracks and the old railway station, two key markers of local identity. In spite of the station's old age and visible neglect, it is still possible to picture the days when hundreds of passengers passed through this once-prosperous railway town. The country's railway industry was headquartered here, and although it employed only two thousand people at its peak, nearly half the population depended directly or indirectly on the railways for wages or for business. The industry attracted hundreds of passengers and workers daily, making Peñarol a vibrant community and commercial center:

> ANTONIO:[2] Peñarol had a mighty economic motor in the railway, with all the activity that came with passengers, freight, people coming to say good-bye to those who were leaving, with the porters, the machinists, all this was in constant motion, and gave the town a purchasing power infinitely greater than it has today; it was another Peñarol altogether.

Across the street from the station lies the canteen of Antonio Pereyra's family. Antoñito, as the neighbors warmly call him, is a popular community activist who was once the most popular local councilor in the entire city. Antoñito is an avid conversationalist who loves to share his extensive knowledge of local history and current politics. As we talk, I come to realize how much the history of his family, like Peñarol itself, is closely intertwined with that of the railways. The Pereyras bought the business in the 1930s during the golden years of Peñarol. In those days, the twenty-two-room hostel located at the heart of town was a busy business that served more than two hundred meals daily:

> ANTONIO: We opened at five thirty in the morning because a ton of people would come to buy cigarettes, deli meat, sandwiches, cutlets,

---

1. In 1915 new street names were added, using the names of famous world poets, such as Shakespeare, Milton, Goethe, Lope de Vega, Dante, Becquer, and Longfellow (Barrios Pintos and Reyes Abadie 1994, 194).

2. The names of people whose quotes are used in the book have been replaced by pseudonyms to protect their identity.

wine to go. Lines of locals waiting for their coffee, which we heated up in pots because the coffee machines were not big enough. The station was a hive of activity that everyone passed through, but all this is gone now.

The trains no longer stop in Peñarol as they did for nearly a century before the government shut down passenger service in 1988. Peñarol is no longer the quintessential railway town and the epicenter of a vibrant railway industry, an identity it maintained until very recently. As I sit for hours chatting with Antonio in the empty pub, only an occasional customer walks in to drink a grappa or two. Sadly, the bar stands as a vivid illustration of the town's demise following the collapse of the railway industry. The only remaining signs of the "good old days" are the impressive countertop made of white Carrara marble, the display of local railway antiques that Antonio's father has collected over the years, and some dusty bottles of liquor from the 1940s that Antonio senior is still saving for a special occasion. Looking through the window across the street, I see the deserted railway station and the occasional freight train slowly passing through. Sadly, the pub and the station shared the same fate, standing today as testimonies of a time that will not return.

Twenty years after my first visit, Peñarol remains a peaceful place, greeting the visitor with an aura of serenity long gone in other city neighborhoods. The pace of life is more reminiscent of the lifestyle of the small towns in the "interior" than that of a capital city neighborhood. People are seldom in a rush here, seemingly enjoying a surplus of time, often willing to interrupt their daily routines to socialize with neighbors. Typically, they walk to local stores to do their daily grocery shopping, housewives spend a good part of their mornings sweeping the sidewalks, and older neighbors sit quietly on folding chairs outside their front doors watching life go by. The occasional street vendor passes by selling groceries door to door, a form of commerce no longer seen in most other neighborhoods. Behind the relaxed atmosphere lies a community rich in social life and with a strong sense of identity, where the street still provides a public space for community socializing.

Early Settlement: Italian Farmers

Antoñito insists that Peñarol had a history before the railways came to town. The origins of Peñarol date back to the mid-1800s when Italian farmers settled in the area to supply fruits and vegetables to the city of Montevideo and grapes to the nascent wine industry. Some of these early settlers came from the Pinerolo, an Italian town to the south of the Piedmont city of Turin, and it is from them that the locality adopted the name Peñarol.[3] Not much remains today of the luxuriant vineyards and farmlands, but some reminders of the period are still noticeable in the outskirts, such as the ramshackle villas, once the dwellings of successful Italian farmers and their families. These villas, which dominated the landscape for over a century, now sit awkwardly among hundreds of modest homes and the occasional industry that sprang up in the area during the past fifty years. The farmlands, which were the raison d'être of these villas, are disappearing fast, though there are still some pockets of green spaces and farming activity that give the area a distinct semirural appearance. The farming lifestyle introduced by the Italians still informs local culture,[4] even though the material basis for such an existence is long gone; in fact, many residents reminisce as often about the *quintas* as they do about the railways.[5]

The Golden Years: British Railways and the Introduction of Modern Capitalism

This quiet farming region changed drastically when the British Central Railroad Company settled in Peñarol in 1890, bringing the modern Industrial Revolution to the heart of the community. Peñarol's life became tied to the fortunes of the railway industry. Purchasing several farms in the area, the company constructed the *talleres*, industrial workshops for building and repairing the trains. Spanning more than ten hectares by 1924, the talleres already employed 1,300 workers, many of whom resided in Peñarol.[6] The

---

3. There are several stories about the origins of the unusual name of "Villa Peñarol," but they all agree that it is connected to the Italian town. Some say that the name comes from one of the earlier settlers, Pedro Pignarolo, whose original last name may have been changed to that of his hometown, Piganorolo, when he entered the country (as happened to so many immigrants). Other accounts attribute the name to Juan Bautista Crosa, an Italian settler who arrived in the region in 1765 and adopted the nickname "Pignarolo," the town where he was born (ibid., 189).

4. In 1882, nearly one-third of the more than three thousand residents of the area were of Italian descent (Barrios Pintos and Reyes Abadie 1994, 191). In 1884, a census of Montevideo showed that nearly half of the 115,500 people living in the city were foreign immigrants, the largest group being the Italians (33,000). See Pi Hugarte and Vidart 1969, 17.

5. The Italian influence is still evident in the country's day-to-day language, culinary culture, norms and values, family life, and music (Vidart and Pi Hugarte 1969, 33–37).

6. By 1950 they employed 1,500 and by 1960 2,000 workers, but not all of them resided in Peñarol; many were brought by train, free of charge, from adjacent towns by the railway company (Barrios Pintos and Reyes Abadie 1994, 189).

company also built the railway station, which became a nodal point in a network of railroad tracks linking different areas of the country with Montevideo harbor. The urban space reflected the centrality of the railway industry and its own hierarchical structure: the town radiated outward from the railway station, depriving local people of the public meeting spaces typically provided by Spanish towns, where the buildings of the main social institutions (church, government, justice, police) are centrally located around a large square. The houses for upper managers were placed together on one street, as were those for technical personnel and lower-level officials a few blocks away. On the other side of the tracks one could see several social, cultural, and sports centers and the technical school that trained future workers for the railway industry. Further away, across from the railway workshops, sat the simpler raw houses for workers.

British culture influenced Peñarol in numerous ways, especially through the introduction of an industrial work ethic and modern leisure activities. The Centro Artesano, built by the British in 1894, promoted multiple cultural and recreational activities, housing the first primary school in the area and offering programs in theater, cinema, music, and art, a pool house, chess competitions, dances, sporting events, and other family recreational activities. Mixing British and local traditions, women organized monthly tea dances as fund-raising events in support of poor children in the area.[7] The British also introduced soccer, which quickly became an important pastime and marker of local and national identity. In 1891, a number of railway executives and workers set up a fraternal sports club in Peñarol officially named Central Uruguay Railway Cricket Club, taking as its colors gold and black, the colors of the railroad company. This club became the first national champion in the country, and twenty years later it adopted the name Peñarol to honor the local town. The club went on to become one of the country's most prestigious and internationally recognized soccer teams, winning three intercontinental cups in the 1960s. As the cradle of Uruguayan soccer, Peñarol provided countless soccer stars to a national squad that was among the most successful in the world in the first half of the twentieth century. The small Latin American nation learned to master the European game, imprinting it with local culture and traditions; Uruguayans were the first Olympic champions in 1926, won the first World

7. In the mid-1930s, two other social centers were created (Peñarol Social Center and Uruguay Peñarol Social Center) as alternatives to the Centro Artesano, which was perceived by many as an elitist British creation serving the needs of older, more established residents.

Cup in 1930, and fetched the World Cup for a second time in 1950, all of which reinforced Peñarolenses' identification with their community.

Internal Migration and the Emergence of Neighborhood Associations

In the 1950s, a new wave of migrants came to live in the areas of the surrounding *quintas*, attracted by low real estate costs, easy access to Montevideo, and the prospect of a railway job. They were part of a movement of people from other parts of the country who migrated to Montevideo hoping to share in the city's economic prosperity.[8] Uruguay, already one of the most urbanized countries in Latin America, became the only country in the region where nearly half of the population had come to live in the capital city. Real estate entrepreneurs parceled out the farms on the fringes of the capital, hoping to attract those who could not afford the rising property prices in Montevideo. They offered reasonable prices for the plots of land, attractive low-interest loans, free construction materials, and a semirural setting that appealed to the newcomers.

Luis and Margarita were among these migrants. Recently wed, they decided to purchase a lot in Peñarol in what is known today as the neighborhood of Oriental Colón and quickly began to build their own house. Over the years, Luis and Margarita and their neighbors developed informal networks of solidarity and mutual help, helping one another to build their houses and working collectively to bring basic urban services and infrastructure—electricity, running water, and roads—to the community. Margarita keenly recalls the earlier times that established the foundations for community solidarity:

> When we moved to the neighborhood we bought a plot of land. The residents were so amazing; when a new person moved in to start to work on his house and had no running water, everyone came by to help hook up to the water supply. The day we put the roof on the house, no one would accept any payment and more than twenty people came to help. . . . We have lost all of that now.

8. Uruguay, however, did not experience the "urban explosion" of other Latin American countries at the time. Early in the twentieth century, it already had a sizable proportion of its population living in cities (29 percent), and by 1963 this figure had increased to 45 percent (Martorelli 1978, 63).

Today, the houses are modest but well maintained, displaying well-kept front gardens and large backyards with traditional, solid-brick BBQs and vegetable gardens. Building activity still goes on, as residents need to add an extra room or a second floor to accommodate the growing needs of their families. But the solidarity of earlier times is not commonly found. In recent years, labor is provided by relatives, close friends, and casual workers but not by the community at large. There are still plenty of open lands, aging vineyards, and fruit farms, as well as the occasional industry, giving the community a distinct feel that distinguishes it from the urban *casco* near the railway station.

Over the years, Luis and Margarita became important community leaders, pioneers in the earlier struggles for urban services. They helped found the Oriental Colón Neighborhood Association, a community-based organization set up in the early 1960s, and thanks to their efforts Oriental Colón now enjoys all basic urban services, such as electricity, running water, and roads, and is integrally incorporated into the community of Peñarol. Through these experiences of securing urban goods, residents developed a strong sense of territorially based community identity, first as members of the neighborhood of Oriental Colón, then as Peñarolenses. In the late 1980s, they obtained funding from an Italian foundation to build a community center equipped with a dance hall, a library, and an outdoor park for young children. Serving as a cultural and social meeting space, the center offers residents free courses and some services, as well as the opportunity to come together to celebrate community events, national holidays, special family days, birthdays, and so forth.

Luis and Margarita could not have known then that these pioneering experiences in community building would catapult them into the center of local politics a few decades later. Luis, now in his seventies, has an impressive resume in community organizing and enjoys widespread respect and admiration beyond the boundaries of his community. "El Viejo" (the Old Man), as he is warmly referred to by his friends, currently serves as the president of the local junta in district 13, which places this longtime member of the Communist Party and community activist at the center of local politics, allowing him to influence municipal decisions in ways that he could not have imagined when he came to the community almost fifty years ago:

> Before it was so much harder. We had to negotiate with the political bosses of the neighborhood in order to get even the most basic things.

Now we don't have to go begging for anything because we ourselves are the government. Now we can decide what we want for the zone and decide how much to invest in public works. This is the big difference.

As he talks to me in his office in his slow, deeply reflective manner, he is constantly interrupted by incoming phone calls from local businesspeople, municipal officers, and neighbors, which makes me realize that interviewing him at work was not such a good idea and that I should have taken him up on his invitation to talk at his home on a Sunday afternoon. Listening to him, I realize that he has a remarkable capacity to consult and to make consensual decisions. I am also pleased to confirm that he remains the humble and sensitive person I met nearly twenty years ago; the power of his office has not "gone to his head," as happened to several leaders in other communities. While he is on the phone, my mind drifts back to the late 1980s, when Luis and Margarita and other community activists were determined to bounce back from the catastrophe created by the collapse of the railway industry.

The Devastation of the Railway

Shortly after World War II, the Uruguayan state acquired ownership of the British-owned railways for £7.15 million. The deal, signed in 1948, was Great Britain's partial payment for the £17 million it owed Uruguay for the provision of beef during the war. In 1952, the Uruguayan government set up the Administración de Ferrocarriles del Estado (AFE), bringing all railways under a single state-run company that enjoyed a monopoly over railway communications. The establishment of a state enterprise was not a novel idea in a country that, early in the century, had turned the state into a central engine of development, providing public utilities, financial and insurance services, production activities, and transport services.[9] Despite the broad consensus in favor of state interventionism, however, Uruguayan governments had consistently avoided nationalizing the railways for fear of reprisals by the powerful British, the main consumers of Uruguayan beef, which was the country's primary export commodity. Searching for a less confrontational strategy, the state built networks of roads alongside the tracks to compete with the de facto British monopoly over surface transportation. Paradoxically, when the railways finally came under

9. See the introduction in this volume.

state control they were no longer profitable, as the British Central Railroad Company had long ago stopped investing in infrastructure and the industry faced fierce competition from trucks and buses, which used the roads built by the state. The economic crisis in the postwar period caused by the decline of the beef industry, the basis of the country's prosperity, reduced state capacity to modernize the railways. Lack of investment and poor management exacerbated the problems, and the railway industry—the heart and soul of Peñarol for more than a half century—rapidly took a downward turn.[10]

The crisis sealed the fate of the community, producing a domino effect that led to the closing of many of the services that Peñarol had gained over the years. The only theater and two movie houses were shut down in the 1960s, the local bank branch closed in 1971, while the police station, the health clinic, the ambulance service, and the post office that operated inside the train station were all lost in 1982. The final blow came in 1988, when AFE eliminated all passenger service, and closed down the railway station and the talleres. Peñarol suddenly looked like a ghost town, a living museum of abandoned buildings that reminded residents of the world they had lost:

> MARIA: When the train quit running, many small towns in the interior died, those through which the train simply passed. It was all the worse here, where the train did not simply pass by, but where it was repaired, and where the railway workers and rail company managers lived. So when they did away with the railway, Peñarol felt it hard. . . . People felt the presence of death, and, even more, as though the corpses had been left behind. What I am saying is horrible but true; the workshops, the station, everything physically located in the neighborhood, all intertwined—it affects you to see, everyday, these monuments to what has ceased to be.

The Community Fights Back: Fostering an Effective School of Community Mobilization

When I traveled to Uruguay in 1987 to conduct research on urban social movements following the transition to democratic rule, the neighborhood

---

10. Peñarol was not an isolated case. In the 1950s the country's model of development based on beef exports and import substitution entered a deep crisis from which it never recovered. The impact of this crisis was also felt in the other communities covered in this study, as we will see in subsequent chapters.

of Peñarol attracted my attention because it appeared to be an island of effective community activism in a sea of disillusionment and demobilization. It was precisely in Peñarol where local activists had avoided the pitfalls of other movements across the city, successfully adapting to the new opportunities created by the democratic context to fight for urban collective goods. Residents of Peñarol had created an umbrella organization called MIRPA (Mesa Intersocial Reivindicadora de Peñarol y Adyacencias), the only organization of its kind in the entire city, uniting numerous local groups around a common project of fostering community development and recovering lost services:

> CRISTINA: With MIRPA we managed to unite the neighborhood associations, and we got them to sit at the table with the school committees, with the women's groups, with the pensioners, with the grandparents, with the business people, with the Church, with the reflection groups of the parish, with the co-ops. . . . That is, we brought together all of organized civil society in the zone. I believe that this was the most important experience we've had in Peñarol: sitting down together.

MIRPA became a vibrant organization, bringing together a wide array of local organizations, including neighborhood associations, housing co-ops, a health clinic, a local health commission, a primary school, several social clubs, the pastoral council of the local church, an artisan cooperative, the railway union, the senior citizens association, local businesspeople, and neighbors. This was no small accomplishment, and MIRPA soon established itself as the principal reference point in the community, mediating between local civil society, the state, and nongovernmental actors. No one would have imagined back then that the experience of MIRPA would have such a lasting impact on the community. MIRPA became a model for an effective kind of community activism rooted in strong networks of trust among local organizations and individuals as well as a proven capacity to use skillful negotiation and lobbying to draw resources to the area. MIRPA established a reputation in the city as an effective organization and became actively involved in MOVEMO (Movimiento de Vecinos de Montevideo), a citywide organization uniting the urban social movements. More broadly, MIRPA produced a school of participation and citizenship unique in the city, and built important stocks of social capital that would be useful for the future development of the community when decentralization opened new opportunities for local movements.

Returning in 1998, eight years after the election of Vázquez to the city government, I was welcomed by many of the local activists whom I had met during my previous fieldwork. They proudly took me on a tour of the neighborhood to show me how much they had accomplished since my last visit. The results were impressive. Community leaders were working on an urban renewal plan for Peñarol in collaboration with architects from the Faculty of Architecture at the country's public university. Their key demands from the 1980s—which included a community health center, a high school, and a cultural center—had already been met, and plans to connect the area to the city's sewer system were well underway. Indeed, MIRPA proved to have a remarkable capacity for capturing resources for community development projects through negotiations and partnerships with multiple layers of governmental and nongovernmental institutions. Not surprisingly, community activists felt empowered by the realization that their collective efforts and their skills in navigating through the changing waters of municipal politics could bring about important improvements in their lives.

Local activists had not only secured new investments but had used their contacts with the railway authorities (AFE) to reclaim some of the unused railway buildings, bringing them back into community service:

> CRISTINA: We have things that other neighborhoods don't; we have access to spaces or facilities that AFE is not using, and the locals have a good relationship with AFE. People from Peñarol have been a part of AFE for many years, so they see us as serious, as peaceful but determined to meet our goals.

Meeting with the AFE authorities, the legal owners of these buildings, to persuade them to support these projects was not a simple task. It required patience, persistence, and clever negotiating skills. In the end, however, the strategy worked:

> AMALIA: We went every day at five in the morning to AFE to sit there; at nine another group went to relieve the first, and at twelve another group came, until the director would come talk to us, and we could ask for the buildings for the high school, for MIRPA. In the end we managed to get together and . . . got the house for MIRPA, the rest of the buildings for the high school, and later another building was made available for the language school.

Convincing the leadership of AFE was not easy. Understandably, before committing to donating the buildings they wanted guarantees that other agencies would invest resources in the project and put those buildings to good use. Navigating the complex bureaucratic networks to bring together all the stakeholders required outstanding negotiating skills and careful strategizing. Residents conducted parallel negotiations with several government agencies, such as the Ministries of Education and Public Health. The challenge was to win the support of each agency and to link these various units of government to facilitate dialogue among them. The main stumbling block was that, before making a commitment, each government agency demanded guarantees from other agencies that they would also support the project; since no one was willing to take the first step, it became difficult to break the impasse and move forward.

The projects to build the local high school and the health center illustrate the tenacity and effective lobbying strategy of MIRPA activists. The case for the high school rested on the premise that Peñarol needed a school to educate its youth locally in order to consolidate community identity:

> CRISTINA: What we hoped to do with the high school is to ensure that kids would stay longer in the neighborhood. Because before, they would finish regular school and have to leave the neighborhood to go to high school because there wasn't one here. And for high school they would go to Colón or Sayago, make new friends there, and start to pull away from here.

What gave more weight to the proposal was their commitment to mobilize the community to help renovate the buildings and build portable classrooms, as well as the guarantee of ongoing parental involvement to support the school. The approach worked, and parents and community leaders secured the support of the minister of education in a single face-to-face meeting with him. Encouraged by this development, they quickly met the national director of secondary education, hoping that she would speed up the process to prevent the project from getting stuck in the web of bureaucratic steps that typically kills many worthy initiatives. The story of what happened at this meeting is widely known in the community, and local activists never tire of recounting the moment when the director made the crucial phone call to break the impasse:

> ANTONIO: There we're going to talk to Dr. Cantonel, who was the director of secondary education, and we proposed the idea. Cantonel

taught Berchesi, who was the president of AFE. She made a phone call right in front of us and said, "Hey there, I need one of the houses on Sayago Avenue because we're going to open a high school in Peñarol." She was a former teacher and now director of secondary education calling her former student, the president of AFE, the two of them of the Colorado Party. Result: in June 1989 the high school opened in Peñarol!

The high school was inaugurated in the former administrative building located near the train station at the corner of Avenida Garzón and Marconi. Unsuited for educational purposes, the building had to be renovated to serve the needs of the 270 local students. The community delivered on its promise, collecting materials and building what became known as *El Gallinero*, a set of portable classrooms at the back of the building, close to the railway tracks, to accommodate the overflow of students. Newly renovated, the school looked attractive in the century-old building, with its outside walls painted white, its antique ceramic tile and white marble floors, and a mature palm tree standing proud and tall at the front gate. The school principal told me that one of the most rewarding aspects of her job was to direct a school that had become the pride of the community and that could count on so much parent involvement, something she had never experienced in other working-class neighborhoods.

The project to set up the community-run Health Center Zully Sanchez is another example of effective community organizing and skillful negotiating. Local activists organized a number of public meetings to gather community support for the initiative. Using the experience of the high school project, they guaranteed that residents would assume full responsibility over the administration of the health center. To get the clinic, MIRPA leaders and the Neighborhood Association Nuevo Peñarol involved relevant government bodies and also local and international NGOs. They brokered a groundbreaking agreement with AFE for the donation of the building, persuaded the municipality to cover the salaries of the clinic's doctors, and secured the support of an Italian NGO to provide the funds to renovate the building. The facility opened its doors in 1996 as a community-run clinic, adopting the name of one of its early advocates, a medical doctor from a housing cooperative in the area who had died of cancer. Located in the refurbished *La Casona*, the large brick building that housed top British managers, the health clinic goes a long way toward compensating for the 1982 loss of health services. It started with the services of a family doctor, a pediatrician, a gynecologist, and two nurses, and has since added services in ophthalmology, cardiology, dermatology, psychology, otolaryngology, and social work. Volunteers from the community perform all the administrative work.

Explaining Success

The experience of community activism in Peñarol is in many respects a success story. A community that was badly beaten got back on its feet and worked to secure resources for the community, inserting itself effectively into the newly created local government structures. Encouraged by these developments, I returned to Peñarol in 2004 to study this example of effective community mobilization within the changing institutional context of municipal politics. My main concern was twofold. First, I wanted to understand how local stocks of social capital (traditions, capacities, etc.) conditioned the ability of communities to seize (or miss) the opportunities generated by the citywide project to decentralize municipal politics and administration. Second, I wanted to see whether the local culture embedded in these traditions and practices shaped the functioning and character of local government itself.[11]

I came to the conclusion that in Peñarol community leaders effectively deployed local resources and skills to take advantage of the opportunities offered by decentralization. Through their active engagement with the project of decentralization, they imprinted local government institutions with the kind of local culture and traditions they had nurtured over the years, providing valuable leadership experience, sharing their traditions with activists from other areas in the district and building bonds of trust and cooperation with them, and adapting to the demands of the new institutional reality. As a result, they helped produce the positive synergy that runs through local government institutions in district 13, allowing them to reduce the potential problems created by the model of institutional design adopted by the city government.

---

11. To do this, I found it more useful to study one community rather than to focus on the larger and more heterogeneous district made up by different neighborhoods. By focusing on a more integrated and cohesive barrio, sharing a common history and similar socioeconomic conditions, I could analyze in greater depth local traditions, levels of social capital, values, and resources, in order to explore how these local associational cultures intersected with the institutions of local government, where activists from different neighborhoods came together.

To fully understand how activists from Peñarol accomplished this, I must first explain the origins of community organizing in the area, the kind of traditions and the specific kinds of capacities and resources that were produced by local militants, and the significance of the umbrella organization MIRPA, to which I now turn.

Forging a Local Tradition of Negotiation, Community Solidarity, and Proposition

I started all my interviews with community activists by asking them to tell me about the three images that first came to their minds when I mentioned the name of their community; typically, the railways and the quintas topped the list, followed by images of a serene, small-town lifestyle as something that set them apart from other neighborhoods:

> CARLOS: Geographic barriers leave Peñarol boxed in, with only three access points, so it is like a little country town in the middle of Montevideo. This explains the small town lifestyle here, without the hurry that you might find in other neighborhoods, where the rhythm of the residents is more urban than in Peñarol, where we are more like villagers.

I found that Peñarol's laid-back idiosyncrasy colors local politics and shapes the nature of community activism in the area. The people of Peñarol are certainly less fervent, but not necessarily less determined, than activists in the other communities I studied, and their debates are less heated, their meetings more orderly, and their conflicts tend to be resolved more easily and consensually:

> CRISTINA: We're more easygoing. How so? We work out our worries, our anxieties in a different way; we're less aggressive, less conflictive, less polemical. And I see this, because when we get together with residents of other zones we are always the most quiet ones; I don't know, we have a different way of putting things.

These deeply rooted local cultural traditions became embedded in the operation of local government institutions, contributing to their success in building effective participatory experiences.

The origins of this local idiosyncrasy may go back to the unique lifestyle brought by migrants who settled in the farmland areas north of the railway tracks:

> CRISTINA: I think it has to do with the zone having a lot of farmland, of green space, in which there is the influence of foreigners who lived a quiet life in the countryside, involving a lot of contact with nature, with the land. The environment has an influence on the people in Peñarol, and this is related a lot to the farms.

Interestingly, the subsequent establishment of the railway industry and the resulting unionization of railway workers did not completely erode this semirural culture. In fact, trade union traditions among railways workers may have been colored by the more relaxed local customs, producing a less radical trade union culture than that of the workers in the other two neighborhoods covered in this book. People in Peñarol do not have strong traditions of union militancy in part because railway workers were dispersed throughout the country, in contrast to the other two communities, where factory and community occupied the same space. Moreover, while local identity recognizes the needy conditions of the community, this awareness does not translate into an explicit working-class identity. Territorial, community-based identity—town rather than class—distinguishes Peñarol from the other two communities covered in this study.

Luis and Margarita offer a living testimony of how the mid-twentieth-century experiences of urban community development on the outskirts of Peñarol produced a strategy, which combined working through clientelistic networks with more hands-on activities that relied on voluntary labor. In the early days, the newcomers helped one another build their houses and worked together to obtain urban services such as electricity, running water, telephone service, roads, and public transportation. Since the provision of these urban goods was the responsibility of state authorities, community activists had to learn to use the clientelistic networks that had been built over the years by the ruling Colorado Party.[12] In fact, most of the more seasoned community leaders, like Luis and Margarita, had their first experiences in community organizing during these times. They established neighborhood associations and learned to work with and manipulate clientelistic networks to get services for the community. For years, they patiently

---

12. The Colorado Party monopolized national and city politics during the entire twentieth century, winning all but two elections before the military coup of 1973.

built networks of contacts and negotiated with people in power, viewing this as the most viable strategy for their community.

Needless to say, these clientelistic networks were based on, and in turn reproduced, dependency relations that tied local communities to local politicians through asymmetrical power relations. According to many studies, these relations discourage the emergence of horizontal linkages and autonomous mobilization among members of poor communities. As they made use of these networks, however, local activists found space to make the system work for them—especially during the more prosperous postwar years when the Uruguayan state had resources to hand out to poor communities—developing outstanding negotiating skills and learning to use to their own advantage a system that rested on power inequalities. In the process, they developed a culture that stressed patience and persistence, and encouraged nonconfrontational and inclusive politics, all of which became embedded in the traditions of local neighborhood associations. This nonsectarian approach to local politics was based on the premise that residents had to band together to exploit every possible contact they may have with people in power, and it acknowledged that those who had the best contacts were affiliated with the Colorado Party.[13]

These experiences convinced local activists that it was possible, and even desirable, to unite around community development projects regardless of political or religious affiliation, a tradition that is still maintained in Peñarol. Sandro, a Communist Party militant who is also the president of a local neighborhood association, explained this to me:

> Our neighborhood committee is made up of residents and in the committee we never discuss politics or religion. It is a rule and in the neighborhood councils you have to respect this, because the councils must serve the neighborhood, independently of political affiliation. If you start doing things for the flag of your political party, not for the good of the neighborhood, then you are blundering.

The capacities fostered in securing urban services during this earlier period became deeply engrained in local political culture and traditions, and

13. While the Colorado Party held the key positions of power in the state administration due to its political dominance throughout most of the twentieth century, the Blanco Party also had access to important posts due to the power-sharing formula established in 1931 (see the introduction in this volume). Thus community activists had to nurture relations with a wide array of political brokers belonging not only to two parties but also to their many internal factions, and established politically diverse neighborhood associations as the best instruments to access the plurality of political power brokers that were spread across public offices.

made up a reservoir of knowledge—like a set of "transferable skills"—that would later be adapted to new contexts of community development. These capacities became critically important, for example, in resisting dictatorial rule, setting up MIRPA following democratization, shaping the character of local government institutions following the election of the Left to the city government, and effectively seizing the opportunities offered by decentralization. The most important activists in the community draw from these experiences:

> JACINTA: Those I have seen work best are the people who have prior experience in community work or in neighborhood associations, because a neighborhood association also has its own regulations regarding who can vote, how a plan of action is to be chosen, how to implement this plan, what things must be done, how to inform the residents of what is being done . . . all this is done well in the case of councilors who have much experience with community work, experience that they apply and adapt to all this.

Railway Workers' Trade Unionism: A Preference for Negotiation

Negotiation, rather than confrontation, also became the preferred mode of trade union activism among railway workers, in contrast to the more radical stance that emerged in the other communities covered in this study. In part, the origins of a less radical tradition came from the kind of labor-management relations established under British ownership. In contrast to the more confrontational approach adopted by American management in the beef industry of El Cerro, British railway managers embraced a more flexible stance, encouraging negotiations and granting concessions as long as the railways kept running and the business remained profitable. Such an approach favored dialogue with the railway union, whose leaders operated more within the framework of negotiation than of confrontation. This preference for moderation, as I pointed out, was also reinforced by the geographical dispersion of railway workers across the national territory and by the decline of railway communications. Unlike the more militant working-class communities of El Cerro and La Teja, for whom home and workplace were concentrated in a single space, railway workers had to make their homes in every town reached by the railways.

The nationalization of the railways changed the industry, making management decisions subject to a political logic rather than the market logic followed by capitalist business. State enterprises became an integral component of the redistributive policies followed by the welfare state, as they facilitated access to services through subsidized rates and generated jobs to redistribute resources through salaries and benefits. Embracing these paternalistic and redistributive policies, AFE authorities fostered good relations with the union and encouraged the continuation of labor relations based on dialogue. In Peñarol, they also cultivated paternalistic ties with the community at large, which would be used by residents to negotiate the use of the abandoned railway buildings several years later. The approach adopted by AFE authorities helped maintain and further consolidate the culture of negotiation and the tendency toward a less radical trade unionism among railways workers.

When the government eliminated thousands of jobs by shutting down passenger service and closing the talleres, the Union Ferroviaria (the railway workers union) did not present the kind of defiant resistance offered by workers in other industries that suffered a similar fate, such as those in the other two communities I studied. In part, potential radical opposition was defused by a clever strategy of closing the industry in small steps. Moreover, since the railways were owned by the state, railway workers were considered civil servants and, as such, they could not be coldly fired, as could workers employed by private companies. Most lost their railways jobs but not their incomes, as they were relocated to other state enterprises or received early retirement bonuses.

Housing Co-ops: Latecomers Bring New Resources to Peñarol

The arrival of the nearly four hundred families who came in the early 1970s to set up the housing cooperative Mesa 2 on the northern side of the railway tracks had a lasting impact on the community. The huge housing blocks that are part of Mesa 2 changed the physiognomy of the community. The establishment of the cooperative also precipitated a shift in the center of gravity of community life: commercial activity moved away from the *casco antiguo* near the train station to the northern side of the tracks, attracted by the "middle-class" purchasing power of the *cooperativistas*.

Mesa 2 belonged to a national housing cooperative movement that emerged in Uruguay in the mid-sixties in response to the rapid decline in living standards caused by the reduction of state-provided social welfare.[14] The Uruguayan Federation of Mutual Aid Housing Cooperatives (Federacion Uruguaya de Cooperativas de Vivienda por Ayuda Mutua, FUCVAM) was set up in 1970 to promote the construction of housing cooperatives, and it erected nearly fifteen thousand housing units in three decades. These cooperatives were set up on cheaper lands with insufficient services near or within established working-class neighborhoods. They were typically large housing complexes of three hundred to five hundred families to make construction and access to services more cost-effective. Since the early days of setting up the cooperative, members engaged in complex negotiations with state agencies to ensure the provision of urban services, thereby developing capacities in negotiation and technical knowledge, and often learning to offer some form of counterpart contribution from the cooperative.

FUCVAM promoted solutions to housing problems, fostering values and practices of solidarity and mutual help, and became an important social movement alongside the trade union and student movements, especially during the dictatorship, when it acted as an important pillar of resistance to military rule. The cooperative housing movement offered a democratic and participatory alternative culture to the authoritarian project of the dictatorship, turning FUCVAM into an important actor during and following the transition to democracy:

> RITA: FUCVAM was a very important social movement, the only one of its kind at the time, I believe. In the period of the dictatorship, it was practically the only one that could take to the streets and this we have retained. And you also learn to self-manage, to follow an administrative protocol and keep everything in order; it is like taking care of a big house, one smaller than the district.

FUCVAM built a highly participatory tradition based on the principle of active membership and mutual help that fostered certain capacities among members. Co-ops required members to participate in planning, building, and running the organization, promoting a participatory culture and securing the ongoing engagement of members in managing all aspects of life in the community. Most cooperatives set up community-run social services such as health clinics, primary schools, day care centers, libraries,

---

14. In this section I draw from Chávez and Carballal 1997.

and gyms, filling the void left by a retreating state and impoverished trade unions, the institutions that formerly provided some of these services. To do this, they developed partnerships with governmental and nongovernmental agencies, retaining responsibility for managing the services and building important stocks of leadership, organizational, and administrative capacities. Cooperatives imparted to members important skills in collective decision making, resource management, and budgeting, and fostered a socially committed approach to community development based on the values of self-reliance, mutual aid, solidarity, and participation:

> CRISTINA: What this cooperativist society teaches you is how to organize. . . . We are masters at organization! Enough to have an issue, and lickety-split, you get organized, you know, this goes here, this goes there, you know, the transportation here, take this from here, the venue at wherever—amazing! This way of organizing you can apply to whatever situation; it's like a—how to call it—natural system. If you're in the school committee but they don't know how to start, you just come out with these things that you know and they catch on right away; these aren't things from outer space, it seems these things are natural; they have to do with life, so they are natural also for those who do not belong to the cooperative. The organizing part we have all figured out.

Cooperatives nurtured public relations and negotiating skills through their ongoing dealings with various government agencies, including the National Housing Fund (the institution that provided the initial loans to build the co-ops), municipal authorities, state-owned utility companies, and various government ministries, such as Education, Public Health, Interior, and so forth. Cooperatives also developed relations with civil society organizations, such as trade unions, student organizations, cultural associations, neighborhood committees, business and professional associations, and NGOs.

The capacities generated through the experience of building housing cooperatives could potentially be transferred to new settings and adapted to pursue different objectives. If diffused beyond the boundaries of the housing project, the traditions, knowledge, and values developed within cooperatives could greatly enhance the organizational capability and the development of the surrounding communities. Such skills in negotiation, project design, and resource management could also help promote a more "propositional culture," overcoming the tendency toward demand making typical of the country's political culture:

> CRISTINA: One learns here inside that you don't go just to make demands; you have also to make proposals. Why? Because we are the ones who decide; we're the owners and we're the ones who have to do everything. Cooperativism is like that. There's no one who is going to just give us things. You learn to design projects because it's you who is going to have to make them happen. These are the little things that one takes from this experience and applies elsewhere. Each situation is different, but the essence, the core of what one learns here, one can take and apply anywhere.

Unfortunately, these potentially transferable capacities often stayed within the confines of housing co-ops and were seldom shared with the communities where the cooperatives had been implanted. Many co-ops remained aloof to the circumstances affecting the wider communities where they were situated, instead turning inward, acting more like gated communities:[15]

> CRISTINA: When we came to the cooperative in '74 things weren't easy. For three hundred eighty families to come to an agreement, draft a constitution and rules about how to live together, this took us a good year of work. We were deeply engaged, very inwardly focused to finish the work. This took us about a year, but then we were done. We were very inwardly focused, very inwardly focused.

This insular stance characterized the leadership of Mesa 2, but it did not prevent a small group of individuals from the cooperative from linking up with community activists outside the co-op. They brought an innovative vision and new resources and capacities that converged with local traditions, helping to strengthen and unify the somewhat fragmented and localized community development experiences in the area. The approach—advocated by two medical doctors and a handful of activists from the cooperative—was relatively simple and effective, leading to the unification of

---

15. When I asked about the contribution of the cooperative movement to the process of decentralization, a high-ranking official in the municipal government expressed disappointment that housing cooperatives had not done enough to support the government's calls to build participatory local government.

local organizations under the umbrella of MIRPA.[16] Departing from a key social problem affecting the community at large—namely, the lack of health-care facilities—they aimed to connect with local organizations to raise awareness about other issues affecting the community. Their efforts to promote a community politics around social issues converged with the existing grassroot work of local activists to facilitate the emergence of MIRPA:

> CRISTINA: MIRPA started here, with the health clinic. It started because comrade Sergio Hernández, the doctor, said we should start our work by focusing on health, because when people have no jobs they lose their health; if you don't have a house, you lose your health; if you have no leisure, you lose your health. From a health perspective, you can address all the needs people have. That's how MIRPA started. It started with the health clinic, when we held the first community meeting with the organizations on August 15, 1985, when we gathered in the co-op's communal room.

The Birth of MIRPA and the Consolidation of a Community Tradition

The origins of MIRPA, therefore, can be traced to the confluence of three strands of local community activism that came together toward the end of the dictatorship and the dawn of democratic rule. One strand came from a small but cohesive group of activists from the Mesa 2 housing cooperative, who provided the impetus and the vision to organize a public community *encuentro* (town hall meeting), bringing together local organizations and individuals from different political traditions to identify the most pressing community problems and to design strategies to address them. These activists provided skills in resource management, proposal making, and self-reliance based on the tradition of cooperativism discussed above. The second current came from the traditional neighborhood associations that had operated for decades within clientelistic networks and had organized community-development initiatives based on neighbor solidarity. This tradition provided seasoned and proven nonsectarian leaders from different political ideologies, all of whom had mastered the art of negotiation

---

16. These cooperative activists had developed contacts with other leftist militants in the community through their political participation in the clandestine struggles against the dictatorship.

through years of dealing with municipal authorities and other levels of government. The third strand came from left-wing political militants who had found a refuge in community activism in the years of repression during the dictatorship. This group overlapped with the other two but was primarily driven by a more ideological perspective and a strong commitment to social justice. Militants from this tradition did not have much experience around territorially based mobilization or even a clear commitment to community-based activism. Indeed, following the return to democracy, many of them abandoned community activism and rejoined political parties, and even paid little attention to decentralization after the election of the Broad Front government. Some of them, however, remained active in community affairs, joining with the more experienced activists belonging to neighborhood associations or the housing co-op.

The task of bringing these diverse traditions together was facilitated by the work of specific individuals with outstanding leadership capacities who persuaded others, especially left-wing militants, to mobilize around social rather than narrowly constructed political demands:

> ANTONIO: MIRPA began with two or three thinkers who had a very clear idea about how to get the thing going. They were social activist types, with far-reaching goals. They raised the demand to get the high school and other groups of people started to get involved. That's what got me involved. And those who got involved in MIRPA started to adopt a particular social vision, a social politics that superseded partisan political positions, and this is what allowed MIRPA to galvanize. It was difficult because we came into it with a leftist, partisan political outlook, but we began to open up a little; we agreed that, if we hoped to achieve anything, we would have to change. . . . MIRPA started to take shape when it proved itself, as it did with the foundation of the high school in 1989; by then, we had twenty organizations behind us, working with us in the high school committee, but MIRPA was the real engine driving that initiative.

Building Links with Others Outside the Community

While strong leadership played a vital role in facilitating the convergence of the traditions of cooperativism, clientelistic community development, and left-wing activism, MIRPA's work received a big boost with the support of NGOs, social movements, and academics:

ANTONIO: There were three or four things that allowed us to succeed. The gals who joined us [in 1987–88] from what was the social work school gave us a working methodology. The work of the Aportes Group [Grupo Aportes, a community development group] helped us understand where we stood. The professional support of the Faculty of Architecture, together with the Universidad de la República, also helped us a lot.

The community of Peñarol, however, was not a passive recipient of outside aid. On the contrary, community activists consciously created the conditions to attract help to the area by putting their networking skills to good use and making sure that their earlier success in mobilizing the community, especially the creation of MIRPA, did not go unnoticed outside the boundaries of Peñarol.

MIRPA activists joined MOVEMO, and began networking with other urban movements in the city and with community development NGOs. MIRPA also received national recognition when a Communist Party MP spoke in Parliament in support of their efforts, precipitating a rush of newspaper articles on the umbrella organization. Such effective "marketing" attracted the attention of academics and NGOs who would provide support through institutional partnerships. It was precisely the success of community mobilization in Peñarol that accounts for the external support they received, which allowed them to further enhance local capacities for effective community mobilization. In other words, MIRPA leaders skillfully used their success as a marketing tool to attract additional support from the university and NGOs.

In 1987, I myself was attracted to the area because of MIRPA's success; I ended up conducting a survey of 250 households, which I made available to community leaders, offering a socioeconomic profile of the area and identifying community needs as defined by residents. At around the same time, upon learning about the outreach programs for low-income neighborhoods run by the Faculty of Architecture of the Universidad de la República, MIRPA leaders approached professors from the Institute of Urban Studies and proposed to work together to conduct a diagnostic study of local needs and design an urban development plan to revitalize the community. Their effort paid off and the architects sent one of their teams to Peñarol to work with MIRPA in what became the first of a series of ongoing projects in the area. The association with community organizations proved so positive that the faculty made a long-term commitment to the area, deciding to allocate to Peñarol, on an ongoing basis, one of their three annual outreach projects in the city. Following the identification of community needs, architects helped design an ambitious urban development project, which included the following goals: "To reverse the process of population loss, to create employment in the zone, to prevent the loss of social services and the deterioration of architectonic patrimony and of public spaces in general; to develop bonds of solidarity, environmental and territorial responsibility, and a sense of neighborhood identity."[17]

Other units from the university, including the Faculties of Psychology and Social Work, also became involved in Peñarol, conducting research and offering professional advice. Social work students, for example, came to Peñarol to offer valuable group work training:

ANTONIO: The school of social work came to MIRPA in the form of three scholarship students, in 1987–88, who helped us to organize our ideas, to elaborate projects, to use a flip chart, things that were basic. That is, the classic flip charts hung on the wall, with various pages that you go turning over and putting in order. To know how to hold workshops, how to undertake projects—methodology for working as a team. Moreover, because we had guests among us who were outsiders, we had to cut back a bit on that familiar form of discussing things and we had to start to show more respect for others, for the ideas of others, to stop challenging them before they even finished speaking, to learn to listen, even to become well-mannered, because there were third parties present.

Grupo Aportes also came to Peñarol offering capacity-building programs. MIRPA activists had developed a good working relationship with the NGO through their involvement in MOVEMO, which persuaded Grupo Aportes to support the work of these activists. The NGO came in the late 1980s and remained in the area after decentralization was put into effect, helping neighborhood councils get off the ground:

ANTONIO: Aportes provided us with the keys to our work, and not just our work at the level of the subzone, where we had things more or less figured out for ourselves; they made us aware of a whole other

17. A group of local architects also helped Peñarol by offering their professional services at reduced rates. This was the case, for example, in the design of the plaza near the train station. The quote provided in the text appears in Barrios Pintos and Reyes Abadie 1994, 201.

universe, a much larger one, and they showed us how we had to co-ordinate all the work being done in the zone as a whole, how to con-nect with the other groups; they opened up for us a whole panorama that we weren't aware of before: how to contact other organizations, how to receive people, how to make a broad proposal, when to do it, how to make it happen. They also instructed us on how to hold work-shops, how to run a meeting, how a steering committee should work, what kinds of issues a thematic commission should take on.

Relations with Grupo Aportes proved crucial because the NGO linked MIRPA with international donor organizations that were to fund several community development projects in Peñarol. Shortly after the return to democracy, the UN-supported Comisión por el Reencuentro de los Uru-guayos (CRU) signed an agreement with an Italian NGO, Cooperazzione per lo Sviluppo dei Paesi Emergenti (COSPE), identifying Uruguay as a potential recipient of community development funding. Wishing to initi-ate a pilot community development project in a Montevideo neighborhood, CRU officials approached MOVEMO to help them identify the best area for the study. MOVEMO recommended Peñarol because of its needs and its proven history of effective community organizing. The Italian-funded project involving CRU, MOVEMO, and MIRPA aimed to support local microenterprises, foster local communication skills, build a social and cultural center, and support the establishment of a local health center. As counterpart, MIRPA committed to contribute voluntary labor and funds it had collected through various community-based fund-raisers. The out-come was the establishment of the Health Clinic Zully Sanchez and the Oriental Colón Cultural Center.

Passing on MIRPA's Tradition to Local Government

The convergence of the three traditions of community activism, with the added support of academics and NGOs, turned MIRPA into an effective articulator of local demands, producing a distinct tradition that still informs local politics after MIRPA disappeared as an umbrella organization:

> MARIA: MIRPA as such practically disappeared; however, the people who learned from it all stayed behind; MIRPA created a school of sorts. Tomorrow they may move on to other things, but they will have

left behind a school of participation, a school of citizenship, that will carry on. It is pretty hard for anyone who lived through this experience to hide away at home alone.

The teachings imparted in this school emphasized a particular approach to community development work:

> GUSTAVO: I'd say, and pardon my lack of modesty, that we created a school. The neighborhood council should not pursue a partisan political project, so when someone came along to the council with a partisan political project to propose, we would say, "Sorry, friend, this is not the place for your proposal; if it is a project geared toward addressing a social demand, it would be welcome, but if it is geared toward furthering partisan political interests, go talk to your base committee." We said this to members of the Broad Front as well, because if we did not we would be undoing with one hand the good that we were doing with the other.

MIRPA produced a generation of local leaders who shared a common vision and were socialized into the values and practices nurtured by the organization. Working side by side over the years, these leaders cultivated solid bonds of trust and friendship rooted in a set of shared values, feelings of solidarity, and a distinct orientation toward community activism and participation. The local culture of community activism produced in Peñarol was transferred to the practices of decentralized institutions, giving them a local character that differentiates them from those in other districts.

The inclusive approach and the negotiating and networking stance that gave Peñarol the high school and the health center was used to speed up the establishment of local government in the district. Residents in Peñarol used their constructive initiative to find a temporary location for government operation even before political parties signed the agreement to move ahead with decentralization:

> CRISTINA: At first there were problems with decentralization; they would not sign the decrees. So we implemented it and that was it. We had called the municipality to say they could implement decentralization here if they wanted. Oh no, they couldn't do that—so what did we do? We called together everyone in the zone, all the social organizations, and we held a town hall meeting in the artisan's center. Sixty-three organizations from all of district thirteen. MIRPA played

a key role in the zone . . . so we went out to find a venue. And where did we find it? In the Club Sayago, by the highway, and that's when it started to work.

Notwithstanding the contributions made by activists from other neighborhoods in the district, militants from Peñarol played a decisive role in building an effective local government system that worked well for all communities in district 13. When decentralization was started up in the early 1990s, Peñarol was well positioned to take advantage of the new opportunities offered by the institutional reforms. Possessing a wealth of experience around territorially based mobilization and strong horizontal organizational networks, the community of Peñarol supplied the leaders who took the central positions in the newly created local government structures. These leaders imprinted local institutions with the down-to-earth pragmatism, unitarian approach, and propositional culture they had nurtured over the years. As they deployed their capacities, sharing their traditions with activists from other areas in the wider district, they enabled the communities in district 13 to effectively capitalize on the opportunities offered by decentralization.

In contrast to the experiences of El Cerro and La Teja, which I will discuss in subsequent chapters, activists in Peñarol adjusted smoothly to the requirements of the new institutional reality, and they helped others learn the ropes of local institutional politics. Thanks to their past experiences, they had already moved a good distance along the path that municipal authorities were now asking them to walk:

CRISTINA: So when this decentralization thing got started, MIRPA helped a lot here in the zone. When decentralization began, MIRPA had already been around for five years and was already working with well-thought-out proposals. We had everything already at a fairly advanced stage. When they asked us to put together a five-year plan, we said, "We already have one; we'll revise and update it." We sat down to work at it again, but we had such a plan in place since 1987, when we held an open workshop with social organizations to identify people's needs in Peñarol. We had already covered this ground, so some of these things were kind of boring for us.

The existing traditions of territorially based activism proved useful in infusing local government structures with rich reservoirs of knowledge, experience, and resources, facilitating the institutionalization of decentralization thanks to the historical experiences of community development embedded in local culture:

> JACINTA: Decentralization has been nourished by this life we have lived in Peñarol. It was nourished by social organizing that was already strong. The residents in Peñarol have been the engine of decentralization; they joined the councils and took action within the process of decentralization. That is, the social work done in Peñarol was carried over into the neighborhood councils, but the process of community development had begun before, it had been started through the work of the residents.

Building Bridges and Trust Across District 13

Ironically, Peñarol's strong bonds of solidarity and effective negotiation and mobilization skills initially became a source of tension when activists met residents from other communities in the institutions of local government. Nearly all council members representing the community of Peñarol, which became the largest contingent in the council, were also leaders of MIRPA and were united by bonds of trust, friendship, and a shared tradition of community activism. Other councilors feared that the more cohesive and more experienced group from MIRPA would dominate local government and use their influence to divert resources to their community:

> GUSTAVO: There were residents who came forward as independents with ten signatures, or who represented very weak organizations, and they felt at a disadvantage. They believed that someone gifted at public speaking, someone with slick skills of persuasion, someone with four or five years of training in these things, was going to transform their neighborhood council into a veritable servant of his subzone.

To overcome this initial mistrust and to calm fears of MIRPA domination, councilors from Peñarol had to build trust and normative consensus among all councilors in the district. To accomplish this, they had to first overcome the parochial outlook most council members, including those from Peñarol, brought to the neighborhood council; further, they had to foster a district-wide identity and vision that could allow them to abandon the narrow territorial confines of their own activism. Antonio describes the practical reasons for the development of deliberative democratic practices:

> We leaders of each subzone came to realize we were coming to the table with a very narrow, local perspective—that it was hard for us to be more open-minded. We began to realize that we mustn't be so confrontational, and that what we needed to do was to come to an agreement on an overall plan; that we were councilors for the entire zone, not just of our respective subzones. We began to develop a broader outlook; we realized that, instead of being concerned merely with filling up the pothole in front of my own house, we should pave a street that needs paving in a squatter settlement in order to allow access to ambulances and fire trucks. This was difficult, but it did us good; it did us good to fight it out at first, so that we could learn to stop fighting. It made us unite, it made us change, because we realized that if we didn't, we were not going to get anywhere.

In order to gain trust and to begin to build a district-wide vision, leaders from Peñarol had to acknowledge that other areas had greater needs than theirs, and they had to demonstrate in practice that they were willing to defer their own demands to help the neediest communities in the district:

> ANTONIO: There were subzones where people lacked certain basic things, and we prioritized these. In the first neighborhood councils, they prioritized the Lavalleja neighborhood, and today they are doing the same thing with Conciliación, which is a neighborhood that is more than one hundred years old and yet its needs have been long neglected. Now this comes easy: figuring out what the priorities are in a subzone. The collective has been trained so that they vote on these things directly, to prioritize this or that subzone, and they select based on a shared sense of urgency, and not because they were influenced by a particularly eloquent speaker at some meeting, or by any other such external pressure.

The approach worked, even if it created tensions between councilors from Peñarol and members of their community, who complained that their needs were being postponed. As a result, the neighborhood council in district 13 started to have orderly meetings and fraternal discussions free of the conflict found in the other two districts covered in this study. Remarkably, the influence of MIRPA's tradition of community participation was also visible when other broad-based umbrella organizations were set up in the two poorest neighborhoods in the district, Lavalleja and Conciliación.

When decentralization was set up, city authorities sensitive to local traditions granted councils the autonomy to define their own statutes and traditions within the broad framework established by the decentralization decree. As a result, during the formative phases of decentralization neighborhood councils spent considerable time establishing norms based on their collective experiences and histories. Often, councils across the city got tangled in never-ending discussions about procedural issues, such as how to operate meetings, set up agendas, keep speakers lists, present and vote on motions, and so forth. Understandably, in the absence of generalized trust among councilors, council meetings turned to formal norms to establish guarantees against possible deviation from collective goals. In some cases, like in the other case studies discussed in the next two chapters, such debates still go on, acquiring renewed strength every time a new council is elected, painfully illustrating the absence of trust or consensus over legitimate traditions, and often producing frustration among neighborhood councilors.

One debate that occurred in most districts centered on whether alternate councilors should act on behalf of the subzone that had elected them or as representatives of the entire district. This issue was strategically important because it potentially affected the voting weight of subzones within the council. A large majority of council members initially conceived of the council as a place where delegates from subzones came to vote en masse to promote the demands of their own neighborhood. Thus, for them, it was only logical that alternates could only replace absent councilors from their respective subzone. As time went by, however, new ways of thinking began to emerge; councilors adopted the view that, once elected, they should act as councilors of the whole district and vote according to the needs of the entire area, rather than the narrow needs of their own communities. This major shift in loyalty and identity was adopted in districts that were successful in building bonds of trust and a shared district-wide vision. In district 13, the council ended up adopting a resolution allowing the first alternate to arrive at the meeting to automatically replace any absent councilor, regardless of subzone. Eventually, councilors came to be seen as articulators of district-wide demands and as promoters of community participation:

> ANTONIO: If you are able to listen to the residents, to talk to them, and also—to work with that social network of cultural, sporting, health,

and neighborhood associations—to motivate them, to organize them, so that they work together in the best, most cohesive way possible, then you will be constantly nurtured by these residents. Because you will be like a sound box for them, conveying their concerns to the council. But you have to be able to filter things. To articulate and defend positions, to interpret them, and this requires experience in relating to others, in communicating with your neighbor. It isn't enough to be a mere transmitter; you have to interact. This way, you can be a proper interlocutor.

Attending the First Meeting of the 2004 Council

Not surprisingly, the 2004 inaugural meeting of the elected council in district 13 was a festive event, colored by a remarkable sense of human warmth and camaraderie that celebrated local activism and its accomplishments. Besides the thirty-eight elected councilors, there were many other people at the meeting, including relatives of the new councilors, former members of local government, local personalities, and community activists. At the start of the meeting it was announced that a local group would play music to close the ceremony. One by one, the elected councilors were called to the front to receive the official certificate issued by municipal authorities recognizing them as members of the local government. As they went up, they were greeted with enthusiastic applause; female councilors received a fresh red rose, while occasional jokes were made spontaneously among members of the audience. The most emotional moment of the entire evening came when a local poet, in her late seventies, read a poem that she wrote to the youngest councilor among the 640 elected in the entire city, who happened to represent one of the poorest neighborhoods in district 13.

The choice of a young female student intern from the School of Communications as master of ceremonies, someone not formally representing local government authorities, helped avoid the rigid formality of the inaugural meetings in the other districts I visited. The director of the district communal center, the administrative head of local government, sat at the back without playing any formal role. The outgoing steering committee presented a brief report of the election results and highlighted the challenges ahead before passing on the torch to the new steering committee. They informed the incoming council that the district's tradition to select the steering committee had been to choose the two most voted candidates from each subzone. Enthusiastically and without discussion, councilors endorsed the nominations and welcomed the new steering committee members with a round of applause. Following the investiture of the steering committee, representatives from the local junta requested time to honor more than twenty local activists past and present. They spoke briefly about each of the activists, highlighting their ongoing contribution to local community development, and gave each a certificate. The language was free of formality, expressing a strong sense of familiarity and comradeship with each of the individuals. Tellingly, the criteria used to select the activists to be honored was not only that they had to have contributed to the cultural and social development of the neighborhoods in the district, but that they had done it working collectively with others. At the end of the meeting, councilors and other community members were invited to look at the flip-chart pages that had been posted on the walls, displaying the various council committees and thematic commissions, their present membership, and the meeting dates and times. People were asked to write their names down for the commissions of their choice.

This opening meeting of the council illustrated how local activists in district 13 had successfully cultivated strong bonds of trust, friendship, and solidarity among themselves, and built smooth relations among all three branches of local government—rare achievements when compared to other districts. The presence at the meeting of many local activists not formally belonging to local government showed the degree to which local government institutions have become a central reference point for a wide network of community development initiatives and projects. The acceptance of normative traditions and practices, such as the endorsement of the procedure to nominate the steering committee, indicated the high level of legitimacy of the practices and traditions of previous councils. Lastly, the choreography of the meeting de-emphasized the rigid formalities that I found in the first council meetings in the other two case studies, instead promoting a more relaxed and less apprehensive atmosphere.

Looking Beyond Municipal Politics

Most councils in the city were trapped by the dynamics of local government and struggled unsuccessfully to broaden their activities beyond the scope of municipal politics. Sympathetic to the plight of the poor and committed

to addressing the social debt created by years of neoliberal national policies, city authorities created expectations that they would address nonmunicipal problems. Councilors in every district felt hard-pressed to channel
all kinds of demands from their constituents through the filter of municipal politics, thereby becoming deeply entangled in the complex web of
municipal politics. Some activists started to express concern about the per-
ils of "municipalizing" local government:

> ANTONIO: We were determined not to municipalize MIRPA; even
> so, in the council we experienced a kind of impulse to municipalize
> everything. The most obvious issue in this regard was electricity . . .
> but health services also became concerns of the municipal govern-
> ment, as was housing and employment. People have access to the
> local government and the councilor, where they know they will be
> heard. Directly or indirectly they inform you of problems for which
> the municipality has been assuming responsibility. We try to change
> things, not to avoid our responsibility, but because you have to locate
> the responsibility for things at the appropriate administrative level . . .
> to understand how to bring demands to these other nonmunicipal
> bodies.

There are, however, several experiences in Peñarol that illustrate effective community development projects involving nonmunicipal actors. The
Villa Peñarol Neighborhood Commission, one of the oldest neighborhood
organizations in the community, offers a good example. As a member of
MIRPA, the organization helped broker the deal that brought the community health clinic in the mid-1990s and it assumed legal responsibility over
the management of the project, thanks to its status as an incorporated
organization. Leaders of the commission joined the council in the early
1990s, bringing their community development experience to the institutions of local government, but they remained focused on local development
pursuits through links with nonmunicipal actors. To their credit, they
contacted the Ministry of Interior on their own and persuaded them to
reopen the police station that had been lost in the late 1980s, drawing on
the same community spirit and solid negotiating skills that had secured the
high school and the health clinic:

> SANDRO: Here, thanks to the association, we had the good luck to estab-
> lish the police station. After the dictatorship, we started struggling

to get them to reopen the station, which was built by neighborhood residents in the first place. It was built in 1959 or 1960, through a "brick" campaign: each resident donated a brick, and they built what is now the station. It was built out of common effort. Thus it was not right that the neighborhood was left without an active police station; that's why we fought and we met with the Ministry of Interior and we were considered one of the most efficient committees to ever undertake this kind of thing. That's why I say that a neighborhood association can sometimes achieve as much or more than a neighborhood council. That is, when things are done the right way, of course.

The commission also negotiated a deal with AFE to renovate the plaza around the train station to create a public recreational space for seniors, to inject some life into the decaying casco antiguo of Peñarol, and to address the lack of public spaces in the community. AFE granted the space on the condition that the commission provided the money and labor to upgrade and maintain the plaza. The commission collected funds from neighbors and local businesses and organized voluntary work brigades to build a playground for children. They also hired a bricklayer to build a police post to guard the plaza, started to erect a fence to separate the plaza from the tracks due to safety concerns, and built tables for senior citizens to play games such as checkers and chess. The commission also enlisted the support of an organization of architects who offer professional support to low-income neighborhoods to draft the design of the plaza for a nominal fee. The plaza is already a big success:

> CRISTINA: We opened the Peñarol station plaza and were amazed at how it filled with people on Sunday afternoons. We never saw so many people in a plaza before! Since the games tables were set up, it is impressive how many people come; on weekdays the schoolteachers come and go, but on Sundays it is surprising how many people gather there, with or without their children; they go there to drink *mate* anyway. The space is becoming too small for all the people who use it.

Another example of effective linking with nonmunicipal actors is the effort of community activists to address an environmental problem. Disagreements over who was responsible for cleaning the areas alongside the railway tracks had resulted in a serious health hazard for the community, as dirt and garbage started to pile up, making it a haven for rats and other animals. AFE, the legal owner of the land and the tracks, claimed that such cleaning was a municipal responsibility, but the city government argued they were only responsible to clean municipal lands. Relations between city authorities and AFE became strained, and eventually the two groups stopped communicating with each other altogether. Local activists from GAP (Grupo Ambiental de Peñarol), an organization created to deal with local environmental problems, took the initiative and got several institutional actors together to address the problem. Their approach was also nurtured by the traditions of community mobilization in the area, and not surprisingly they aimed to educate and persuade potential allies rather than antagonize them:

> FRANCESCA: With the GAP group, we got together with the teaching centers, the local police chief, residents from the housing co-ops, businesspeople, the managers of AFE, et cetera. . . . What we tried to do was to educate these people, and we thought that you don't educate by protesting, that we needed to improve the social environment by educating.

With the typical pragmatism of community activism in Peñarol, they sought the help of an unusual ally: the military battalion headquartered in Peñarol:

> SOFIA: We went to the military headquarters to talk to the commander, because there was a lot of conflict between the municipality and the AFE, and to discuss the issue of sanitation, we needed to bring to the table the district's authorities, AFE and the Ministry of Defense. We went to talk to the commander and he told us how to prepare the letters we would need. We went to the Ministry of Defense with the letter and we got an appointment with the ministry, AFE, and the municipality, and we got to organize a cleaning day.

It was a risky decision, as the wounds opened by the military repression remained unhealed, but the initiative produced an unusual outcome: the army mobilized the troops to clean the track lands with the help of neighbors, many of whom were supporters of the leftist Broad Front, while children, under the guidance of an art teacher from MIRPA, painted colorful murals to beautify the walls. The event turned out to be a great success, building bonds between a reclusive and feared army battalion and the community at large:

> FRANCESCA: If you go to the railway tracks you will see that all the walls of the battalion are covered with paintings by the kids from the educational centers, authorized by the battalion. They cut the grass for us, they set up the ladders, and on the final day we got together with all the soldiers who had participated. I always felt an aversion to soldiers, which I later realized was wrong, that I should not be that way. With these people I learned to think differently about soldiers, and in fact when we spoke of political matters I found that many of them thought the same way that I do; many are in the service out of need. Out of concern for being a full member of my community, I learned to relate to them.

Another example of the community hands-on approach is the experience of addressing the need for a primary school. When the Mesa 2 housing cooperative was established in 1974, they constructed space to accommodate commercial businesses and a day care center. The Ministry of Education, however, lacking the facilities to respond to the infusion of so many children into the neighborhood, asked the co-op to lend this space for the temporary operation of a primary school. More than twenty years later, the ministry finally announced it had the funds to build a new school and asked residents to help them find a suitable space. The residents contacted the key stakeholders and found a local flower grower of Japanese descent who donated an ideal lot:

> CRISTINA: When they proposed that the funds are available, we went to figure out where to put it. And the place we found was this field, a little garden where a Japanese man grew flowers and vegetables. So anyway, he gave us this place, the field; we had to go talk to him and he agreed. We had to do all the paperwork.

Something similar occurred when the Ministry of Education, recognizing the inadequacy of the buildings that housed the high school, decided to build a brand-new high school in the area. Residents supported the initiative but also requested that the refurbished buildings continue to be used for educational purposes. They again started negotiations with AFE and the ministry to discuss how best to use the facilities. In the end, the ministry set up a language center offering free Italian, Portuguese, and French language training courses, one of only ten of its kind in the country:

> CRISTINA: When we convinced them to build a new high school, we asked that the old building not be returned to AFE but that it continue to be used for educational purposes as well. We talked to the secondary education people and the director there told us that they had this plan for a language center and it sounded good to us. We consulted with the residents and it seemed wonderful to us that the kids could learn a language on top of studying in high school. . . . And that was it, we put the language school there.

The Crisis of Participation

In spite of these successful experiences in community mobilization, activists often complain that people are less willing to participate, and they long for the early days when it was easier to get neighbors to join community improvement projects:

> MARGARITA: Some months ago we cleaned up the bus stop in our neighborhood. We went with the rakes, the trimmers, the shovels, with everything, and there were only three of us to do it all. Everyone that passed by would say, "They're cleaning the bus stop for us," or "It's going to look nice." The time is over when we would say, "On Sunday, we are going to do this or that," and the residents would show up to help.

This drop in participation is connected to nationwide structural and political changes rather than local government shortcomings. Many activists insist that bonds of trust still run strong in the community, but some have started to observe a disturbing trend:

> SILVIA: There is less trust. The distrust comes from above, from the system itself, from society at large. It is not a distrust that arises out of the neighborhood of Peñarol; it comes out of the very structure of Uruguayan society. For at the level of government, certain issues have arisen—of corruption, of things Uruguayans are not used to, and we have begun to distrust organizations, everything to do with organized groups.

This change in perception of public officials and community organizations has filtered down to the level of the community, prompting local organizations to be more transparent:

> SILVIA: So we had to take measures that we had not taken before. To go out monthly to explain what we were doing, what we were not doing, why we were not doing certain things, in order to maintain a degree of trust. . . . It is a thing that must be done by anyone who holds any responsibility in a neighborhood association, or in a parents' school committee for the high school, or in a pensioners movement, or a seniors club. Constantly you are receiving reports on what they do, what they don't do. Before, we didn't do this. It wasn't needed; there was trust and that was it. The distrust now is notable.

Local leaders argue that the downturn in participation results from the severity of the economic crisis that hit the country following the collapse of the Argentinean economy in 2002. The impact of the crisis forced people to devote more and more time to economic survival:

> JORGE: If, in my home, I have nothing to feed my children, I am going to go out to try and get food for them. I can't go about trying to help others, get politically active, if in my house I don't have food, no power, no water. I can't participate if I don't have what I need to survive, the basics.

Paradoxically, the success in building consensus and trust among councilors from across the district may have contributed to the decline in participation. While redefining councilors' roles as representatives of the whole district was an important step forward in building local government institutions, it was not always understood by community organizations, who complained that their councilors had stopped representing their interests. In addition, running local government placed more demands for time on the busy schedules of local activists. As activists from Peñarol shouldered a disproportionate share of responsibilities in local government institutions—which required them to familiarize themselves with problems in the entire district, study community development projects, draft the annual budget, and prepare five-year plans—they were left with little time to devote to the community organizations they once led.

Peñarol paid a high price when MIRPA, which provided the foundations for their success, disappeared as an umbrella organization and became a community center. The organization had its own quarters, housed in one of the former railway row houses next to the high school and across from the health clinic, which they obtained as part of the high school–health center deal with AFE. No longer aiming to act as an umbrella organization, it had become one more organization among the many that existed in Peñarol. It offered important services to the community, including a library and courses in arts and crafts, community radio broadcasting, sewing, and electricity, and it lent its space to other community organizations for their meetings and activities. Many of the former leaders were no longer active in MIRPA, and most of them had become active in local government.

More recently, MIRPA was appropriated by militants from the Movimiento 26 de Marzo, a radical faction of the Broad Front that chose to abstain from participating in local government. Interestingly, the same political faction decided to participate in the councils of El Cerro and La Teja. Over time, this group turned its back on MIRPA's community service orientation, transforming it into a partisan organization that became increasingly less central to the lives of residents.

Some people I interviewed suggested that low participation may be connected to the style of militancy assumed by local organizations and decentralized institutions, which is drawn from the tradition of left-wing militancy that revolves around the face-to-face meeting as the privileged site for making decisions. This style may have clashed with the preference of many residents, especially women, to become engaged in concrete activities of community improvement rather than to participate in seemingly endless discussions and debates:

> ANTONIO: It also happens that you burn out. I experienced this too, with the constant militancy; it is exhausting and sometimes pointless, like when you have a meeting just to have a meeting and for no other reason. . . . There is a need for self-criticism; political militancy can't be just for the sake of militancy. This problem adds to the burnout produced by the crisis.

None of the councilors I interviewed explained the drop in participation in relation to possible inadequacies in the model of decentralization. In contrast to the other two districts I studied—where local activists were very critical of such a model, arguing that high desertion rates and low participation were the direct outcome of the councils' lack of decision-making power—leaders in Peñarol tended to see this differently:

GUSTAVO: I have not changed my fundamental values, but I do have a different vision in terms of how to conduct politics day to day. I arrived at the conclusion that the arguments we sometimes made to defend participation are not so valid. Participation for participation's sake—without some basic knowledge of how to do things—is not the best way to go either. You can't leave to councilors decisions that are suddenly going to have repercussions in the zone or on a group of residents. Are you going to entrust political control of the zone in the hands of a body that will disband every two years, that will be made up of people of varying qualities, that was never coordinated in the way it should be? There were times we ran the neighborhood council in a symbolic way, just so that the three pillars of decentralization would still be in place. So you start to wonder; you want people to participate, to get involved, to make decisions, to have control, but these people—are they ready for things to be this way, or is this just your wish?

The main concern centered on the initial need to fine-tune the often overlapping and ill-defined attributions of each level of local government. Indeed, the first local juntas had difficulties delimiting their roles and learning to exercise wisely the decision-making power they were invested with by the model. They struggled to build legitimacy for this unelected body that appeared to have all the power. In district 13 this problem was aggravated when the second president of the local junta, a former leader of MIRPA, was charged with abuse of power and corruption. Interestingly, the district recovered from this setback with only minor bruises, and even today it is still very difficult to get activists to talk openly about what occurred. As the years passed, the decentralized system produced a generation of councilors trained in the running of local government who would subsequently move upward as they were appointed to the local junta, ensuring continuity and granting this body greater legitimacy. Having former councilors in the junta facilitated relations between the social and political bodies of local government:

RITA: The junta in this zone was made up of people who used to be councilors. It's good, good because they bring with them all that prior knowledge of neighborhood work, and they keep working in the neighborhoods.

In the introduction I identified a design flaw in the model of decentralization that gave significant authority to the secretary of the local junta, who was appointed directly by the mayor and whose power was magnified because they were full-time paid employees with regular access to the mayor's office. As a result, the individual approaches to teamwork and the personalities of each secretary had a significant impact on the running of local government in each district. Washington González, the secretary in district 13 for the 2000–2005 period, got off to a rocky start when Mayor Arana appointed him over a locally sponsored candidate from Peñarol. While in other districts this kind of disagreement would produce a great deal of conflict, Peñarol reluctantly accepted the appointment and moved on.

Washington came to the position equipped with a wealth of experience in territorially based urban movements, thanks to his involvement in MOVEMO, and he quickly earned the respect of local militants. I asked activists about their perceptions of the local junta and the secretary in order to gauge both the level of support for individuals occupying formal office positions and the degree of legitimacy of local government institutions; the responses were overwhelmingly positive:

> JACINTA: The secretary has organizational and work skills, an impressive political mind. You need a person like that. Beyond the fact that he is a politician and I am practically in the antipodes of the Broad Front, still I have to acknowledge that he does his work perfectly well. He works hard and I don't see him getting caught up in silly political divisions. He is serious about what he manages, and being in a paid full-time position, he is much more well-known in the zone than we are. . . . They respect him because he is also always straightforward, he is always frank with you. We might argue with him for hours, but he has true leadership qualities.

The process of building a local park illustrates the workings of synergy between community organizations and local government institutions, and shows the important role of a secretary embedded in the community, facilitating the realization of a community initiative. Residents of two subdivisions of Peñarol (Peñarol Norte and Jardines de Peñarol) started to work on a project to build a small park on vacant lands. They first presented their project to two neighborhood commissions, both of which endorsed it and advised them to approach local authorities for support and guidance. They met Washington, the junta's secretary, who liked the project and promised to support them. He linked them with urban planners from the Faculty of Architecture, who helped them design the park and see the project through and secured support from various levels of municipal government: city workers leveled off the site, and the municipal authorities purchased the games and a dozen young trees. I was fortunate to be in the city to attend the last day of volunteer work that carried the project to completion. The event illustrated the successful deployment of synergy among residents, academics and university students, local government officials, and event students from an upper-class, private Catholic high school who volunteered to work for one day as part of the school's outreach program. Everyone seemed in good spirits, planting trees, setting up benches, and putting the final touches on the park. The inauguration of the site was marked by an emotional ceremony:

> ALBERTO: Boys from the Juan XXIII private Catholic school, authorities, local personalities, councilors, residents, friends, members of neighborhood associations—they all came. I consider it a successful, a positive activity. It brought me much happiness and satisfaction at seeing a personal dream fulfilled, because I was born and raised in this neighborhood and we never had the chance to have anything like this, but today the kids in the zone do.

The two neighbors who initiated the project went on to be elected to council one year after they came into contact with Washington, showing the expansive effect of successful community initiatives. Their experience also shows that while people's initial decision to participate may be motivated by very practical concerns, they may also remain involved for social reasons. Alberto explains the immense fulfillment he receives through his participation in the council's Culture Commission:

> A great deal of trust has developed among the people I have become involved with lately. Maybe it is the moment, our passion, our way of being, our way of treating the other with respect, which gains us a small place in the trust of the other, which builds like a chain. In district 13 interesting things happen . . . there is a special committee on cultural affairs, but it is more like a family than a committee. There's a human warmth there that is very important: we share a mate, a joke, meals. Like a family. The committee brings the symphony, we try to bring theater productions, to do theater workshops;

through decentralization, we hold poetry, dance, percussion contests. There's a lot we do.

Conclusions

The case of Peñarol shows that—despite the constraints on community participation created by major institutional design flaws, a deepening economic crisis, generalized demobilization across the city, and a tradition of political party dominance over civil society—local actors in this district successfully took advantage of the opportunities created by participatory decentralization. Their relative success in building effective practices of local government was due to the particular interplay of three sets of factors: local associational cultures and the particular stocks of social capital they produced, the absence of deeply entrenched divisions resulting from socioeconomic conditions within the district, and the grassroot orientation of local government officials who had previous experience in community organizing.

The local associative culture found in Peñarol supplied a reservoir of well-seasoned leaders who had forged the kind of skills required by participatory local government: the predisposition to favor pragmatic and constructive engagement with authorities over more radical and contentious oppositional politics, the capacity to manage resources through projects of community development, and an orientation toward collective mobilization based on an inclusive and nonsectarian approach. The community of Peñarol brought to local government in district 13 a powerful tradition of territorially based mobilization for urban goods, which began operating within the confines of the clientelistic networks of the ruling Colorado Party and had continued to build a tradition of community solidarity and self-help. The experience of building an inclusive umbrella organization like MIRPA fostered exceptional conflict-resolution and community mobilization skills, and contributed to the fostering of solidarity and trust within the neighborhood (bonding social capital).

Thanks to these attributes, activists from Peñarol quickly became recognized as leaders across the district and came to occupy key positions in the structures of local government, sharing their traditions of inclusive and democratic mobilization with activists from other neighborhoods. They helped consolidate trust and democratic participatory practices that produced bridging kinds of social capital, thereby enabling the entire district to capitalize on the opportunities offered by participatory decentralization. Thus the values and practices produced in Peñarol—the MIRPA school— became embedded in local institutions, infusing them with the slowly paced lifestyle typical of this former railway community; the less radical working-class traditions of railway workers, an identity that adhered more strongly to community and territory than to class belonging; and a type of community participation based on negotiation and inclusive politics.

The potential of these predispositions to produce synergy with other levels of local government was amplified by the leadership style of the local junta secretary. His pragmatic and inclusive approach, developed through his personal involvement in urban social movements in the city, helped foster collaboration among all levels of the decentralized system and produced trusting relations between communities and local government officials. The case of Peñarol, I argue, illustrates the potential of decentralization to foster synergy between community organizations and local government officials, and to enable poor communities to advance their interests and turn participatory institutions into vital articulators of local mobilization. It shows how the bonding forms of social capital found in one community were extended to relations among activists from various neighborhoods to produce bridging social capital, which in turn fostered synergies with local government officials.

While the particular stocks of social capital found in Peñarol and the personal attributes of the local junta secretary were essential to facilitating the relatively harmonious operation of local government institutions, such cooperation across all levels was also made possible by the comparatively less severe and more uniform socioeconomic conditions found in the district (I will return to this point when I compare the socioeconomic conditions in each district in the concluding chapter). Underscoring the importance of material conditions, the next chapter examines the case of a community with very powerful traditions of collective mobilization and high levels of bonding social capital. Despite these advantages, this community's efforts to build district-wide bonds of solidarity and synergy with local government officials were undermined in large part by the divisions produced by the overwhelming poverty and marginality affecting most district residents.

CHAPTER 2

El Cerro: Participatory Decentralization Among Former Militant Meatpackers and Recent Squatters

El Cerro is my life; I grew up here, this is where I am bringing up a family, this is where I am making myself into who I am, this is where I will die. Because I am of El Cerro, in my soul and wherever I go I will always say that I am Cerrense.

—Susana

The image of El Cerro is one of people who put up a fight, of a place that is organized and combative, thanks to the meatpacking industry, of very solidary people.

—Pablo

Community Profile

It takes me less than half an hour to drive to El Cerro from the upper-middle-class neighborhood of Pocitos, which is located on the south-central coast of the city. Driving the coastline, halfway through my journey I pass the harbor, from which point I can see El Cerro (which literally means "the hill") overlooking the city on the other side of Montevideo Bay. The physical landscape changes suddenly when I take the *accesos,* the freeways alongside the bay that were built to facilitate access to the port and to the city center from the western and northern parts of the country. Instead of the palm trees and luxurious high-rise buildings found along the south-central coast, I now see warehouses and industries announcing the entry to the western industrial corridor, which used to extend from the harbor all the way to El Cerro. As I drive by the state-owned oil refinery, ANCAP—whose future was the subject of intense public debate since citizens had called a referendum to stop a government plan to privatize the plant—I start to see dozens of garbage pickers pulling their carts alongside the road on their way to salvage glass, cardboard, or anything of value from the trash of middle-class neighborhoods on the other side of town. The distinctive putrid odor of the polluted Miguelete River tells me that I am near El Cerro.

Villa El Cerro was erected in the mid-nineteenth century on the southeastern slopes of El Cerro de Montevideo. It is located in the western part of the city, separated from the city center by Montevideo Bay. Largely surrounded by water on its southern and eastern sides, El Cerro enjoys a privileged location, offering a stunning view of the harbor and of the Ciudad Vieja, the colonial downtown area across the bay. The top of El Cerro hosts what was once a major tourist attraction—a fort built by the Spanish colonial forces in the early nineteenth century to defend their hold over the northern shores of the River Plate from the threat of British invasion. From the fort, which is now a museum of colonial history, I look toward the foot of the southwestern slopes and see the century-old golf course, built for the exclusive use of the managers of the American-owned meatpacking plant that settled in the area in the early twentieth century. When I turn to my left, looking toward the bottom of the southern side of the hill, I see the white sand of El Cerro's public beach and the recently upgraded Rambla Suiza stretching along the coastline, two popular sites in summertime where residents come to enjoy a refreshing swim or a quiet walk on the banks of the river.

I also cannot fail to notice three colossal cement structures, skeletons of the former plants of the powerful frigoríficos, the meatpacking plants that employed thousands of Cerrenses for almost a century. As in Peñarol—where the British architecture and the railway tracks point directly to former times—these buildings are like eternal ghosts of the age of splendor, when El Cerro was a vibrant meatpacking town and home to the most combative working-class community in the country.

One of these abandoned plants that used to belong to the American-owned Frigorífico Artigas, ironically adopting the name of the country's national independence hero, is now the headquarters of local government in the district. Strangely enough, when I come to interview the bright and spirited president of the local junta, I realize that she now occupies what used to be the office of the American president of the frigorífico. The eleven-foot ceilings, fine wood trim, and worn oak floors still show signs of the room's former prestige. I gaze through the large windows overlooking the yard, imagining the days when the plant's managers monitored workers from their second-floor quarters. Sitting on a white plastic lawn chair behind an oversized oak desk, the lonely survivor of the original furnishings, Alicia introduces me to the intricacies of local politics. Though only in her mid-thirties, she is already a respected family lawyer and an established community leader, and her analysis of local politics is crisp and insightful. She helps me understand the multiple layers of complexity found in this fascinating community, starting with some history:

> The history of El Cerro is like the country's history in microcosm, for this is a country that received a significant influx of immigrants from Europe, and all of them came to El Cerro. Villa El Cerro was first called Villa Cosmopolis, which is precisely the right name for such a cosmopolitan place. It was founded one hundred seventy years ago as Villa Cosmopolis in order to receive this wave of immigrants coming from Europe, immigrants who came to define the population of the country, and especially of this neighborhood.

European Immigration and the Emergence of a Multicultural Community

Villa El Cerro was established in the mid-nineteenth century as part of a government effort to attract European immigrants to work in the meat-processing industries that had settled in the area and constituted the heart of the country's beef-export economy. Thousands of European immigrants settled in El Cerro between 1880 and 1940, drawn by the beauty of the natural surroundings, the growing job opportunities in the beef industry, and the provision of free housing by employers. To underscore the spirit of cosmopolitanism, the streets of El Cerro were named after countries, mostly European, something that remains a distinctive feature of the neighborhood to this day.

Over the years, migrants of various European origins—Spaniards, Italians, Lithuanians, Yugoslavians, Poles, Greeks, Russians, Germans, Armenians—built a vibrant multicultural working-class community devoid of the divisive ethnic segregation found in other countries.[1] These immigrants set up their separate ethnic associations and congregated with other newcomers at work and in the community, creating a distinct identity from the unique mix of cultural traditions:

1. There was also a small group of black runaway slaves who had escaped from the quarantine warehouses, which had been built in 1789 near El Cerro, a "safe" distance from the city center. See Valia 1998, 34.

ALICIA: This is what contributed to the formation of a distinct Cerro identity. Because all at once people of different languages and cultures and cuisines and ways of dressing and of thinking, by force of circumstance, had to get together and forge a common way of life. They had to go to the same school, work in the same meatpacking plants or in the same slaughterhouses. So suddenly and without choice this multicolor gamut of cultures had to find a language and a way of living together that would let them unite, and in doing so they created a new identity.

Aware of this history, I was not surprised to learn that the esteemed, white-haired president of the electoral commission that oversaw the last elections for neighborhood council was a second-generation Greek. The soft-spoken Kostas, born and raised in El Cerro to parents employed in the meatpacking industries, is an open book regarding the community's history. Behind his mild demeanor and courteous manners I discover a principled man who was involved in radical politics in his younger days, like so many residents in this militant working-class community. I also learn that he spent fourteen years in jail, accused of belonging to the legendary urban guerrilla organization Tupamaros. Kostas proudly recounts the days when Avenida Grecia, not Calle Estados Unidos or Calle Inglaterra, was the principal center of commercial and cultural activity in the community:

Sundays in Grecia Street there was a continuous parade of happiness, of mixed dialects and languages. There were a number of important social clubs in the zone as well as four or five cinemas, and all of them kept busy.

Indeed, by the first quarter of the twentieth century El Cerro had become a lively town, hosting several theaters, dance halls, cultural and ethnic associations, and mutual aid societies, as well as two successful first-division league soccer clubs, a vibrant local press, and a thriving network of local business. Such rich social and economic life, reinforced by the community's geographical segregation from the rest of the city, made El Cerro a compact and nearly self-contained community, something that Julio, a member of the local government for over a decade, is old enough to remember:

The images I have of the past here are of a splendorous Cerro, one that was rich, in economic and cultural terms. El Cerro was a self-sufficient city unto itself; you did not have to go anywhere else; all the needs of the locals were taken care of right here. Grecia Street was a regular beehive, a real marvel! This I experienced firsthand.

Monopoly Capitalism, Foreign Ownership, and the Meatpacking Industry

The material foundation of this prosperity came from the El Cerro meatpacking industries. Located on the waterfront at the foot of the hill, these large enterprises became the bloodline of the country's economy, producing the wealth that funded the high levels of social development that set Uruguay apart from many of its neighbors during most of the twentieth century. El Cerro became the quintessential meatpacking town, and the community's fortunes—intertwined with the country's beef-export economy—were subject to the vicissitudes of the industry. In fact, the history of this community offers a paradigmatic illustration at the micro-level of the failure of the country's beef-exporting development model. Ultimately, as occurred in Peñarol, the community's prosperity ended with the collapse of the industry that had made it thrive for nearly a century; but the impact of the crisis that followed was much greater for the people of El Cerro than it was in Peñarol, as we shall see below.

The early meat-processing plants—called *saladeros* because they used salt to preserve meat—settled in El Cerro in the nineteenth century, exporting low-quality salted meat, called *tasajo,* to feed slaves in the Caribbean. The invention of refrigeration and the rise of monopoly capitalism in the late 1800s facilitated the emergence of the frigoríficos.[2] If the country's economy in the nineteenth century was dominated by the saladeros, the twentieth century became the age of the frigoríficos, and most of them, to the pride of Cerrenses, were based in El Cerro. Local entrepreneurs set up the first plants in El Cerro in the early twentieth century, but their hold on the industry was short-lived and soon succumbed to powerful American meatpacking industries. Swift and Armour—two American companies belonging to the "big four" Chicago-based meatpacking giants—seized control of the

2. In 1876, the French engineer Charles Tellier and two Uruguayan businessmen (Francisco Lecocq and Federico Nin Reyes) sent the first ship with refrigerated meat from Burdeos. After one hundred five days on the high seas, *Le Frigorifique* arrived in Buenos Aires with perfectly edible meat. See Bernhard 1970, 17.

industry in El Cerro, leaving the Frigorífico Anglo, in the city of Fray Bentos, to the British.[3]

The frigoríficos were the first truly modern capitalist industries in the country, exporting refrigerated meat to satisfy the rising demand in Europe. These large-scale enterprises employed thousands of people, using the latest technologies and modern, Taylorist management methods. They brought together under a single production site all the manufacturing phases required for cutting, processing, and commercializing meat. In a short period of time, these foreign companies acquired control of the country's meat industry and used their power to lower the prices they paid for cattle, thereby upsetting local cattle producers.[4] Seeking to appease the powerful landowning classes, the government responded in 1929 by setting up the publicly owned Frigorífico Nacional (FRIGONAL).[5] Influenced by the early ideology of state developmentalism, this move aimed to make the internal beef market more competitive in order to increase beef prices paid to producers. To ensure the economic viability of this frigorífico, the government gave it the exclusive right to supply meat to Montevideo city.[6] The new plant was also established in El Cerro, in the facilities of the former Frigorífica Uruguaya, sealing the community's position as the home of the country's meatpacking industry.

The Making of the Cerrense Working Class: Community Identity and Labor Militancy

At the peak of the beef-exporting bonanza during World War II, the three meatpacking plants in El Cerro employed nearly ten thousand people,

3. The American companies came to Uruguay and Argentina to avoid rising production costs and antitrust legislation at home, enticed by government incentives and the availability of livestock and cheap labor on the shores of the River Plate. Recognizing the centrality of beef exports to the national economy, as well as the lack of adequate capital, technology, and transportation to market the product, Uruguayan governments passed legislation to attract foreign capital—including a law that guaranteed 6 percent return to companies investing more than half a million pesos and waived taxes on imports of meat-processing machinery and industrial inputs. Swift set up Frigorífico Montevideo in 1911 on the former site of the Saladero Cibils, while Armour bought Frigorífico Artigas in 1917, only two years after it had started operations (ibid., 19–20).

4. During the World War I period, Swift controlled nearly 50 percent of the country's meat exports, displacing British capital as the key player in the industry, but by the 1930s Swift's dominant position weakened following an agreement between Britain and the United States over export quotas.

5. Although FRIGONAL started operations in 1929 with a capacity to slaughter 2,500 cattle and 4,300 sheep daily, it had inadequate technology and financing (Bernhard 1970, 24–25).

6. See Solari and Franco 1983, 120–21.

mostly Cerrenses, in a community of under fifty thousand—which meant that it was nearly impossible to find a local family not dependent, directly or indirectly, on the industry. In contrast to the case of the railways in Peñarol—where workers were dispersed over a larger territory—most Cerrenses lived and worked within the boundaries of their neighborhood. Labor, the basis of collective identity, operated as an overriding marker that linked the plurality of cultures that coexisted in the community. El Cerro was, above all, a community proud of its working-class identity at a time when jobs were plentiful and workers earned very decent salaries:

> MANUEL: What united the family of El Cerro—because the neighborhood was like a big family—was work. Here, people worked, and because they worked they had money, and this income stirred up Cerro society, in every sphere, whatever you care to mention. In El Cerro there were shops, businesses of all kinds, restaurants, cinemas, theaters, churches, nothing was missing. This generated a strong feeling of belonging among us.

The meatpacking plants, however, did not mechanically create the Cerrense working class.[7] Rather, the proletariat in El Cerro made itself from the raw materials of its daily life—a geographically segregated community where workplace and residence blended within a multicultural framework provided by European immigration—and over the course of hard-fought struggles. The high concentration of workers in a few enterprises facilitated the growth of worker organization and consciousness, which were in turn reinforced by the residential concentration of these workers on the slopes of El Cerro. In this manner, workplace and community became intertwined, as daily life in this multicultural town recreated and shaped the collective identity emerging on the plant floor. Paradoxically, elements of this consciousness remain deeply engrained in the community, even though the frigoríficos are long gone.

7. I follow the argument by E. P. Thompson (1968, 9–10) regarding the making of the English working class: "The working class did not rise like the sun at an appointed time. It was present at its own making. . . . The notion of class entails the notion of historical relationship [that] . . . must always be embodied in real people and in a real context. . . . Class happens when some men, as a result of common experiences (inherited or shared), feel and articulate the identity of their interests as between themselves, and as against other men whose interests are different from (and often opposed to) theirs. . . . Class-consciousness is the way in which these experiences are handled in cultural terms: embodied in traditions, value-systems, ideas and institutional forms. If the experience appears determined, class-consciousness does not. . . . Consciousness of class arises in the same way in different times and places, but never in just the same way."

Immigrant workers played a major role in constructing this identity, adapting their European traditions and trade union experiences to the context of El Cerro. The newcomers contributed their skills and strong work ethic, as well as the more radical traditions of European socialism, trade unionism, and anarchism. As they set up roots in their new home, these immigrants fostered union militancy, promoted social and cultural activities, and taught their children the value of education:

> GRACIELA: El Cerro is a neighborhood with a lot of character, with a long history of struggle, from children of different immigrant families being raised side by side when the meat-processing industry was developed. Lithuanians, Russians, Italians all came and brought up new generations with the traditions they brought from Europe. These were people with a history of labor struggle, many of them were anarchists, and they made sure that their children were well trained, that they studied, and that they loved this place, this cosmopolitan city.

These immigrant workers creatively adapted European ideas and traditions of struggle to the reality of a foreign-owned industry and an export-dependent economy. Influenced by anarchist and socialist ideals, these mostly self-taught workers created a working-class culture that spilled beyond the factory gates. They built a rich network of popular theater companies, libraries, local press, and *ateneos* (clubs that encouraged debate and popular education), all of which nurtured pride in the laboring classes; these workers also searched for alternative forms of social organization and practiced various forms of solidarity, mutual help, and self-reliance.[8] These immigrant workers produced a strong working-class culture rooted in a specific territorial community where diverse ethnic groups came together by the centrality of their class experience.

Since the dawn of the twentieth century, Cerrenses distinguished themselves for their powerful militancy and class-based solidarity, unusual in a country characterized by centrist politics. Workers struck countless times—for better salaries, to improve working conditions, or in solidarity with other workers—always counting on the unconditional support of the entire Cerrense community.[9] The first major worker victory came in 1916, following

---

8. See Barrios Pintos and Reyes Abadie 1994, 112–13; and Zibechi n.d.

9. As early as 1905, for example, seven hundred meatpackers in El Cerro struck in solidarity with striking port construction workers from La Teja.

a march through the streets of El Cerro by more than four thousand residents in support of striking meatpacking workers. As a result, workers gained a 10 percent salary increase, implementation of the eight-hour law passed by Parliament, and reinstatement of all striking workers who had been replaced by scabs. The following year, however, the government dispatched the military to break a strike by more than six thousand meatpackers, closing down trade union locals and imprisoning their leaders.

Military occupation of the villa became a common occurrence in El Cerro during the first half of the twentieth century, but it never weakened the community's resolve to confront their American meatpacker bosses. During the 1950s—when the import substitution and beef-export economic model began to show signs of exhaustion, and the country witnessed widespread labor conflicts—the most combative strikes took place in the western region of Montevideo, among workers in Montevideo harbor, and in the communities of El Cerro and La Teja. It was during these times that El Cerro secured a place in the national consciousness as a bastion of trade union militancy. Not even the harsh repression unleashed by the government in the early 1950s to quash strikes in El Cerro—declaring a state of siege and ordering the massive imprisonment of labor leaders—succeeded in damping labor militancy. The strikes resumed in 1955, and again in 1956, and meatpackers gained important concessions from their American managers. It is noteworthy that in contrast with the railways, where British and state management encouraged dialogue and negotiation, the American bosses were much less inclined to negotiate at first, often pushing workers to strike. Differences in management stance contributed in part to the distinct trade union traditions found in Peñarol and El Cerro.

The meatpackers' determination built their reputation for uncompromising politics and placed them at the center of the most radical wing of the trade union movement that emerged along the territorial axis of El Cerro–La Teja–El Puerto (the harbor). Calling for direct action, class independence, and socialism, this current became an important reference point in the history of the labor movement in the region. Their May Day marches were massive, as thousands of proud and militant workers descended from El Cerro to join their brothers and sisters from neighboring La Teja:

> KOSTAS: Every first of May, the marches would start at the Autonomous Meat Federation by Greece and Holland streets, led by the cattle drovers mounted on horseback with their most luxurious harnesses, with their ponchos, their headbands; it was they who would

lead the march to Lafont Square in La Teja, where they would hold the "meetings" that were held back then.

Over the years, El Cerro produced a combative, non-accommodating radicalism rooted in labor militancy and a strong sense of class solidarity. This culture was implacable in its hostility toward strikebreakers, whose actions undermined the collective spirit that united the community and made the strikes possible:

> KOSTAS: When there were strikes, the strikebreakers were persecuted. I saw them cut off the hair of women scabs. And I recall vividly one extreme instance, because the image is so powerful, of a scab that they stripped naked and who ran down the street, knocking door-to-door seeking refuge; people would open their doors and when they saw who he was, they'd close the door again. These are extreme cases, right? But they are revealing.

The meatpackers' union solidarity went far beyond the factory floor, constructing links of trust and loyalty across the community:

> SUSANA: During the time of the strikes in the meatpacking plants, I had hepatitis but I never went without a good steak dinner, because the union would make sure that people who were sick still got meat, and quince jelly, and cans of peaches in syrup—everything that you needed. When someone was in need, nothing was held back: we never went hungry.

Working-class militancy in El Cerro was so powerful that I can still see traces of it today. Remarkably, Cerrenses fashioned an identity, centered on the image of "El Cerro combativo" (combative El Cerro), that still frames local culture long after the plants and the meatpacking jobs vanished:

> PABLO: The image of El Cerro is of people who put up a fight, of a place that is organized and combative—thanks to the meatpacking industry—of very solidary people. Unfortunately, the children of these working people have been left without work, since the close of these huge monsters of El Cerro: the meatpacking plants.

Even though there has not been a major strike in El Cerro in more than three decades, the values underpinning the image of "El Cerro combativo" are embraced by second-generation Cerrenses who still use the language of radical proletarian solidarity that emerged during the time of the frigoríficos:

SUSANA: "You must always be a decent person; never be a scab and never suck up to your boss"—this is what my mother taught me. And I just don't understand scabs.

Worker Resistance and the End of Meatpacking Jobs

The supremacy of radical trade unionism in El Cerro came to an end with the collapse of the meatpacking industry in the 1960s. Swift and Armour closed down operations in 1958, leaving behind dilapidated installations and a considerable debt of unpaid social security and pension benefits. In a desperate attempt to save jobs, the government bought the American plants and opened a new meatpacking operation, Establecimientos Frigoríficos del Cerro. In the end, the new enterprise succumbed to the domestic and foreign pressures that had brought the industry down in the first place, and the government could not stop the permanent closing of the outdated meatpacking plants. The availability of modern technologies, and a desire to curtail labor militancy, had produced a shift in the structure of the meatpacking industry, favoring new systems of production based on smaller and more decentralized plants that were scattered all over the country. Cerrenses struggled courageously against the loss of their jobs and hard-earned gains, using the radical repertoires of collective action that had served them well in their previous struggles against American companies, but their militancy was not sufficient to curb the formidable economic and technological forces they faced.

The last major battle took place toward the end of the 1960s when Cerrenses massively took to the streets to protest management's decision to suspend the daily allocation of two kilograms of beef that each worker received as a complement to his or her salary. Vivid memories of this conflict come to my mind as I cross the Pantanoso Bridge on my way to El Cerro. The bridge, which is the main gateway into the community, was the site of brave battles as workers regularly set up barricades to prevent police access. During the famous struggles of the 1950s and 1960s, the bridge became popularly known as "the 38th Parallel Bridge," in reference to the line that separated North and South during the Korean War. I recall the pictures on the front pages of daily newspapers depicting a veritable war zone, the air darkened by thick black smoke from burning tires, stone-throwing workers behind makeshift barricades facing hundreds of well-armed soldiers. Only the army and the police equipped with riot gear, tear gas, armored vehicles, and charging horses dared to cross the bridge to enter the community and battle the unarmed workers.

> ERNESTO: When I think of El Cerro, the first thing that comes to mind are the strikes by the meatpackers and by the students, back in 1969 when I was in high school. Everyone was a worker and it was an amazing thing, those street battles, because El Cerro was like a fortress. They'd close off the Pantanoso Bridge and I remember one day the soldiers tried all day to gain control of the neighborhood. There were even barricades set up—it looked like a war zone!

Although the workers lost this battle, it is still remembered as the last major combat in El Cerro, a battle that ensured that the image of a gutsy community that went down fighting would live on in the country's collective memory. A former Tupamaro commander recalls those days:

> I never saw anything so broad-based as this struggle; there were fire-pits in all the houses of El Cerro. Every home was in solidarity with the struggle . . . and all of El Cerro rose up to demand a national meat-packing industry. We were all united . . . all of El Cerro rising up, and nobody could get into the neighborhood. And we were all comrades, all brothers: kids, women, men, students, everyone together in this fight, it was so beautiful. It is sad that we lost, but beautiful because of the shared struggle, the joining of students and workers. That Cerro was an example that will never, never be forgotten.[10]

The Aftermath of the Crisis: Reconfiguring the Community

The closing of the meatpacking plants had a devastating impact on El Cerro, much deeper than the effects brought about by the closing of the railways in Peñarol. All the movie theaters and most major businesses went bankrupt, turning Avenida Grecia into a nearly deserted street, and the few bars and cafes that remained open thanks to a few loyal customers

10. Quoted from transcription of radio interview with Esteban Jorge Pereira Mena, CX36 Radio Centenario, Montevideo, April 14, 2005, available online at http://www.radio36.com.uy/entrevistas/2005/04/180405_pereira_mena.htm.

saw their business shrink to a bare minimum. As residents found jobs in other parts of the city, El Cerro slowly became a dormitory neighborhood. Thus, once a successful working class community, El Cerro is currently one of the most rapidly declining areas in the entire city, characterized by high rates of unemployment, violence, crime, and drug use. More recently, it gained the sad distinction of having the highest suicide rate in the city.[11]

The disappearance of jobs drove a dagger through the heart of the community, affecting its collective self-esteem and undermining a central axis of local identity—namely, the centrality of work as the basis of human dignity. Julio—a former trade unionist who became a community activist, was elected to the neighborhood council for three consecutive terms, and later took a seat in the local junta—experienced this situation firsthand:

> That we have arrived to where we are now is completely screwed up, a total regression. The degree of degradation to which people here have arrived—the carts of the garbage pickers, the garbage, having to eat garbage—is terribly sad. And I have seen it for myself; I worked since 1968 but didn't make it to 2000 with a job, and so this decay also affected me. What we are going through is very sad, and at my age it is very hard to get work.

The crisis undermined one of the central pillars that had sustained this community for nearly a century: class solidarity:

> MIGUEL: We have been utterly destroyed, not as politicians but as human beings. We suffer from every need: we have no work, no good health care, no good schools in which to educate our children. . . . This neoliberal world has brought us here, to individualism, to a loss of any sense of collectivity. Yes, we lost our sense of solidarity because when you have less, you start to think, "If I give away this cup of sugar, tomorrow I will be without." I think that people are still solidary deep down, but this sentiment has gone dormant because economically, we have been beaten to a pulp.

Intensifying the Cerrenses' understandable sense of injury, a panoramic look from the fort at the top of the hill reveals that squatters now surround this once proud and nearly self-contained working-class community.

---

11. Instituto Nacional de Estadística 2004.

Pushed out of the city center by high rental prices and poverty, squatters arrived by the thousands to illegally seize vacant lands to build their dwellings on the northern and western parts of the hill. The massive influx of newcomers explains why district 17 experienced the highest rate of population growth in the city between 1996 and 2004.[12] According to the latest figures from the 2004 census, in fact, three of the six neighborhoods with the most population growth were located in district 17.[13] Such an increase comes on top of an even greater spike in population growth that had occurred between 1985 and 1996, when the communities of Casabo and Pajas Blancas doubled their population, and the population in the neighborhood of La Paloma and the other areas surrounding El Cerro increased at a rate between 25 and 39 percent—much higher than the 2.3 percent average population growth in the city during the same period.[14] As squatting in the area accelerated in the 1990s, by 1997 nearly one-sixth of the three hundred asentamientos in the capital city were found in district 17.[15] According to the 2004 census, 43 percent of all people living in asentamientos were in district 17.

This population explosion that brought an avalanche of squatters to El Cerro occurred without much planning, producing high-density communities that lacked basic urban services.[16] When Carmen, a longtime resident of El Cerro, visited the asentamientos for the first time in 2004 as a census officer, she was shocked by what she saw:

> They piled themselves up! They did not respect the need every human being has for a certain amount of space in which to live. They lost all privacy. They left these tiny little passages that nothing can enter; no car can get in, nothing can. And it's horrible because there will never be streets or sidewalks there, it's disastrous. And what's more, they occupied land that later, out of financial need, they further subdivided and sold. It is horrible; you can't believe that people live all piled up together like that!

12. A rate of population growth of 8.1 percent in a city with a negative average growth of 1.5 percent. Ibid.

13. Casavalle, 26.0 percent; Casabo/Pajas Blancas, 22.4 percent; La Paloma Tomkinson, 22.0 percent. Ibid., 10.

14. See Avila et al. 2003, 11.

15. See IMM 2004c, district 17, 7–9.

16. According to the city government, average population density in asentamientos is more than twice as high as the average for the city of Montevideo. See IMM 2004a. Data from the 2004 census shows that there are 3.8 persons per household in the asentamientos, compared to the average figure of 2.9 for the rest of the city.

In the haste to claim a piece of land, squatters grabbed some of the most treasured public spaces:

> MIGUEL: I remember how it was before; my old man would get the mate ready and we would go to watch the neighbors play soccer, but the need for housing was so intense that now, here in El Cerro, even these recreational spaces have been taken over. They took over the playing fields to make houses!

While a few asentamientos in the district date back to the 1950s, squatters started to settle in significant numbers in El Cerro in the early 1970s, precisely at the time when Cerrenses experienced the collapse of the local economy, the loss of jobs, and the erosion of their proletarian community lifestyle.[17] The mix proved challenging, to say the least:

> SUSANA: Before, El Cerro had industry, theaters, cinemas; it had everything but, bit by bit, they tightened the economic belt and filled the zone with poverty. There are tons of people who came here to live who are excellent. But there are many other people who moved here en masse, as a whole neighborhood at once, and created Cerro Norte.

Indeed, one such asentamiento is Cerro Norte, an agglomeration of several smaller settlements, with a reputation for crime and violence. Set up in the 1970s, Cerro Norte is one of the largest of the more than fifty squatter settlements in the district. In contrast to the migration wave that brought migrant workers from smaller towns to Peñarol in the 1950s and 1960s, the people who built Cerro Norte came primarily from impoverished neighborhoods in the center of Montevideo. The newcomers belonged to the so-called marginal masses, people with little formal education, no steady jobs, and certainly no history of organized trade union or political activity. Their experiences and lifestyles clashed with the more cohesive, militant, working-class culture that had been fashioned in El Cerro over the years. Not surprisingly, Cerrenses did not welcome the newcomers, and perceived their arrival as an invasion by people whose values and traditions were alien to the ones they had built through hard work and struggle. Cerrenses

---

17. Some describe the mixing of the "historical" residents and the newcomers as a process of *mestizaje*, a term traditionally used to describe the racial miscegenation that occurred in Latin America since the time of the conquest (between the Indian, African, and European people) but that has been adapted to refer to class intermixing.

experienced the growth of asentamientos as another act of aggression by a society that had turned its back on their community. They resented the intruders, feeling that their once proud and prosperous community had become the dumping ground for "antisocial" elements that were not wanted in other parts of the city:

> KOSTAS: And to Cerro Norte came antisocial people who moved in and created this new neighborhood. It is practically a pigeon shed, because it really lacks dignity, although it's true that compared to today's asentamientos it looks luxurious.

Feeling besieged by squatters, Cerrenses justified their fears of the newcomers on social and political grounds. Socially, squatters were labeled as bums and criminals who would eventually destroy the solidarity, family-centered values, and community lifestyle of El Cerro. Politically, squatters were considered easily manipulable by right-wing political bosses, who would ensure their political loyalty through patronage handouts. As evidence of this, they pointed to the fact that the wife of Bordaberry, the right-wing president who dissolved Parliament in 1973, opening the period of military rule, sponsored the first settlements in Cerro Norte.[18] "Original" Cerrenses even resented that the name El Cerro was appropriated by the residents of Cerro Norte. To them the squatters were muddying the heritage of this proud community and they emphatically insisted that there was only one El Cerro, which they now call "El Casco del Cerro" to distinguish it from the surrounding settlements.

Back in the offices of local government, Alicia complains that these distinctions between El Casco or the asentamientos matter little to a mainstream society that stigmatizes everyone in El Cerro by labeling the entire district a red zone—rampant with crime, violence, prostitution, and drugs. She argues that this discrimination is perversely connected to the history of militancy in the community:

> El Cerro's bad reputation is not based only on poverty; it stems also from part of the neighborhood's history. The dominant system has

---

18. This perception runs against recent findings that show that the social configuration of asentamientos has changed over time. Although the majority of squatters remain poor and socially excluded, their levels of formal education and labor market participation increased when compared with those in the 1970s. This may indicate the deepening and broadening of poverty and social exclusion across the city, as people with formal jobs and higher levels of education are turned into squatters.

to destroy anything that, in some way, subverts the status quo, and that old Cerro of rebellion, of unions and strikes, was a threat to the status quo. So there is continuity in the way we are stigmatized. Before, the rebels, the so-called antidemocratic ones, were stigmatized; today, it is the thieves, killers, and rapists who are stigmatized.

Alicia speaks with authority on this issue because she has been a squatter for more than twenty years. Surprisingly, Alicia, the educated lawyer and the current head of local government, is a resident of San Rafael, an asentamiento on the edges of Cerro Norte. Located a few blocks to the north of Avenida Carlos María Ramírez, the dividing line between El Casco and Cerro Norte, her family lives in one of the older and more established subdivisions of Cerro Norte. To the untrained eye, the modest houses on her block do not look like squatters' homes. In contrast to the makeshift dwellings further north, these houses enjoy access to basic urban services and are built with solid brick walls, cement roofs, and glass windows. This particular community was settled more than half a century ago. The asentamientos, most certainly, are internally stratified.

From her standpoint as a resident of a squatter settlement, Alicia protests a pervasive logic of discrimination affecting residents of asentamientos:

> ALICIA: We were victims of a double-stigmatization: the internal and the external. Because there is also a form of internal marginalization or stigmatization that's perpetrated by the overwhelming majority of residents in the old core—or *casco*—of Cerro toward the new residents of the asentamientos. They say that in those new neighborhoods live the no-gooders who pay no taxes and expect everything from the state: "I pay my taxes, and they don't fix the streets here, but they do for those on the other side, those who just arrived and who are not really from Cerro." There is a certain hypocrisy around this, too; you won't find many people who will tell you this openly, but this is how it is, how they feel.

I actually found many activists and councilors from El Casco who expressed this view openly, without much probing, like Manuel, a medical doctor recently elected councilor to represent El Casco:

> They call us, from El Casco, the "bourgeois," but it is us who pay property taxes and the taxes to cover the cost of the new sewer system;

it's us who provide the municipal revenues! I understand that there is this whole social problem to address, but because there is always such a rush to take care of the social sectors of the periphery, who truly have urgent needs, the needs of the core are being eternally neglected!

Building Bridges Across the Two Divides

Torn between these two opposing logics of solidarity/discrimination and altruism/selfishness, residents of El Casco and squatters came together in the institutions of local government in the early 1990s. The underlying tensions and mistrust that existed between them combined with the profound economic and social problems affecting residents in the district to make the workings of local government awfully difficult. In fact, this was what attracted me to El Cerro. Neighborhood councils in district 17 have a reputation for ongoing internal strife, which I had earlier hypothesized to be directly connected to the history of combative working-class struggles in El Casco; the confrontational politics nurtured by meatpackers in El Cerro, I presumed, would not easily adapt to the realities of decentralization, which required skills at diplomacy, consensus building, and negotiation.

Longtime Cerrenses and squatters came to local government institutions with their own traditions, expectations, and agendas. The stance of people from El Casco was framed by the sense of urgency and entitlement that they felt due to the devastating losses they suffered after the closing of the frigoríficos, including the ensuing disappearance of jobs and trade unions, key pillars of their community identity and cohesion. Understandably, they were not inclined to defer their own demands in order to attend to the needs of others who they thought had illegally invaded their community and, on top of that, did not pay taxes. Solidarity and trust would have to be constructed:

> CATALINA: We councilors from the core felt a little frustrated because we wanted something to be done for El Cerro and they would argue and say, "But you already have everything." So we would say, "OK, so we have everything but still we pay the taxes, so it's only right that our requests get some attention!"

The squatters felt that their needs were more urgent and more legitimate than those of El Casco. Most settlements, they argued, lacked basic urban services, something that residents of El Casco had enjoyed for over half a century. They also faced the formidable challenge of building a sense of community from the fragments that each squatter had brought to this alien and unwelcoming territory. The squatters could not understand why a community that had earned a reputation for solidarity across the city was so reluctant to defer its own demands when making decisions about the allocation of municipal resources in the district. For some, Cerrenses had become an inward-looking, selfish, and privileged group of people who were unwilling to extend solidarity to people beyond the confines of their narrow borders.

The potential for internal strife and misunderstanding was much greater than in district 13—an area with fewer asentamientos and less-pronounced social cleavages—making it virtually impossible for Cerrenses and squatters to reproduce the same kind of trust and solidarity. Exacerbating the problems, the confrontational repertoires of collective action from El Casco were not easily adaptable to the exigencies of decentralization. Thus, lacking a tradition of propositional and inclusive collective action centering on urban goods, such as the kind that existed in Peñarol, councilors from El Casco grew increasingly frustrated as they realized that they were ill prepared to lead the rest of the council.

First Meeting of the Local Council

Sitting at the center of a lot larger than ten soccer fields, stretching from the banks of the Pantanoso River to the edges of Cerro Norte, the aging building of the former Frigorífico Artigas ominously overlooks the community. In 1995 the building became the headquarters of the local government, hosting council meetings and multiple community activities. While everyone is pleased to have these facilities (none of the other districts in this study have their own meeting place for council meetings), the space still evokes contradictory feelings among some people, as I discovered when I interviewed a councilor from El Casco in the building:

> SUSANA: Many times when I come in here I have to brace myself so as not to cry, because when we were on strike against the meatpacking plants my whole family worked here: my uncle was the floor chief, my other uncle was the grease chief, my father-in-law was one of the plant's three knife sharpeners, my husband also worked here.

Later, it all changed; they closed this plant, they closed the other, and we slowly started to suffocate.

I go to observe the first session of the newly elected council, as I had done in district 13. I arrive at the large hall on the second floor of the building, where I see several people slowly setting up for the meeting, scattering more than sixty white plastic patio chairs in the hopes of a big turnout. At the center of the hall, a huge wood-burning stove built in stone and black iron holds an open fire that battles in vain against the cold draft filtering through broken windows and the open door. Even though I secure a spot close to the fire, as the meeting unfolds I become painfully aware that even my three decades of coping with Canadian winters have not prepared me for the bitter, humid cold that settles over working-class neighborhoods in Montevideo. I also sense that, in contrast to the celebratory and relaxed atmosphere I had witnessed at the inaugural meeting in district 13, the meeting of the local council in district 17 is going to be tenser and more conflictive.

A full hour behind schedule, the secretary of the local junta stepped to the front to call the meeting to order and to invite special guests to take their seats at the front of the hall. The personalities included two representatives from the city government, the coordinator of the western region of Montevideo and a city councilor who was a former official with the district's local government; members of the local junta, including its president and secretary; and Kostas, on behalf of the electoral commission that had organized and supervised the recent elections for neighborhood council. Two members of the team of social workers and an urban planner stationed in district 17 were also in attendance but did not sit at the front of the hall.

The first part of the meeting was chaired by the secretary of the local junta, who introduced the guests and invited them to speak briefly about the importance of local government, the gains made in building participatory democracy, and the challenges ahead. The formal speeches ended with an emotional plea from Kostas urging councilors to put a stop to the feuding that had worn out previous councils.

As soon as the councilors moved on to the first order of business, it became evident to me that leaving past conflicts behind would not be easy. A new councilor from El Casco, who had garnered the highest number of votes in the district, was assigned the daunting task of moderating the meeting. In spite of his good efforts and his determined attempt at being fair, his authority was constantly challenged from the floor by councilors who raised questions of order or refused to acknowledge his position. Frustration mounted within less than an hour over a minor procedural misunderstanding about a motion, when an angry councilor from an asentamiento challenged the chair to a fistfight. Fortunately, the chair remained composed and with the help of other councilors they calmed down the angry councilor and the meeting resumed, though no less chaotically than before.

To facilitate the running of the meeting, returning councilors tried to convey to the newcomers how things had worked in the past, a passing of traditions of sorts. With nearly 70 percent turnover in the council, these more experienced councilors were in the minority and found that the traditions they invoked were dismissed by incoming councilors who insisted that they would chart their own course. This insistence precipitated a flurry of unruly debates about how the council should operate, what it could and could not discuss, who should and should not vote, and so forth. The experienced social worker assigned to the district, wise enough to let councilors figure things out by themselves, would only intervene in exceptional circumstances to help move things along, explaining procedural issues like what a motion is and how to present, discuss, and vote on one, or summarizing the main arguments before a vote.

Adding to the confusion, multiple small-group meetings took place simultaneously on the sidelines as the meeting went on, making it extremely hard to follow proceedings from the floor. Many councilors stood up the entire time, moving from one end of the hall to another, engaging in conversations with other councilors, while their fellow council members were addressing the meeting. These ambulant councilors would intervene from time to time in the general discussion, only to return to their side conversations at the edge of the hall without bothering to listen to the responses from other councilors. Not surprisingly, very few decisions were actually made; after more than three hours the meeting ended, leaving councilors feeling frustrated and bewildered.[19]

The dynamics of the meeting underscore the formidable problems that activists in district 17 faced in their efforts to build solidarity and trust across neighborhoods and to ensure a smoother operation of local government. The chair's fragile hold over the meeting highlighted the absence of trust

19. This description differs from that offered by Baiocchi in his discussion of such discussions at meetings in Porto Alegre, where he found that the conversations on the sidelines allowed people to talk over their differences and get things moving.

and vividly illustrated the lack of consensus over basic norms and traditions among elected councilors. Not surprisingly, in this context, there was little room for handing out certificates or flowers to local activists, and no time for poetry or jokes, as had occurred the week before in district 13!

Following the meeting I hitched a ride to the bus station with five of the six councilors from El Casco, all newcomers to the council. Cramped in a small car, the newly elected councilors were stunned after their first meeting of the neighborhood council. They complained about the hostility they felt from other councilors and the absence of basic rules of communication. One of them, a social worker by training, made the understatement that it would be very useful to organize workshops to improve group dynamics and collective decision making among councilors, and offered to start with the small group of councilors from El Casco. As I rode back in the bus I started to wonder whether the poor operation of local government in district 17—which I had previously imagined grew directly out of the history of radical labor militancy in El Casco—could not be explained by other factors.

Leadership Capacities in the Neighborhood Council

Soon after I started fieldwork in El Cerro I realized that activists from El Casco never had the same capacity to influence the workings of their neighborhood council when compared with their counterparts from Peñarol in district 13. While community leaders in Peñarol successfully brought their experiences into the heart of local institutions, in district 17 leadership did not come from El Casco but rather from activists belonging to the older squatter settlements. These settlements had brought migrants from the interior of the country and impoverished residents of inner-city neighborhoods together with second- and third-generation Cerrenses who could not afford to remain in El Casco. This third group put to use some of the collective mobilization traditions of El Casco to build new communities, spreading the traditions of solidarity beyond the boundaries of El Cerro:

> GRACIELA: All this history and experience with organizing was passed on. The people who lived in El Cerro had children that they raised in the neighborhood. Some lived in extensions they built onto the houses of their parents, but not everyone could do this. So the asentamientos of Casabó, La Paloma, and La Boyada were organized by

these children or grandchildren of the organized workers. In the case of Casabo, beginning in 1968 they organized themselves and occupied land; they divided the land and built flimsy homes at first, but within a year they would have a solidly built kitchen, bathroom, and bedroom, and they would all get together to put the roofs on. And this way of doing things came from a long history of organizing in El Cerro.

These pioneer squatters built their homes and improved their communities, relying on solid bonds of solidarity and mutual help, as Luis and Margarita had done in Peñarol one decade earlier:

> PABLO: When we were trying to finish the house and put the roof on, neighbors would appear from everywhere to lend a hand. A neighbor would pass by and ask, "When are you making the cement roof?" Or, "When are you setting up the bathroom?" And then there they would be, on Sunday at 7:00 A.M. with a bucket and a shovel and a bunch of people who, on a completely voluntary basis, came to lend a hand. And it is a real source of pride to help a neighbor, to see him get ahead—but also to see the neighborhood progress at the same time.

Some of the first squatters set up neighborhood associations that became virtually the only institutions in these communities, providing the groundwork for community development and filling the vacuum created by the absence of state institutions. The associations organized urban planning, ensuring that squatting proceeded in an orderly fashion, reserving areas for the future construction of roads and community recreation, and granting every family an equal amount of land on which to build its home. The legitimacy earned by these associations allowed them to act as mediators when conflicts arose among residents or in relations between squatters and the state.

Many of these neighborhood associations remain active today, even though there was an overall decline in the number of active associations in the asentamientos. Still, when I asked activists to identify the organization that had contributed most to their community, leaders from the asentamientos did not hesitate:

> PABLO: Oh, the neighborhood associations, no doubt. It is the specific work of the association that people respect so much—neighborhood improvement, the legalization of land titles—and what's more,

sometimes the association has to play the role of judge or arbiter of problems among residents.[20]

It was in these neighborhood associations that community activists gained their first experiences in collective organizing, a tradition they passed on to future generations. Pablo, for example, has lived in one of the earlier asentamientos ever since his parents joined the group of squatters that built what is today the community of Casabó.[21] A second-generation squatter, Pablo followed the footsteps of his parents, joining the local neighborhood association, where he got his early schooling as a community organizer:

> Yes, I got started in the neighborhood association, following somewhat in the footsteps of our parents, our neighbors. It was they who undertook to bring electricity and running water to the neighborhood, and then we continued by bringing bus stops, paved streets, streetlights. And when I say "we," I mean a bunch of residents who carried forward the legacy of that generation, the generation of our parents, in order to continue making the neighborhood better.

Similar to the case of Peñarol, the capacities developed in these associations proved valuable when decentralization was set up in the early 1990s, allowing activists from these asentamientos, like Pablo and Alicia, to quickly become leaders of local government. Pablo joined the neighborhood council in 1995 and was reelected in 1998, earning a spot in the local junta in 2001, a position he has held to this day. Alicia became an alternate member of the local junta in 1993 before she was elected to the council for two consecutive periods and became president of the local junta in 2001. They brought to the local government a wide array of capacities developed through participatory community development activities and years of experience in negotiating urban goods with state agencies. Building these capacities was facilitated by the emergence in the 1960s of a more conciliatory

20. In contrast, activists from El Casco had difficulty identifying a single community organization. Instead, some named trade unions, while others pointed to senior citizens clubs or cultural associations.

21. Casabó occupies what used to be the area of La Tablada, the open grasslands on the western slopes of El Cerro where the stockyards were located. This area became available after the collapse of the frigoríficos, attracting people from across the city and from El Cerro itself. Today, more than twelve thousand people make their home in Casabó. The community is internally stratified; in some areas residents own their lots and have access to basic urban services, while in others residents do not own the lots where they erected their houses and they have few urban services. See Universidad de la República 2002.

stance among state authorities toward illegal land occupations, encouraging negotiations with squatters over urban services.

Thanks to these previous experiences, leaders of the asentamientos adapted more successfully to the institutional exigencies of local government when they were called on to help foster participatory democracy:

> PABLO: Of course, we came with the experience of creating a neighborhood, with proper infrastructure and public spaces. The resident of the asentamiento knows that it's here, to our council, that you have to bring any proposal for neighborhood improvements. There are also strong neighborhood associations, because it is through the association that you can make requests for neighborhood improvements.

Thus, since their repertoires of collective action were more adaptable to the institutional reality of decentralization than those from El Casco, activists from the asentamientos with more experience with collective mobilization found it easier to position themselves as leaders of local government and to seize the opportunities opened by decentralization.

As in Peñarol under MIRPA, the squatters had already moved beyond the narrow boundaries of each community before decentralization arrived, setting up in 1985 an umbrella organization of representatives from neighborhood associations from the asentamientos in the district. Commonly known as the Cordinadora de Tierras, the Commission for the Legalization of Asentamientos in El Cerro and Surrounding Areas (Comisión Para la Regularización de los Asentamientos del Cerro y Adyacencias) worked to obtain the legalization of land titles, to encourage community organization, and to offer conflict resolution in troubled areas:

> ALICIA: The land commission was a strong organization; in it were concentrated the representatives of the asentamientos of the zone and there we would make collective proposals. We would also resolve issues that were internal to the neighborhood associations. There was a conflict in that neighborhood, within its neighborhood association, and so they sought the intervention of the commission. We also sought to encourage the formation of neighborhood associations in neighborhoods that hadn't any.

The Cordinadora de Tierras facilitated networking and communication among leaders of asentamientos (including Pablo and Alicia, who were founding members), encouraging them to design community development plans to address their common problems. Like MIRPA activists in Peñarol, they had already started the work they were asked to do when they joined local government institutions in the early 1990s:

> ALICIA: Before Tabaré's government, there were already structures in El Cerro very similar to the ones required by decentralization. Before they started the institution here of the five-year plan, we were already accustomed to bringing the associations together to make collective plans; we'd been doing this for four or five years. For the first five-year plan we met with the neighborhood associations in each subzone and put together collective proposals. We were already accustomed to consulting in this way.

Even though the commission was dissolved after most of its leaders joined local government, the collective experience of this organization lived on and helped determine the tempo and character of the first councils:

> ALICIA: The land commission was created in 1985. And I was in it until decentralization took place, then the commission more or less dissolved. Almost all of us who were in the commission ended up being councilors. That's why the first neighborhood council had such a strong and respected land commission, a commission that truly came up with proposals and even legislative projects. So, the first and the second councils were characterized by having a land commission that set the tone, the rhythm for the rest of the council.

Thus, contrary to what I had assumed, leadership in the first councils came from the asentamientos, especially from those with organizational and collective mobilization experience, rather than from the militant El Casco. Not surprisingly, the demands and mode of operation of local government tended to reflect the interests and experiences of people in these communities. As we will see below, however, and in contrast to what occurred in Peñarol, the ability of these leaders to imprint their more pragmatic leadership style onto the council and to contain clashes therein was undermined by the conflicts arising from the overwhelming socioeconomic conditions affecting residents in district 17.

Representatives from El Casco found themselves in unfamiliar territory when they joined the council, and they initially had a hard time adapting to the institutional dynamics of participatory decentralization. They arrived equipped with more contentious repertoires of collective action that were not easily adaptable to the operation of the council. They had little, if any, recent experience of mobilizing for urban goods, since their community had enjoyed urban services for decades. To make matters worse, with only seven out of forty councilors in the district, they were an absolute minority in the council. Ironically, the district with such strong traditions of trade union militancy did not elect a single trade unionist to council in 2004:

> PABLO: We have not had many unionists in the council. What's more, there are no strong unions in the area now; there is no work around which to organize and bring workers together. There is a strong representation of the asentamientos in the council because it is there that they have the greatest need. Everyone has troubles and things to advocate for.

The Erosion of Traditional Cerrense Solidarity

Another factor weakening the traditional strength of El Casco was the sudden destitution that afflicted most residents in the community. According to several people I talked to, poverty and unemployment undermined the community's collective solidarity:

> MIGUEL: The custom of working collectively has been lost. Everything is worn out. Here in El Cerro the social fabric that produced strong social organizations that we wove through the workers' and students' struggles has been worn out. Today we are suffering the worst flogging El Cerro has ever undergone; we must be forty-five percent unemployed. When you have no work, you worry about your immediate personal or household problems, about your home, and this leads you to put aside other matters.

The powerful bonds of solidarity that used to unite the community of El Cerro were overshadowed by emerging feelings of insecurity produced by rising crime rates in the area. These feelings built on the culture of fear that emerged during the dictatorship to push people away from public life and into the safer environment of the home:

> CATALINA: Solidarity has changed, because with all the insecurity now your neighbor has turned more inward. Before, he was more solidary;

we left our door open because we knew that the neighbor would look out for us. Now you are being robbed and your neighbor stays inside his house watching and does nothing. Before, your neighbor would take risks to protect your things; he might even have looked after your things more than his own.

PABLO: When economic hardship came, people started to really retreat into their homes. Also because of the whole situation under the dictatorship—it was like a habit that was instilled in people to stay at home out of fear and insecurity, it stayed on after the end of the dictatorship. This fear and insecurity just kept growing, and this is so now more than ever because of the current situation, all the theft and violence.

Cerrenses complain that alarming manifestations of day-to-day violence are further undermining community cohesion, as residents are more edgy and more prone to violence than ever:

CARMEN: We're more touchy, more violent, we can't tolerate anything. You see this at the soccer matches, in children's games, in the schools, in the places where people go and get into trouble. Also in cases of domestic violence. In the offices of the local government there is an office for women, that's where women go to denounce abuse, and there you can see all this violence.

Paradoxically, most activists that I talked to from El Casco still list solidarity as one of the defining features of their community. The changes described above may have weakened community solidarity, but they have not erased it altogether from the collective memory.

Decline in Participation?

Activists often complain that people do not participate in community affairs as they used to, opting instead to delegate community development tasks to a few overburdened activists:

JULIO: Five years ago, this was a beehive of associations; now it's like there has been a decline in participation; the decrease has been notable. I think it's a consequence of the crisis itself, that people are tired, dispirited; they have no time and no expectations.

MIGUEL: The few *compañeros* that participate in anything now are over-burdened. Today, when you are in the neighborhoods, in the asentamientos, the residents elect an association and they say, "Just take care of everything." But it can't be like that. . . . Residents stay calmly at home, or not even calmly because they have their own problems to worry about, but they won't give you so much as an hour of their time to participate as an individual and to help build the collective.

This attitude—which undermines collective mobilization and weakens civil society organizations—also encourages more individualistic leadership styles and resurrects practices that the Left criticized for years:

MIGUEL: There are now some sixty-plus asentamientos and not even ten of them have a neighborhood association. What you have are individual contacts in those neighborhoods. You know these individuals because they used to belong to the old neighborhood association that no longer exists. So when you want to deal with that neighborhood, you do so through this individual resident. What we are doing, then, is resurrecting the old *caudillismo* of Uruguayan custom, and this is wrong!

Ironically, when opinion polls showed in 2004 that the Left had a strong chance to capture the national presidency in the elections scheduled for November of that year, political activists complained that left-wing militants were not participating in the *comités de base,* the network of neighborhood clubs established by the Broad Front coalition to unite all sectors of the Left in a single, territorially based organization:

ERNESTO: The neighborhood clubs also disappeared, those clubs from 1971. Some remain but these are heavily defined by political party affiliation; you have the MPP [Movimiento de Participación Popular] club, the Socialist Party club, but you have none of those clubs that brought everyone in, that were full of members and that worked with the neighborhood association.

Readily acknowledging that residents are less inclined to join traditional political structures or the institutions of local government, some activists insist that to argue that there is a generalized crisis of participation is to miss a key point. According to them, people participate in numerous community activities, but not in the structures set up by parties and governments to channel citizen participation:

> CARMEN: In El Cerro, there is probably a crisis of participation when it comes to the neighborhood council. There is a crisis of participation in those old structures that we keep trying to reproduce, but people still participate in many things—in baby soccer, in old folks' organizations, in women's groups, in sports clubs.

> ALICIA: When we say that no one participates in the neighborhood clubs set up by the Broad Front, it's true. But if you go to the soccer field on Sunday you'll see three hundred parents there; during *carnaval* when it comes time to choose the carnival queen of Club Calamochito you'll find five hundred parents there with their kids; if you go to the seniors association when they hold their spring festival you'll see one hundred veterans there, dancing. Life gets expressed somewhere; people participate in some things, because they have to participate, because it is impossible not to participate, and this is all the more true in this neighborhood, where you have to obtain everything through collective effort. So life goes on in other places. . . . Or that is to say, participation happens, but not within the conventional structures.

What is in crisis, they argue, is the traditional model of participation of the Left that privileges formal meetings as the central locus of resident involvement, something that does not resonate with many residents, especially women:

> ALICIA: Somehow, from generation to generation we keep passing on certain structures from the 1960s that are resistant to changes in the way people can get involved. The oldest militants reproduce in today's assemblies the old way of holding meetings—of interjecting, of raising your hand, of being given five minutes to speak, of having a speakers list. We just can't seem to make certain social or political organizations change or adapt.

They stress that people participate in less formal activities and that they are more inclined to join other neighbors in ad hoc, short-term endeavors when their community is affected by a particular problem that can be solved through collective action:

> PABLO: Then you have the kind of participation that comes about in moments of neighborhood crisis, when there is something looming there that will affect everyone, then you see a big group of residents getting involved so that the thing can be resolved. That's how it was in our neighborhood when people had to pay a minimum fee for the installation of public streetlights. According to an agreement with the municipality, we had to pay part of the expense to install the lights. So we went house to house, door to door, and people got involved, each paying a small contribution, and with everything we collected from all the residents we were able to purchase the materials to bring public lighting to the entire neighborhood.

Participation, therefore, emerges as a complex, multilayered phenomenon that cannot be measured by residents' formal engagement in local government, whether by voting or attending council meetings. The institutional setup established through decentralization combined with the ongoing infighting in the neighborhood council to effectively discourage resident participation in decentralized institutions. Nevertheless, many people remained active in a wide array of social organizations even though local government institutions were not on their radar screen. The crisis of participation alluded to by many activists, therefore, may be an expression of the failures of local government rather than a generalized absence of trust and sociability running through the district. It also shows that for many residents, the council does not constitute a key referent for community initiatives, as it does in the case of Peñarol.

The Evolution of Neighborhood Councils: Weakening Links with Local Organizations

The launching of decentralization in the early 1990s generated great enthusiasm across the city, enticing numerous grassroot organizations and activists to embark on a common effort to shape the reform project of the incoming leftist administration. This initial period is remembered by activists as the most rewarding, a time when the creative energies of residents were unleashed in the hope of democratizing local politics and increasing access to urban resources. District 17 was no exception:

MIGUEL: When all this about decentralization got started there was a whole big boom, because it was something new, a new tool through which residents were going to be able to voice different concerns, proposals, and plans. People were eager because they understood that with this new social entity they might be able suddenly to accomplish many things that they had been working on for many years without success.

The enthusiasm, however, was not sustained, and as time went by neighborhood councils in district 17 grew increasingly more detached from local organizations. Tracing the character of the different councils in the district since 1993 showed me that there were marked differences among them. There were two distinct periods in the ten-year history of neighborhood councils: the first was typified by the experience of the first two councils (1993–98), and the later period was exemplified by the operation of the 2001–4 council. The 1998–2001 council, combining practices of both, marks a transition between these two periods.

Meetings of the earlier councils were very well attended and acted as popular assemblies where passionate debates and intense political clashes occurred:

ALICIA: The first councils were very politicized, especially by different sectors of the Left. Old political battles were carried over into the council. The different political tribes expressed themselves, but in another way: confrontationally. There were very heated discussions, very sharp, but well reasoned, each one with a lot of validity. They were huge assemblies, where people came to harangue.

These councils enjoyed relatively high levels of legitimacy because they got things done, in spite of these confrontations; at least at the level of the working commissions of the council, ideological debates faded as residents focused on concrete, immediate problems:

ALICIA: These councils attained a kind of legitimacy with other residents. If there were disputes over land, residents knew that they could go to the land commission that met on such-and-such a day; if there was some problem with the roadways, they went to the commission that met on Wednesday nights, because that was the commission that dealt with roadway issues. And the heated debates that went on in the larger assemblies tended to quiet down in the thematic commissions because there they dealt with concrete issues. At the same time, those commissions also took you out in the street, brought you into more direct contact with people.

Unfortunately, relations deteriorated in subsequent councils, causing these bodies to become increasingly inward looking, submerging councilors in a sea of endless infighting. Visible gains diminished, dropout rates skyrocketed, and debates over ideas often turned into personalized attacks:

JULIO: In the first councils, we were a wide spectrum of comrades of different political stripes and we were all true debaters. Compared to the discussion in those councils, the quality of discussion in today's councils has dropped way down. Before, a lot was worked out through debate and, despite the arguments, good things resulted. In the recent councils this has not been the case; they have not come up with things, with results at the end of the debates, in the way the earlier councils did. As much as we argued—because at times the debates were quite violent—good things used to come out of those discussions.

Paradoxically, the overwhelming presence of partisan politics in the councils may have had a positive impact on the workings of local government in district 17. The clashes among political cadres may have diverted the councils' attention from municipal issues, but they also helped frame the debates on programmatic terms, shedding light on the root causes of the problems affecting communities in the area. Moreover, political parties of the Left had a footing in all the local communities and used these connections to facilitate communication and to mediate the differences between residents from El Casco and the asentamientos. In fact, it was precisely when local leftist party structures entered a crisis in the late 1990s, as occurred in other neighborhoods as well, that relations within the councils started to deteriorate. With the decline in influence of political cadres in the council, the clashes that had occurred around clearly defined political strategies became fuzzier, and councilors' loyalties and groupings started to be driven by other factors:

ALICIA: Then, groups were created more on the basis of custom or territorial affinity than on the basis of those ideas held by the earlier groups that set up the council. This had to do with the weakening of political party structures.

Raquel, a three-time council representative from El Casco, has fond memories of the time she spent in the second and third councils, when political conflict did not preclude the emergence of strong feelings of camaraderie among councilors. Her experiences in the fourth council (2001–4), however, convinced her not to run for another term in office:

> The people in this council that just finished up were completely worn out. I don't know how some people came to be councilors, because they didn't represent any organization. They had drug problems, and they stole things, so people quit going. It was a disaster. The problem was the people involved. Unscrupulous people; you can't work with them. It truly made me feel ashamed. They weren't from El Casco, but from very conflictive areas from the asentamientos.

This new group of councilors that changed the character of the councils came from the newer asentamientos. The entry of councilors with weaker ties to community organizations came about as a result of changes in the electoral regulations introduced by municipal authorities in 1998. Aiming to increase the number of candidates running for council and to facilitate representation of non-organized sectors, municipal authorities lifted the requirement that individuals be sponsored by a local organization to be eligible to run. Under the new regulations, residents could run as independent candidates if they obtained only ten signatures supporting their candidacy. The new regulations effectively opened councils to previously disenfranchised sectors, but they created other problems:

> ALICIA: Before, the facts of how things were forced you to become connected to society, to the community. In the first council, the most supported councilor received eleven hundred votes. Now, since they divided neighborhoods into subzones—and here in El Cerro the zones are very small—and allowed for candidates to run just with ten signatures, there are councilors who have been elected with no more than thirty votes. So now it's problematic to have a vision of "a representative" or "the represented," or to make decisions for a zone as big as this one, when there you have no real popular support. So

this council has less legitimacy. The more recent councils have had less contact with their constituencies; they have been more cut off.

In effect, the new regulations may have contributed to weakening the ties between councils and grassroot organizations, undermining the potential of the council to act as a catalyst to reactivate civil society:

MIGUEL: In the council of 1998, most of the comrades represented neighborhood associations or had experience in social activism, so it was easier for us to work together despite our differences. But since then, the social organizations as such no longer participate in the neighborhood councils. Everything has changed. The council doesn't go out into the neighborhood; it doesn't hold meetings where residents can present their demands or complaints, so a distance grows and the council becomes out-of-touch, and this destroys the thing you always supported—the grassroot organization—even if you don't always realize that this has happened. And sometimes when you realize, it is too late.

Ironically, as the councils became more detached from community organizations, they adopted an increasingly narrower vision of their role and an exaggerated sense of their own importance that further undermined the potential of local government institutions to promote participation:

ALICIA: They weren't capable of attending the other issues in the neighborhood or the zone that had been organized with complete autonomy from the council. For example, a group of artisans came up with a plan to hold a crafts fair but the council didn't support it because the request was never taken to the council; but really, it should be the other way around. It's the council, as a representative body, that should be going to those groups, to that space; not to take it over, but to accompany these groups and to keep the council relevant, to ensure it is doing its work as it is supposed to. Instead, somehow it has come to pass that if a proposal is not taken to the council, then the proposal is considered to lack legitimacy!

Toward the end of 2003 a dwindling, internally divided, and demoralized neighborhood council dissolved itself six months before the end of its term. Decentralization in district 17 had come to a critical juncture, facing the worst crisis since its inception one decade earlier. The formal dissolution of the council was prompted by a decision by the city government to set up the new citywide office of the neighborhood ombudsman (*defensor del vecino*) to advocate on behalf of city residents vis-à-vis municipal authorities. Many activists in the city opposed the decision on the grounds that the ombudsman's office would weaken neighborhood councils, whose raison d'être was precisely to advocate on behalf of city residents, but they vowed to continue working in the councils. Councilors in district 17, however, took the unprecedented step of resigning in protest. At first glance, this decision appeared to confirm El Cerro's reputation for radicalism and intransigence. A closer examination, however, shows that the council was already disarticulated and most council members had already deserted well before the city's decision. The resignation, therefore, had as much to do with the demoralization and internal infighting that preceded the city's decision as with a principled stance in protest against the perceived shift in responsibilities from the council to an ombudsman's office.

The factors identified above—erosion of community solidarity, decline in participation, weakening ties between local organizations and decentralized institutions, influx of inexperienced councilors—were not unique to district 17. Most areas experienced similar problems, even the more successful district 13, but the impact of these factors on the operation of local government varied across the city. In the following section I will explain why these pressures had such a devastating effect in district 17, focusing on the local contingencies that earned this district the reputation of being a tough and problematic place to build local participatory government.

Rising Expectations Amid Dwindling Resources and Increased Poverty: Impact on Participation

One factor that undermined the operation of local government and the consolidation of norms of reciprocity and bonds of solidarity among councilors was the deep social and economic crisis impinging on the district. El Cerro sits in one of the most rapidly impoverished districts in the entire city. The redistributive discourse of the city government and the mayor's famous pronouncement that he would "rather feed a hungry child than build a road" created high expectations among the urban poor. Thus they brought to the orbit of city politics an avalanche of demands that could hardly be addressed by the city's social policies in the absence of national policies and programs:

CARMEN: The demands that residents make nowadays are for things they have not been able to get taken care of by city hall. And what they are asking for mostly is employment. Last year, city hall promoted an initiative called "solidarity workdays." In our zone, six thousand people signed up and there were only five hundred positions available. So, no matter how much you want the municipality to help, people's needs are always too great; you can't resolve them all.

The overwhelming influx of demands that swamped local government officials was not experienced with the same intensity in any other district in the city. While other districts, including the ones covered in this book, were hit hard by the crisis, they never experienced the kind of social problems found in El Cerro. This proved to be a crucial difference that partly explained the different levels of success I found among the three case studies, a point to which I will return in the book's concluding chapter. When successive local governments in district 17 failed to respond to resident's greater needs and expectations, coinciding with intensified internal bickering in the councils and dwindling resources in city coffers, widespread demoralization followed and participation dropped:

MARIA: When you lose trust in things, you pull out. In the neighborhood councils there was a high desertion rate; participation is dropping and this is the product of people not believing, of seeing no results and still being unemployed, so they get dispirited and start feeling low.

Julio's experience illustrates the dilemmas confronting many councilors. Growing increasingly frustrated by the widening gap between local needs and the municipal resources made available to address them, he chose not to seek reelection after his term as councilor ended in 2001:

In the first councils, they set up municipal health clinics, and the lighting division always worked well. We had many needs to address and, little by little, we were getting things done. The accomplishments were not huge, but we were basically trying to lift people up out of the mire. In the roadway committee, we had a budget for El Cerro. The director of roadways came and said, "For Cerro, I have this much money," and it came to about a million dollars. "You guys prioritize which roads need work and then we'll see," and they built streets, and you felt like you had a role in managing that budget. But this came to an end later. For particular reasons the budget was cut, and this left me disillusioned and led me to drop out of the last council.

As happened in district 13, councilors tried hard to leave behind their parochial loyalties and imagine themselves as representatives of the entire district, placing district-wide needs ahead of their own or prioritizing the most needy areas in the district when drafting their budgets or their five-year plans. Even councilors from El Casco, upon learning about the deplorable conditions in squatter communities, slowly came around to be willing to postpone their own demands. But the advances made locally in building solidarity were often undermined by the responses of city officials, who were struggling to cope with shrinking resources. Miguel's disappointment illustrates the feelings of many councilors:

> What always generated the most conflict was when we ran out of funds; when we made up a list of demands and the demands were never met. We made up, for example, a list of ten or fifteen streets that needed work. To do this, we negotiated with the residents, we fought among ourselves (and I mean "fight" in the good sense), and when we finally all agreed on what we were going to ask for, along comes the city hall official to tell us there was no budget, that we had to cut back on our plan. Well, that was a big waste.

With fewer resources at their disposal, city officials angered local activists, as they were seen as eliminating the space of negotiation over budget resources that had become one of the central pillars of the decentralized system:

> ALICIA: There are many bad feelings because now we are less able to negotiate for things from the municipal government. Many times the council will work on making up plans, requests for budget commitments from city hall, and these requests usually come after a period of initial negotiation. But now the councilors make their presentations of these requests in city hall but no one responds, or they simply say no . . . they don't actually do anything. So the opportunity to negotiate for things is narrowing.

Afraid that meager municipal resources were being used inefficiently, the neighborhood council set up a commission in 1999 to monitor the implementation of public works in the district. The commission also aimed to raise awareness among neighbors that city hall was not the only governmental unit responsible for addressing the district's problems:

> MIGUEL: Neither have we channeled the demands as we should, because we always have to go to the same place with our demands—to city hall. Before, the council set up a commission to coordinate and monitor all municipal and governmental projects, because we residents also had to make demands of the state. The ones who are in debt now are the Ministries of Housing and Public Health, plus we have rural areas in El Cerro and the Ministry of Agriculture and Fisheries does not pay any attention. We have in El Cerro asentamientos without potable water and the OSE [Obras Sanitarias del Estado] is responsible, not the IMM [Intendencia Municipal de Montevideo]. We have asentamientos without electricity, and it's the responsibility of the UTE [Administración Nacional de Usinas y Trasmisiones Eléctricas], not the IMM.

City authorities praised the initiative, presenting it as an example to be emulated in other districts. They understood that it could improve efficiency and help redirect resident demands toward other governmental agencies. The efforts of the commission, however, did not produce tangible results, and to my knowledge none of the other districts in the city set up similar monitoring bodies. In fact, the commission could not even get municipal authorities to respond to basic complaints from neighbors on the poor performance of municipal crews. For example, when members of the commission spotted a municipal crew taking a long siesta while on duty supposedly upgrading a small plaza, they reported it to the authorities responsible for supervision of local crews but no action was taken. Their subsequent complaints to higher authorities also fell on deaf ears, even after they denounced the incident through local media. Understandably, councilors became discouraged and dissolved the commission soon thereafter.

Although monitoring is defined as a central responsibility of neighborhood councils, not all districts carry out this role on a regular basis. El Cerro is no exception. When I asked for a list of municipal works in the district, I was told that the list did not exist, at least in the offices of district 17. Indeed, the council does not keep an up-to-date record of what gets implemented from the annual plan established through the participatory budgeting process. The control commission was a first attempt to fulfill this role, addressing the key principle of community control over the use of public resources.

To make matters worse, councilors grew increasingly uneasy when they became the ones who, as frontline members of local government, had to take the brunt of their neighbors' rage:

> MIGUEL: The crisis of recent years was so harsh that many times we wondered what we would say to people if we were to go into the neighborhoods. That there is no budget for the roads? That there will be no budget for public lighting? That there will be no titling process to formalize ownership of property in the asentamientos? That the public utility offices don't give us the time of day when it comes to our requests, and that they are bringing nothing to the neighborhood? And no matter how much you try to explain the situation, the residents are going to blame you—and they're right!

Local activists often found themselves in a difficult predicament in their roles as members of neighborhood councilors, as Miguel pointed out:

> The neighborhood associations became a buffer between the residents and the municipal government. The councilors considered themselves representatives of social organizations of the zone, but in the end they had pretty much become the face of the city government for residents. So their very purpose and roles had changed; they were no longer doing what they had joined the council to do, which is why councilors did not run again to join the council.

Feeling squeezed between their loyalty to the grass roots and to the city government, councilors faced a difficult challenge:

> MIGUEL: I go to the neighborhoods to talk to the residents, and if they start ripping into city hall, I become defensive like I'm a public official, even though I have a million problems myself with the municipal government! I have to explain to them that city hall brought us the health clinics, that they provided land for the schools, that they subsidized students' bus fares. I have to explain why some things don't get attention and that city hall does many things that it doesn't

have to do because they're actually the responsibility of other government agencies. But I also get critical when the municipal authorities come and give speeches here. I don't hold back with them! Because you can't forget which side you're on; you're of the people and for the people.

Indeed, El Cerro became legendary for the merciless reception it gave to city officials when they dared to come to the district to face the angry mob. Seemingly drawing from the radical legacy of El Cerro, they confronted city representatives with the intransigence that Cerrenses had demonstrated when dealing with meatpacking managers in the past:

> JULIO: During the first government of Tabaré Vázquez we were really tough, we made really tough demands. Tough, because we just laid out our needs without holding back, and our needs were pretty serious.

To my surprise, it was the activists from El Casco—the sons and daughters of militant meatpackers and the inheritors of their traditions—who distanced themselves from these confrontational tactics, especially in the most recent councils:

> RAQUEL: Sometimes city officials would come and I'd be embarrassed because some residents would make embarrassing statements. It was insulting, because in order to speak the truth you do not need to resort to that; there were residents that don't contribute a dime because they live in an asentamiento and they want streets and electricity but they pay no taxes. It can't be!

Contrary to what I had assumed, I found councilors from El Casco to be more pragmatic and moderate than councilors from other communities in the district.[22] Those who advocated for more confrontational tactics were the more recent squatters, the new poor whose angry protests superficially resembled the repertoires of protest embedded in the culture of El Casco. In fact, these squatters seem to have appropriated the "El Cerro combativo" myth, adopting the language of radicalism to express their frustration at the lack of response to their pressing needs.

---

22. They were also better educated. Among the six councilors elected in 2004, for example, there was a medical doctor, a teacher, and a social worker.

Councilors' Evaluation of Local Government

The most positive evaluations of local government come from leaders of
the most established asentamientos:

> PABLO: It's a huge change. You work now in a planned way and from
> year to year you go along fulfilling program goals. It's a radical change.
> Because since 1991 we have managed to get buses, to pave the most
> important streets of the neighborhood, to get ANTEL [Administra-
> ción Nacional de Telecomunicaciones] to install telephones in the
> zone, to get garbage collection services, and to move ahead with a
> sanitation plan, which will be finished this year. Where we have not
> been able to advance is in the titling of land, but the neighborhood
> has changed, really changed during these ten years.

Julio, who lives in the impoverished but more established community
of La Paloma, readily acknowledges the many improvements he has seen
over the years:

> During the first administration we got lighting for the neighborhood.
> We got it through an agreement in which we provided the labor and
> the light bulbs, and the administration provided the rest. We got a
> street, a plaza, a bunch of things, all thanks to the fact that the peo-
> ple and the association struggled and supported us. Now we have an
> entryway into El Cerro that is a beauty; we have a pedestrian street
> that's also lovely; we are improving the quality of life here with a
> sanitation system that will soon be ready. These are the good things
> of the period, the flipside of the abject poverty that Uruguayans have
> been suffering.

Not everyone, however, praises local government as much as Pablo and
Julio. Activists in the district are much more critical of local government
than their counterparts in Peñarol and almost never incorporate the pal-
pable improvements identified by Pablo and Julio into the language of
gains. When I asked them to list the concrete gains brought about by
participatory decentralization, they came up with a very short inventory
that paled in comparison to the impressive list drawn by activists in Peñarol, where people even included as accomplishments of local government

things that had been obtained through nonmunicipal institutions or that had come to the district prior to the election of the left-wing city government.

For a while I assumed that El Cerro had indeed accomplished less—most likely the result of poor local government performance—until I examined city expenditures by district and realized that overall the city government had invested considerably more in district 17 than it had in district 13. Seemingly out of sync with municipal expenditures, local perceptions of benefits are certainly not directly connected to the size of public investment in the area. Rather, whether these improvements get incorporated into the discourse of gains depends on the character of local cultures, on the distance between levels of investment and expectations, and on normative assessments of the processes through which improvements came about. In El Cerro, perceptions of success are typically shaped by a local culture that places a premium on participation. Many local activists had a hard time identifying as gains the outcomes of projects whose means and ends they did not contribute to define, and they assess these projects in direct relation to the level of community engagement. Many of the most expensive and visible infrastructural accomplishments in their district, such as the upgrade of the Rambla Suiza, the construction of an impressive bus terminal, or the newly built rotunda at the entrance of El Cerro (recently renamed the Plaza of the Meatpacker Martyrs to honor the workers who had fallen during the earlier working-class struggles) were designed and funded by the city administration without the involvement of local government. As part of a general development plan for Montevideo, these works, like many others in the city, were defined centrally and remained off-limits to local governments. Funded by a different source in the city's central budget, the projects were not subject to participatory budgeting processes, and as a result many local activists often opposed them and did not easily recognize them as gains until years later:

> ALICIA: Then there's the issue of the bus station that's being built, despite the opposition to it expressed by everyone: the businesspeople, the council, the previous local junta. Everyone was opposed to the pedestrian boulevard too! There was even graffiti and flyers protesting these projects. But now some people are talking about these things as gains won. In some zones, this process takes more time. People's time lines are different from public time lines, from political time lines, and so, too, time lines are different in Peñarol, in El Cerro, and in La Teja.

Alicia may be right. The process of incorporating gains into local discourse may be slower in El Cerro than in Peñarol. Perhaps local residents
more readily appreciated city expenditures in Peñarol and in all the neighborhoods belonging to district 13, although smaller in monetary value,
because they had provided comparatively greater input in designing and
monitoring these projects. Paradoxically, this may be an unforeseen consequence of the fact that, compared to El Cerro, district 13 received fewer
public funds through centrally allocated projects, the kind that fell outside
local participatory processes and had alienated many Cerrenses. As a result,
the projects that were implemented in district 13 were subject to participatory processes, giving residents proportionally higher opportunities to
engage with city projects in the district, strengthening their sense of ownership over the outcomes. Differences in gain recognition between activists
in the communities of El Cerro and Peñarol may also be connected to the
gap between actual investment and perceived needs. Since El Cerro and
the whole of district 17 suffered comparatively more severe problems than
the communities of district 13, public investment in the former, although
higher in absolute terms, may still be comparatively lower vis-à-vis actual
needs. These factors may explain the puzzling question of why so many
successful community development experiences addressing gender equality, access to culture and medical care, and job creation failed to come up
in the discourse of gains among local activists in district 17.

Successful Experiences of Community Organizing and Synergy

One such experience involved the creation of a women's organization
housed in the district's local government office. Comuna Mujer (CM) offers
a space for women to come together to reflect on women-specific issues,
to organize workshops on domestic violence, health promotion, and education, and to offer legal advice to women. One of only eight such organizations in the city, Comuna Mujer came to fruition as a result of the work
of a group of women in the district. They pressed local authorities to include
the project in the district's five-year plan, a precondition to receiving municipal support, and once the project was approved in principle they contacted
the city's Women's Commission and other NGOs to secure support.

Offering a good example of synergic relations among local women, city
officials, and NGOs, Comuna Mujer is part of a broader municipal plan to
facilitate women's participation and to address the problems they experience

at the community level. The CM in district 17 is run entirely by the volunteer work of seven specially trained women. It receives various forms of support from the municipality and from NGOs contracted by the city government, including physical space, professional support, and training in legal matters, intake and referral skills, and counseling:

> GRACIELA: We have a team that has an agreement with the Women and Society Institute, which provides us with a lawyer, a social worker, and an attorney. The women in the neighborhood have been trained in legal first aid and now they help other women when they arrive. And in this you have real participation by neighborhood teams, who take their work very seriously.

It was not easy to obtain support to set up the CM, especially in the council, which was not a hospitable place for women's participation:

> ALICIA: Neighborhoods like these that—precisely because of how they came to be, because of their history, the union struggles against the meatpacking plants, and blah blah blah—have this very masculine, very macho imprint, it's a hostile neighborhood in this sense, even tough on a day-to-day basis it's the women who keep the social organizations, neighborhood-based and otherwise, running. It's a hostile environment to the extent that the boys here are all expected to live up to this unionist tradition, to be rude and rough, to be fighters and all that.

Interestingly, in such male-centered cultural context, women occupied the presidency of the local junta in two out of three periods while in district 13, where women did not report experiencing the same kind of discrimination, no woman ever rose to the presidency of the local junta. Over time, women won the respect of male councilors, securing a place within the council and making up nearly half of elected councilors. The running of local government, however, was clearly gendered: council meetings tended to be dominated by men, who felt more comfortable debating in public and addressing larger crowds, while the concrete, day-to-day work of the council took place in the thematic commissions where women played a prominent role. It was thanks to their contribution to these commissions, where things actually got done, that women in El Cerro carved a space for themselves at council meetings:

CATALINA: We women have come along, winning our space. It would happen before that it would be our turn to talk and a man would cut us off and just erase us from the map. But we began to make ourselves heard, because in the subcommissions we really did the work and the *machista* men would want to present our work to the council, but we just told them, "You present on the things you worked on and we'll present on the things that we have done."

Women in CM decided to educate councilors to address these problems, especially after discussions at council meetings turned increasingly harsher. They designed a project offering councilors gender sensitivity training that was funded by an outside agency, which started shortly after the inauguration of the 2004 neighborhood council. The setting up of Comuna Mujer constitutes an important accomplishment, offering evidence of a positive experience of community participation to attend to the needs of women in the district. The creation of the organization was a catalyst for the growing assertiveness and self-confidence of women, projecting gender awareness through local government. Surprisingly, gender issues remain marginal and unacknowledged, and the experience of Comuna Mujer seldom came up in conversations about gains among male or even female activists.

Another noteworthy initiative is the Florencio Sánchez Cultural Center (FSCC), which has all the ingredients for success and for synergy, with resident participation, embedded local officials, and a proactive and sympathetic city government coming together to promote popular culture.[23] The FSCC opened its doors in 1997 in the building of the former Apollo Theater, the vibrant cultural center that had served the community from 1915 to 1962.[24] The project enjoyed wide support among residents and received backing from the city government and a former secretary of the local junta. An advisory commission comprising local individuals and organizations was consulted on all aspects of the project, including the building renovations. Residents decided that they wanted a multiuse cultural center rather than a traditional theater. The city funds the basic cost of operating and administering the FSCC, including the salaries of all full-time employees.

---

23. Florencio Sánchez was a Uruguayan writer born in 1875 who became one of the most important figures of Latin American theater during the first half of the twentieth century. He was also a person of advanced ideas and a clear commitment to the disadvantaged.

24. In 1962 the municipal government purchased the theater and renamed it Teatro Florencio Sánchez, and it ran until 1982.

Wanting to learn more about this experience, I set up an interview with the FSCC coordinator Elder Silva, a nationally respected writer, journalist, and cultural advocate, who is the backbone of this project. A passionate spokesperson of the FSCC, Elder tells me that it reclaims the right to culture for residents of El Cerro. The center brings "high culture" to disadvantaged areas, but most important, it also envisions the poor as legitimate producers of culture, encouraging their participation in cultural production through music workshops, popular plays, and literary competitions, and by fostering local identity through these activities. The FSCC mounts theatrical productions, readings, and concerts by well-known popular artists, and even hosts performances by the city philharmonic orchestra.[25]

The theater's outstanding facilities and rich cultural production would be the envy of many communities in the city. But the project was originally opposed by many councilors, who argued that it constituted a "luxury" they could ill afford given the immediate needs in the district. Supporters of the project responded by arguing that every citizen—rich or poor—should have the right to produce or consume culture. The conflict between these two positions was settled with city assurances that funding would come from the central municipal budget, and therefore monies allocated to address the urgent needs in the area would not be reduced. In the end, the neighborhood council unanimously passed a statement supporting the project.[26] Nevertheless, neighbors engaged in the FSCC complain that cultural issues seldom come up on the agenda of local government. In fact, I found only a handful of councilors who listed the FSCC when asked to identify the gains of decentralization.

A third example of a positive experience in community development is the case of the dental clinic known as Policlínico Odontológico de la Villa del Cerro. Set up in 1993 when decentralization got underway, the primary oral-care clinic brought together residents, the Faculty of Dentistry at the Universidad de la República, and the city government, becoming the first of its kind in the city. The idea came to light when residents came into contact with people from the Faculty of Dentistry wishing to start a project

25. In the first two years of operation, the FSCC reported that it had organized more than three hundred cultural events, attracting fifty-three thousand people (with admission either free or at modest prices).

26. The statement read as follows: "We reaffirm the role of culture in the integral development of human beings. . . . Anyone who thinks that cultural and material needs are in contradiction with each other is mistaken. Those who believe that by spending money on the FSCC . . . we are 'turning our backs on the most needy' place themselves on the side of those who believe that the poor don't need theater, books, or music."

in El Cerro through the university's community outreach program (APEX). When APEX settled in El Cerro in 1992, one year before the elections for the first neighborhood council, it was supported by the city authorities and by the social workers and activists who were engaged in setting up local government in the district. These social workers facilitated the initial contact between the university and local organizations, and brokered a deal that allowed the Faculty of Dentistry to purchase space in the building of the former Frigorífico Artigas, the home of the district's local government.

The Faculty of Dentistry donated ten used dental chairs and other dental implements and offered the services of upper-level students and dentists. The city government agreed to fund the salary of dentists and other professionals working at the clinic. A small user fee charge to residents helps collect the additional funds required to run the clinic. Neighbors made the long-term commitment to manage the clinic through voluntary work, a promise they kept for over a decade. All the administration and management of the clinic is carried out by volunteer work provided by members of a local neighborhood commission that has the legal status to enter into the required legal agreements with the municipality and the Faculty of Dentistry.

The clinic provides dental care targeting children, pregnant women, and adolescents and imparts preventive oral-care knowledge to residents, hoping to turn them into oral-care advocates within the community. The clinic's outreach program also brings dentists, students, and health promoters to day care centers and schools through regular visits.[27] The Policlínico Odontológico is an example of a successful experience of synergy involving the city government, the university, and local organizations. The residents, in collaboration with professional staff and students, define the clinic's operating guidelines and specific projects in regular plenary meetings that are open to the community. To promote participation, access to the clinic's

27. APEX–El Cerro has built an impressive network of outreach programs in the area, including: programs in childhood, adolescence, and adulthood supported by child psychologist services, a youth center and a youth clinic, and a seniors' center and a geriatric clinic; and programs in oral and family care housed in local municipal and neighborhood clinics. In addition, APEX set up six neighborhood development programs through operational neighborhood teams made up of upper-level social work students and community members (APEX n.d.). In 2004, APEX initiated a series of summer courses offered to the community free of charge. The courses are open to everyone and cover a wide array of topics, including regional economic changes, trade unions and the university, the university and society, human rights, violence against women, sexual diversity, education, arts, nursing, literature, history, communications, and various topics in health. During the duration of the summer courses, the FSCC offers special concerts, movies, plays, and art displays, also free of charge.

services is tied to engagement of local organizations in the running of the clinic, each receiving a quota of tickets in relation to their contribution, producing impressive results, including the active participation of more than thirty community organizations:

> GRACIELA: The commission for a dental clinic in El Cerro had lots of support. There's an assembly of social organizations that work with the clinic that meets every fifteen days. They keep a record of attendance, and it is from this they determine the share of appointments that are given to each organization. The people also take care of the maintenance of the clinic. If you work there for so many hours it is worth a molar, so then a resident of the neighborhood can get a molar fixed up for free.

Surprisingly, in spite of its resounding success only one activist whom I interviewed mentioned this experience when listing the gains of participatory decentralization in the district.

The last successful experience involves the Industrial Technological Park of El Cerro (Parque Tecnológico Industrial, PTI). Set up in 1998, the PTI is part of a municipal effort to reactivate the western industrial corridor by recycling abandoned facilities in depressed areas. It aims to create jobs by attracting small- and medium-sized industries employing innovative and environmentally friendly technologies.[28] The PTI initiative originated in the Economic Development and Regional Integration unit of the city government, which invested nearly three million dollars to purchase and recondition the facilities. The city provides the facilities, free of charge, to selected businesses, which are in turn responsible for the costs of upgrade, maintenance, security, and other support services. The PTI provides material and technical support, business networks, support services, and know-how to seventeen businesses that settled in the industrial park, and it pays the salary of the executive director, who happens to be a widely respected former secretary of the local junta, who was also instrumental in providing support to the Florencio Sánchez Cultural Center.

The companies range in size and specialization but most are in the food processing or recycling businesses, using environmentally friendly technologies. Five of these businesses are organized as cooperatives. Three of

---

28. It is estimated that microenterprises constitute 97 percent of all business and contribute nearly 50 percent of the country's GNP. Each year, however, thirteen thousand of a total of seventeen thousand such businesses set up each year go bankrupt (Costa 2003).

them were set up by workers of companies that went bankrupt,[29] while another (Cooperativa de Trabajadores Artigas) was established by former workers of the frigorífico, who used their knowledge of the facilities and the area to provide security and maintenance services to the PTI. The PTI even attracted the high-profile, Brazilian-owned Sacotem, which supplies paper bags to key fast food chains, including McDonald's, from its plant in São Paulo. The new plant in the PTI will supply the Golden Arch company in Argentina, Bolivia, Venezuela, Colombia, Chile, and southern Brazil.

Unlike the experiences of Comuna Mujer, the Florencio Sánchez Community Center, and the Policlínico Odontológico, the PTI did not involve the neighborhood council or local activists. Instead, it was a centrally defined project linking city hall and local entrepreneurs. The PTI constituted a relevant initiative to address the lack of jobs in the area and to search for alternative local development strategies through new partnerships between public, private, and collectively owned enterprises. But the neighborhood council failed to embrace the idea and search for ways to support it from the offices of the local government. Despite its novelty and relevance, the PTI never came up in conversations of about gains of decentralization.

Assessment of Local Government

Notwithstanding the colossal difficulties that residents faced in building local government, most people I talked to had not given up on the reform project. On the contrary, they generally offered measured and relatively positive comments on decentralization. Carmen told me that decentralization was "one of the best policies" to come out of city hall, a surprising statement coming from someone who, sickened by the infighting and politicking, had decided not to run for council. To her, in spite of all the problems, the participatory project produced an irreversible change in local political culture:

> It was a very ambitious project and it still is. The days are over when those in office were positioned way up there above us. No way! That doesn't pass muster anymore. Now that we residents have got a little taste of what it is to co-govern, we want our opinions always to be taken into account.

29. Niboplast, Spiller, and Cristalerías del Uruguay.

Raquel, another activist who chose not to seek reelection after three terms in the council, also offers lots of praise for participatory decentralization. For her, the key benefit of decentralization was to narrow the distance between city officials and ordinary residents:

> When you went to city hall it was impossible to do anything, because you could only talk to the secretary of the secretary of someone. Now you can raise issues personally. There is still bureaucracy in parts of the municipal government, but now you can go talk directly to a city official about your needs and this is a beautiful experience that inspires enthusiasm in people. Things are different, because now you have city hall inside El Cerro.

Several councilors spoke of their own political education resulting from their involvement in local government. They told me that they had acquired new knowledge and skills, stressing how much participation in the councils pushed them to look beyond the boundaries of their narrow political outlooks, to learn how to work collectively, to figure out how the state operates, changing their vision of politics forever. Alicia best summarizes what I heard from many councilors:

> Neither the high school nor the university taught me to have a citizenship vision. That is something I learned in the council: to have a more global outlook, a longer range perspective, one that takes me out of the little shell of my own neighborhood. First I learned to see all of El Cerro, the whole zone in its full magnitude, and then to see the city. I didn't have such a perspective before. I also learned the inside stuff, the small details, like how many square meters of resistant material are needed to make a road; what it costs to build a street; what ballast is, a ballast of concrete; what an asphalt carpet is. And I learned how to take a stand on how my neighborhood or my city should be built.

These positive evaluations are coupled with criticisms of the practice of local government and the shortcomings of the institutional model. In contrast to the overwhelmingly positive assessments in district 13, where people had nothing but praise for decentralization, Cerrenses point out the urgent need to make changes to improve the model and the practice of participatory decentralization:

MIGUEL: We must continue to deepen decentralization and to keep changing it in various ways because, although it is a very useful tool, it has become rusty of late.

The most serious problems in the workings of participation, according to most people I talked to, arise from deficiencies in the model adopted by the city government. Julio, a strong advocate of decentralization, points to Porto Alegre as an example of a better model:

Participation is meaningless without economic decentralization. Things are still centralized really, because you can decentralize services, but if each zone doesn't have a budget—as I think is done in Brazil—managed by the local government, then it won't work. We haven't seen this happen yet, but it will have to happen.

Manuel's criticism is much harsher. For him, the main problem lies in the democratic deficits of the model of decentralization adopted in Montevideo, an argument I often heard in El Cerro and more so in La Teja, the next case study:

The neighborhood council is a popularly elected body, people elect it by secret ballot. But what happens? Well, the council is a democracy because we are chosen by the people, but the local junta is an example of "handocracy," because its members are handpicked by politicians. The neighborhood council is in charge of presenting proposals, of elaborating the five-year plan, but these all have to pass through the filter of the local junta, which is an unelected political body. I don't agree with this arrangement, and one of my projects is to eliminate this dichotomy, that a popularly elected body should be subordinated to a body appointed by members of the political parties.

Other councilors felt less strongly about the unelected local junta but vehemently opposed the idea that the secretary of the local junta, the most powerful position in the architecture of local government, be appointed by the mayor. Some went further, calling for the elimination of the position, which they saw as the real "bottleneck" in the system. The secretary's appointment frequently produces tensions and dissatisfaction among local activists. Ultimately, when the mayor appoints the city's eighteen secretaries—balancing the recommendations of local political forces with the need to include representatives from the multiple groupings that make up the coalition—someone is bound to be unhappy. This was the case in district 13 when the mayor appointed Washington against the wishes of local activists. In this case, however, although the appointment was initially resented, it did not produce open conflict since Washington's virtues quickly gained him the respect of local activists. El Cerro was a different story. The appointment of Gustavo as secretary of the local junta coincided with rising tensions in the council and fed the growing polarization within local government:

> CARMEN: El Cerro was always a very political place. The unions, the meatpacking plants, the high schools—always, always you are having to pick between one side or another. Now, nobody said the council had to be an apolitical entity, but it should be nonpartisan. However, some in the council have become partisan in their defense of the junta's secretary, because they belong to the same political organization. Understand? The council became divided.

Many councilors spoke candidly about the poor relations between them and Gustavo, the current secretary of the local junta, blaming him for the misunderstandings and the poor operation of local government. Speaking directly about his individual shortcomings, they often mentioned his lack of knowledge of the district, repeatedly calling him an outsider, for living and working outside the district, and for being a school principal who had little understanding of the difficulties affecting people in the district. Such distance was exacerbated, they told me, by his poor work habits and lack of dedication to his job:

> MIGUEL: The current secretary is nothing like the previous one. He works full-time, but not full-time. Well, we pay him to work full-time, but if there is no one keeping track, a person can do whatever he likes. He doesn't participate in the plenary meetings of the neighborhood council unless you send him a written request that he do so in advance. The previous secretary always came to the plenary meetings, even if it was just to lie to us or to be insulted. If a director from any part of the municipality came by, he was always there, and he'd always pass on information; with Gustavo, you always have to ask for it. I have a good rapport with him but he is what he is. He's

more like a schoolteacher; everything has to be presented in a written note.

Some of the criticisms resonated with my personal experience in trying to interview Gustavo. In fact, he stood me up three times without ever offering an apology or an explanation. Such practices on his part ended up alienating councilors from his own party, who were initially among his most loyal defenders.

The case of district 17 gives ammunition to the numerous criticisms that have been raised about the role of the secretary in the model of decentralization and the manner in which secretaries are appointed. The experience left me wondering how an individual with so few skills and credentials was placed in such a strategically important position of responsibility. I am certain that when appointments to this position rely exclusively on the political imperative of distributing posts among the various groups in the governing coalition, regardless of local preferences and needs, the potential for conflict increases. This was most clearly seen in the next case study.

Looking beyond the present Broad Front administration, Miguel has other reasons to worry, highlighting how much the character of participatory decentralization rests on political variables rather than institutional design:

> MIGUEL: Look, I always dreamed about the Porto Alegre experience, because one has this ideal notion about decentralization from Porto Alegre and its participatory budget. And we have aimed for this, and fought for it—to have a genuine participatory budget here. . . . But then it could also come to pass that a government of the day would tell us, "Hey, we only have three hundred pesos for you," and they'd throw that to us and we'd fight like wild beasts over these three hundred pesos, then they'd say to us, "There, we are giving you participation; that's all there is, so make do."

Indeed, Miguel's insightful remarks highlight the fragility of many participatory experiences underway in Latin America that rest, primarily, on the political will of those who hold power at city hall. It is quite likely that a new city government with a different political outlook may turn decentralization upside down, using it to transfer responsibilities without the corresponding delegation of resources and power, turning the entire project into an instrument to shift state responsibilities away from social citizenship and the provision of collective goods.

Conclusions

The experience of district 17 reveals that Cerrenses had a significantly tougher time than people in Peñarol in adjusting to the reality of local government. Their associational traditions included a rich heritage of radical labor politics that had effectively secured relatively high salaries and generous benefits during the country's beef-export bonanza. But these traditions proved less adaptable to the exigencies of decentralization. Participatory local government called for specific capacities that were in short supply within the El Cerro culture of collective mobilization, namely, skills in conflict resolution, consensus building, constructive engagement, and resource management. Further, their class-based traditions clashed with a new system of local governance that asked them to engage in urban development projects around territorially based issues and identities. Thus Cerrenses had struggled, not always successfully, to make the fundamental adjustment of putting aside their long-standing posture of protest and opposition, the heart and soul of El Cerro, and taking the initiative to design, propose, and carry out concrete community development projects.

Other community activists in the district, however, possessed some of the skills that were lacking in El Cerro, especially among people who came from the more established asentamientos. Although they may have had a less impressive pedigree in radical politics than their Cerrense brothers and sisters, they possessed capacities that positioned them well to lead local government in the district. The squatters' early history of community development and their experiences in negotiating urban services at a time when city authorities had more resources at their disposal provided them with similar skills than those I found among activists in Peñarol. In district 13, such capacities had been crucial to inject a dose of pragmatism and inclusivity into the day-to-day workings of local government that fostered robust democratic participatory practices.

But the experience of Peñarol was not replicated in El Cerro, as the capacities brought by community leaders from the older squatter settlements failed to influence the operation of local institutions to the same degree. Unfortunately, their efforts to do so were undermined by the formidable socioeconomic conditions found in the district—widespread poverty and destitution and the massive influx of squatters, who were heaped in crowded spaces without basic services—in the context of a city government with dwindling resources. Such conditions exacerbated the deep mistrust and resentment separating residents from the community of El Casco and those from the more recent asentamientos. Thus, in the case of district 17, the primary obstacle to the smooth operation of participatory decentralization was not the absence of capacities per se, even though the skills of the older squatters did not match the more wide-ranging reservoir of capacities found in Peñarol, but rather the perverse logic of conflict and mistrust generated by the overwhelming economic conditions affecting everyone in the district. Under these conditions, the formidable challenge of building links of solidarity across neighborhoods, or bridging social capital, proved insurmountable.

The naming of the secretary of the local junta, someone clearly unqualified or uninterested to work with community activists in the district, further exacerbated tensions. This was certainly a case of a local official who failed to become embedded in the district, and who undermined efforts to build bonds of trust across the district and synergy between communities and the offices of local government. The confluence of crushing economic conditions, deep divisions and mistrust, and poor leadership from local government officials overwhelmed activists, many of whom left the council demoralized. Thus the conflictive reputation of the neighborhood councils in district 17 that had attracted me to El Cerro in the first place turned out to be less directly connected to the community's history of radical militancy, as I had assumed when I started my research, than to the consequences of the overwhelming poverty affecting everyone in the district and the less-than-desirable orientation of local government officials. If anything, it was a cohort among the more recent squatters who appropriated the discourse of radical militancy embedded in El Cerro to express their frustration at the failure of municipal and national governments to address their desperate needs.

The next chapter discusses the case of La Teja, a community with similarly strong militant traditions and with little experience of territorially based mobilization that also faced tremendous difficulties adjusting to the logic of participatory decentralization. Unlike the case discussed in this chapter, however, the next chapter examines a district that was more uniformly poor, with comparatively fewer cleavages along socioeconomic lines. Nevertheless, the experience highlights the difficulties of building solidarity and coordinated action within and across neighborhoods as well as synergy among the different layers of local government, due to divisions framed in ideological and political terms. In a context marked by strong ideological polarization and in the absence of developed consensus-building skills and pragmatic predispositions to mitigate these tendencies (as in the case of MIRPA activists in district 13), the next case illustrates yet another distinct experience of participatory decentralization.

CHAPTER 3

La Teja: Participatory Decentralization Where Radical Politics Mix with Soccer and Carnival

In La Teja we are more like warriors. It's in our blood. Not that we are rebellious; it's just that we yearn for justice and when it's time to shout, we shout.

—Silvia

Community Profile

The communities of La Teja and El Cerro are literally a stone's throw from each other, spread out on opposite sides of the Pantanoso River. It only takes me a few minutes to reach one from the other by crossing the famous 38th Parallel Bridge, witness to many of the epic meatpackers' struggles. The overpass is today a busy crossway, crowded with pedestrians, cyclists, even an occasional horse rider, crossing alongside countless noisy cars, motorcycles, public buses, and heavy trucks on their way to the highway.

I often cut through the city to go to La Teja, starting my journey driving up one of the most beautiful avenues in the city. Named after the country's national independence hero, Boulevard Artigas begins in the Punta Carretas neighborhood by the exclusive golf course on the shores of the River Plate, picking up traffic as it runs northbound for about five kilometers, suddenly ending on the western shores of Montevideo Bay near the ANCAP oil refinery. Shortly before the end of the boulevard, I take Agraciada Avenue toward the neighborhood of El Prado, home of the official presidential residence occupied by Tabaré Vázquez, the former mayor who introduced decentralization in the city and who became the country's first socialist president following a highly contested second-ballot runoff election in 2004. El Prado has lost its former flair since many of the upper-class families who lived there lost their wealth or migrated toward newer upscale neighborhoods, but the stunning, aging mansions remain as testimonies of the neighborhood's former days of grandeur. The edge of the famous Parque del Prado—a striking, century-old park whose lush gardens, stocky trees, grand fountains, and monuments make it a favorite spot for tourists and city residents alike—tells me that I am near the boundaries of district 14.[1] I enter the district through Paso Molino, a neighborhood that used to have a bustling commercial center before the arrival of shopping malls and the economic debacle of 2002.

The community of La Teja is only five minutes away from El Paso.[2] Driving along Carlos María Ramírez, La Teja's main commercial artery, gives me the first impression of the community, which feels livelier than sleepy Peñarol and less disheartened than El Cerro. Carlos María Ramírez is a noisy, clogged avenue. It is lined with small businesses—grocery stores, bakeries, pubs, hardware stores, hairdressers, and gas stations—that cater to the needs of Tejano families, and it also hosts the historic Plaza Lafone, the site of many working-class rallies, as well as the headquarters of local government and several social and sports clubs. The avenue runs all the way to El Cerro, on the other side of the bridge over the Pantanoso River.

I search in vain for architectural markers that might provide a sense of the community's history, like the aging railway buildings or the imposing meatpacking plants that struck me the moment I set foot in the other two neighborhoods. La Teja, I realize, is made up of simple one-story houses that look remarkably similar to one another and not too different from those found in adjacent communities. The one distinctive sign of the community is ANCAP, the commanding oil refinery sitting on the shores of Montevideo Bay. The histories of the plant and La Teja are undoubtedly intertwined, but the refinery seems detached and isolated since it was cut off from the community when the coastal freeway was built. Lacking distinct physical markers, I will need to dig deeper into the community's history to discover what makes La Teja unique and what gives Tejanos their strong sense of identity.

The Making of a Working-class Community

Spanish, Italian, and French Basque family farmers and members of a Jesuit order settled present-day La Teja more than two hundred fifty years

1. The following neighborhoods belong to district 14: La Teja, Prado Norte, Sayago Oeste, Paso Molino, Belvedere, Pueblo Victoria, Tres Ombúes, Nuevo París, and Villa Teresa.

2. Situated on the western part of Montevideo city near the shores of the River Plate estuary, it is enclosed by two rivers (the Miguelete and Pantanoso) on its southern and northern ends and by the freeway running alongside Montevideo Bay to its west.

ago. In spite of their earnest labor, the Jesuits' stay was short-lived because they were expelled from Hispanic America in 1767, caught in the conflict between the Spanish monarchs and the Vatican. When the Jesuit lands were publicly auctioned off, enterprising businessmen rushed to buy them, attracted by the industrial potential of the area, which was strategically located on the shores of the River Plate between the port of Montevideo and El Cerro. A young entrepreneur from Liverpool named Samuel Lafone set up the first modern industry in 1833.[3] The job opportunities created by Lafone's saladero—the earlier meat-processing plants that produced tasajo, salt-preserved meat to be exported to feed slaves in the Caribbean—plus the company's offer of free housing for its employees, attracted the first wave of workers to the area. The industry's one-story white houses with terra-cotta clay tile roofs, reminiscent of the ones first produced by the Jesuits, became the community's signature—hence the name La Teja, which literally translates as "the clay tile."

Recognizing the strategic importance of the area, the city government set up the town of Villa Victoria in 1842, in honor of the queen of England, only ten years after the founding of Villa El Cerro. The villa developed quickly during the last quarter of the nineteenth century thanks to im-provements in communication, such as the construction of several bridges over the Miguelete and Pantanoso rivers and the laying of railway lines that passed through the area on their way to the harbor.[4] Villa Victoria also prospered with the increase in economic activity linked to the building of Montevideo harbor in 1883, attracting nearly seven thousand rock diggers, many of Yugoslavian descent, who came to labor in the quarries to extract and transport tons of rocks used to build the port.

The saladeros and the quarries sealed the fate of the community as an industrial area, and in contrast to the case of Peñarol, traces of the earlier farming life were quickly swept away. La Teja's nascent economy, like the one that had emerged in El Cerro, depended on meatpacking and extractive industries. Local saladeros in La Teja, however, did not evolve into modern frigoríficos as did their Cerrense counterparts, and were eventually pushed out of business by the more powerful, foreign-owned meatpacking plants of El Cerro. Lafone's original plant gave way to the state-run oil refinery ANCAP, built in the 1930s in southern La Teja, quickly becoming a key

3. Samuel Lafone is considered the founder of La Teja. Ironically, the name of this pioneer-ing capitalist was used for the community's historic Plaza Lafone, which would later become the site for countless labor rallies and demonstrations organized by Tejanos.

4. Regent 2004, 17.

source of jobs for Tejano families. A large part of the area's manufacturing, however, remained dependent on the meat industry for raw materials, including leather tanning, wool washing, textiles, and soap and candle making. Subsequently, La Teja attracted medium-sized glass, steel, and vegetable oil industries, and by the mid-twentieth century it had become a well-established working-class community, similar to other surrounding neighborhoods like Belvedere, Nuevo París, Paso Molino, and Capurro. In contrast to El Cerro, it developed a more diversified industrial infrastructure and, thus, a working class that was structurally weaker and less concentrated. Lacking the industrial development of El Cerro, many Tejanos found jobs in industries in neighboring communities, such as the port and the frigoríficos in El Cerro, where they helped create the militant working-class traditions found there.

While in the annals of Uruguayan working-class history La Teja does not figure as prominently as neighboring El Cerro, Tejanos nevertheless built a strong tradition of proletarian militancy, becoming close allies of Cerrenses and central protagonists in the historic working-class struggles waged in the industrial corridor alongside Montevideo Bay. Tejanos proudly identify with the saying *"La Teja vive y lucha!"* (La Teja lives and struggles!), despite the disappearance of the neighborhood's industrial infrastructure. La Teja's reputation for militancy and solidarity was forged during the early part of the twentieth century, but it was sealed during the struggles at the state-owned oil refinery ANCAP following the end of World War II, at around the same time workers struck in nearby El Cerro. In 1951, union leaders at the plant were suspended from their jobs and jailed for refusing to load a vessel in an act of solidarity with a boycott organized by workers at the docks. This measure was met with widespread outcry, leading thousands of workers in other industries—meatpacking, public transport, textiles, and public utilities—to go on strike in support of their brothers and sisters at the oil refinery. The thirty-day solidarity strike, the longest of its kind in the country's history, ended in victory when Parliament granted amnesty to the imprisoned leaders, who returned to their posts amid jubilant celebrations. The strike proved the effectiveness of worker solidarity, a value that remains engrained in Tejano culture to this day, and boosted calls to set up a single national union federation, leading to the founding of the Central Nacional de Trabajadores (National Workers Central, CNT) in 1964.[5]

5. Rodríguez 1965, 52–58.

Workers at ANCAP would once again be at the center of popular struggles in 1973 during the historic fifteen-day general strike against the military coup. Outraged by the military takeover, the overwhelming majority
of Uruguayans responded to the CNT's call for a general strike in defense
of democracy, occupying their workplaces and paralyzing the country for
a tense two weeks, risking imprisonment, torture, and the loss of jobs.
ANCAP workers were among the first to strike and remained unyielding
until the end, keenly aware of the strategic importance of the oil refinery:
if the military forced workers in other industries back to work, they would
not be able to operate without oil so long as ANCAP remained on strike.
Thus ANCAP became a test and symbol of the country's determination to
protect democratic traditions. Understanding that the refinery was indeed
the country's nerve center, the military occupied the plant, forcing two
hundred workers to keep basic services running at gunpoint, under the
vigilant watch of soldiers and police dogs. Still defiant, the workers secretly
instigated an "accidental" short-circuit that brought the entire plant to a
halt, extinguishing the flame that typically crowns the plant's chimney, one
that had burned continuously for forty years since the plant was founded.[6]
Indeed, the extinguished flame of ANCAP became a metaphor for the
suppression of Uruguayan democracy. Such an unprecedented act of cour-
age inspired thousands of other workers and helped to keep the general
strike alive, offering another example of worker militancy to be incorporated into Tejano mythology.

Thirty years later, when I returned to Uruguay, ANCAP was once again
in the headlines. An ardent national debate engulfed Uruguayans over the
future of the plant following the approval of a law that ended the state's
monopoly on the import and refining of crude oil. Countering that the law
would effectively be the first step toward privatizing ANCAP, a broad coalition of citizens—led by the Broad Front, union leaders, and prominent
citizens—set up the Commission in Defense of ANCAP to oppose the law
and organized a legally binding referendum to repeal it. They contended
that the government proposal had nothing to do with lowering prices for
consumers, as defenders of the law had argued, pointing out that after
state-owned oil refineries in Argentina and Brazil had been privatized, gaso-
line prices had doubled. They also argued that the real reason behind the
government's decision to end the national monopoly on fuels was that this
was mandated by a secret condition attached to a $743 million loan from

6. Lustemberg 1978, 99–108.

the International Monetary Fund, a staunch supporter of privatizations. The conflict over the future of ANCAP showed how much, long after the demise of the developmental state, Uruguayans still valued public enterprises. Since the rise of neoliberal economics, Uruguayan citizens had stubbornly, and successfully, resisted several attempts to privatize state-owned businesses, shielding them against the avalanche of privatizations sweeping across Latin America through the use of referenda.

The campaign in defense of ANCAP struck a chord with Uruguayan citizens, galvanizing public debate about the merits of privatizing public enterprises and turning the vote into a referendum against the overall free-market policies of the country's two traditional parties. When the results were announced in November 2003, it became clear that Uruguayans had sent an unequivocal message to government officials: close to two-thirds rejected the government law. Thousands of ecstatic Uruguayans poured to the streets to celebrate late into the night and many waved the traditional flags of the leftist Broad Front. Such a resounding victory, they thought, was a harbinger of an impending victory of the Broad Front in the presidential elections the following year.

The End of Import Substitution: Closure of Industries and Increased Poverty

In spite of these important victories against privatization, Uruguayans could not halt the overall demise of the country's import substitution industrialization model, a process that had begun decades earlier. The downfall of this model had dire consequences for Tejanos, who suffered in the face of the downward spiral of poverty caused by the collapse of the Uruguayan economy. Most of the two hundred industries that existed in La Teja by the early 1980s had prospered under protectionist policies that granted them privileged access to the domestic market.[7] Unable to compete with the flood of imported goods following the opening of the country's borders to foreign imports, and without government incentives, these industries went bankrupt. Indeed, one by one, the factories that had employed thousands of Tejano workers started to close their doors: the large steelmaker INLASA closed down and its building was taken over by squatters;

7. These factories covered thirteen different industrial activities, according to a study conducted by the Department of Geography, Faculty of Humanities and Social Sciences, Universidad de la República. See Barrios Pintos and Reyes Abadie 1994, 137.

the glass factory CODARVI also went under, as did the entire glass industry in the country; and in a matter of only twenty years, the renowned soap
maker BAO reduced its staff from eight hundred to fewer than fifty workers.[8] To make matters worse, the scope of operations at the ANCAP plant
in La Teja was reduced in 1977 when it stopped acting as the reception point
for crude oil; since then, large petroleum ships deliver the oil to a station
on the eastern coast, closer to the Brazilian border.

The closing of these industries—which, as we have seen, were smaller
and less concentrated than the frigoríficos in El Cerro—stretched over a
longer period of time, which may explain why Tejanos did not have an
easily identifiable cathartic moment of resistance to the disappearance of
their jobs, as had their brothers and sisters in El Cerro. In addition, La Teja's
weaker manufacturing economy never generated the kind of prosperity produced by the powerful railway or meatpacking industries in Peñarol and
El Cerro, which may explain why Tejanos are less nostalgic about the past,
never evoking a foundational golden age as do people in El Cerro or Peñarol.
Given that, relative to the other two communities, La Teja was already poorer
before the closure of the industries, it is possible that Tejanos may not
have experienced the fall in living standards produced by the economic crisis as traumatically as Cerrenses and Peñarolenses.

Still, the loss of industries caused Tejanos widespread poverty, insecurity, and serious psychological hardship:

> MAGDALENA: The neighborhood has become poor. They closed the
> factories and the men were left without work. The women who until
> then were homemakers now have to go out and work, but the pay is
> frighteningly low. People are in disbelief, hurting; mothers are in
> anguish, and many men in the area are morally crushed; they feel
> badly because their wives are the ones who have to bring home the
> bacon.

"La Teja was always poor," a community activist told me, "but we
suffered no hunger like we do today." Indeed, today's Tejanos must cope

---

8. In a 2004 article in the local paper *El Tejano*, Susana Regent, a community activist who
has been involved in local government since the initial phases, lamented the closing of many
industries: "The cooperative CODARVI . . . also closed. The Montevideo Oil Company is no
longer with us. . . . Victoria Oil is also gone. The following companies also went out of business: INLASA (steelmakers), SEDALANA (textiles), Emporio Cerrense (cracker factory), Man-
zanares (soap and candles)."

with unprecedented levels of poverty, disease, and indigence. Most of these problems are concentrated in northern La Teja, where residents face more serious environmental and social problems than their neighbors on the southern side of Carlos María Ramírez. Northern La Teja houses most of the neighborhood's asentamientos, which mushroomed alongside the shores of the Pantanoso River, a highly polluted waterway that for years served as a garbage dump for local industries. Northern Tejanos cope daily with lead poisoning—vestiges of the industrial past—and illegal garbage dumps found alongside the river basin or in abandoned industrial buildings. In this part of La Teja I find pockets of poverty like the ones I found in many of the squatter settlements of El Cerro, some of which are visible on the opposite shore of the Pantanoso River. Several studies have also reported dangerously high incidence of typhoid, infant diarrhea, hepatitis, and bronchial disease in this part of La Teja.[9]

Radical Solidarity, Soccer, and Carnival

The disappearance of jobs shook up the community's sense of identity as a bastion of working-class militancy. Nevertheless, Tejanos remain unmistakably clear about their proletarian origins, evoking images of working-class life, proletarian struggles, and class solidarity when they shared with me the images, places, and events that came to their minds when they thought about their community:

> JOSE: There is a union culture, a workers' culture of solidarity in the area. From the beginning there has been a culture of solidarity and of working life here that you don't find in other parts of Montevideo.

Tejanos are keenly aware that the material foundations of this working-class culture—the factories that shaped their proletarian identity—are gone for good. Still, they stubbornly hold on to their strong sense of class belonging, uncompromising class politics, and solidarity. As I walk around the community in this intense preelection year, it strikes me that the only visible political signs posted on people's houses belong to the various parties of the leftist Broad Front, which reminds me of the words of an activist I spoke with when I first arrived: "In La Teja, you have two options: you either belong to the Left or you belong to the Left. There is no other option!"

9. Barrios Pintos and Reyes Abadie 1994, 137.

Interestingly, working-class politics intersect with other, less markedly political local institutions. To the extent that the frigoríficos and the railways were central to defining the soul of the communities of El Cerro and Peñarol, La Teja did not have such key markers of community identity. ANCAP came close, but it paled in comparison. Whereas in El Cerro the influence of meatpacking unions spilled beyond the plant floor, becoming central pillars of community life, the weaker, more dispersed, and numerically smaller unions of La Teja had to share the task of shaping and giving expression to Tejano daily life with other local associations, such as social and sports clubs and carnival groups. The blending of a vigorous trade union culture with the traditions arising from cultural and sports associations shaped a unique Tejano identity. Community life in La Teja centered around a dense network of more than twenty social, soccer, and bowling clubs that articulated a distinct sense of belonging to a territorially bounded working-class culture. Apart from their traditional athletic and cultural activities, these clubs also acted as conduits for community solidarity, organizing fund-raisers for striking workers and the unemployed, local political events, soup kitchens, and community health clinics.

Prominent among these associations is the Progreso Athletic Club, a bastion of Tejano identity since it was founded in 1917 by a group of Spanish anarchists who worked in the quarries, and the club's colors are faithful to its origins: yellow and red, inspired by Spain's national flag, and red and black, the traditional colors of anarchism. In contrast to Peñarol, whose pride for giving birth to the most celebrated team in the country was shattered when the team moved out of the community, Progreso remained in La Teja thanks to the support of thousands of loyal Tejano fans who backed it in victory and defeat. The faded proverb painted on the wall at the club's canteen, "*Quien es rico en recuerdos nunca esta solo*" (He who is rich in memories will never feel alone), rings true for Progreso, a club with so many glorious soccer memories and so much community support. The three-time second division champion (1947, 1979, 2001) joined the country's first division league in 1980 and was crowned national champion nine years later under the leadership of a popular Tejano physician. The two teams from neighboring El Cerro never managed to achieve such a feat.[10] Community support for Progreso, however, does not come exclusively from its soccer glories. Since it was founded, the club has been a pioneer in

10. Progreso also twice earned the right to participate in the Libertadores de America tournament, the equivalent to the European Champions League.

community work, putting into practice the strong values of Tejano solidarity and supporting all kinds of grassroot initiatives. The club, for example, has offered a free hot lunch to two hundred schoolchildren and has operated a free medical clinic for over twenty years, thanks to voluntary efforts of its members and donations from local institutions.

Another local club with deep roots in the community is the Arbolito Bowling Club, set up in 1958 by a group of young Tejanos.[11] Throughout its fifty-year history, Arbolito ("little tree") became a beloved Tejano institution strongly identified with community struggles. Located at the heart of La Teja, across from the famous Plaza Lafone, Arbolito lent institutional support to a wide range of social and cultural organizations and community initiatives. Among these are a *comedor* that offers a daily free snack of warm milk, bread, and jam to nearly four hundred children, and a community health clinic that has been offering free medical services to Tejano families since it opened in 1965. These initiatives, like those of the Club Progreso, are carried out by the collective effort of volunteers and community donations.

Given the community development work offered by these institutions, I am not surprised to find near unanimity when I ask residents to identify the institutions that have done most for the community:

> NESTOR: No question, the Arbolito Club with its medical clinic and the Progreso Club with its cafeteria, run by women who have given many hours to it. It has taken the effort not only of the people who work in the cafeteria, but also that of the management of the two clubs, with all the support this has signified for the neighborhood over many years.

During the dictatorship Tejanos used the infrastructure of these local clubs not only for solidarity activities but also to organize political resistance. Aware of the militant history of the community, the military was unrelentingly ruthless with Tejanos, targeting union leaders and political activists and repressing any sign of collective activity. Many Tejanos were forced into exile, others were jailed and tortured, and some were disappeared by the military. Today, a powerful sculpture commissioned by city hall and created by a local artist and councilor sits at the heart of the community

---

11. Local folklore recalls that these youngsters set up the club when they rebelled against the local priest, who started to demand attendance at mass as a requirement to play on the local Catholic school soccer team.

as a tribute to the Tejano martyrs from this period. When the military banned political and trade union activities in the 1970s and 1980s, social and sports clubs provided refuge for hundreds of militants, offering safer contexts for organizing to address the troubling social problems affecting the community. These socially oriented activities, in turn, became acts of political condemnation of the unpopular policies of the dictatorship.

The social and sports clubs also became the home to another Tejano institution, the widely popular carnival groups called *murgas*. A form of popular musical theater associated with carnival season, the murgas came from the city of Cádiz in southern Spain, a Moorish-influenced Mediterranean seaport that, along with Seville, acted as one of only two Spanish gateways for the tons of precious metals and raw materials that were taken from Latin America during colonial times. Carnival in Cádiz was a truly popular fiesta with a subversive touch, as commoners hid behind masks and colorful costumes, assuming identities that transgressed social norms and resisted prohibitions. Carnival was brought to Uruguay by Spanish immigrants more than a century ago and has since blended with local culture and Afro-Uruguayan traditions to become a central feature of popular culture.

During carnival, murgas go about the city in elaborate, colorful costumes and clown-like painted faces, performing musical plays that include singing, dancing, and recitation in *tablados,* popular stages organized by local neighborhood associations. Like the Brazilian "samba schools" that express the collective spirit of the poorest communities in Rio or Bahia, each Uruguayan murga is associated with a particular popular neighborhood, asserting and shaping community identity through music and performances. Rehearsals—held in local clubs like Progreso and Arbolito, trade union locals, or housing cooperatives before the month of carnival in February— are usually open to the community to try out the performance in front of a familiar crowd and to receive input from residents, turning the final performance into a truly collective creation.

Murgas use the language of popular culture, drawing on popular wisdom, idioms, and proverbs to convey a message that is purposely ambiguous, loaded with double meanings, and impossible to translate literally without reference to context. Murgas rely on parody and burlesque to become powerful weapons against established norms and social institutions, using a coded language that is inaccessible to people who are not familiar with the culture of the popular classes, like the elites or military censors. Mastering the arts of metaphor and insinuation, murga lyrics offer satiric commentary on current affairs, make reference to day-to-day life and public passions such as soccer and politics, mock public figures, and critique social conditions. Traditionally, murgas entertained their audiences by celebrating the country's fame for its remarkable accomplishments in international soccer or in social welfare, or by picking on neighborhood archetypes, like the womanizer, the bully, the immigrant, or the local police officer. Over time, as the country fell deeper into crisis and became more politically polarized, the murgas added to their targets authority figures, national politicians, and social and political institutions, turning celebration of past events into humorous but poignant critiques of current conditions. The most popular themes became the high cost of living, rising unemployment, mass migration, and humiliating soccer performances.

Whereas carnival under Franco's Spain was banned in 1947, Uruguayan murgas survived repression and became central articulators of national protest during the dark times of military rule in the 1970s and 1980s. As the threat of repression made direct political discourse virtually impossible, opposition to the regime by necessity relied on indirect language, the privileged field of murgas and popular culture. It was precisely the murgas' use of metaphor, parody, and double meaning that provided a platform for popular resistance. Military censors worked incessantly to silence these groups—demanding that their lyrics be approved in advance; prohibiting the use of certain words, like liberty, working class, equality, future, and harmony; and even jailing murga performers—but they could not muzzle *murguistas,* who outsmarted them through their skillful art of saying what one was permitted to say in order to insinuate that which one could not say.[12]

Over time La Teja became a community of soccer aficionados and murguistas. If Cerrenses could boast about the glorious struggles of meatpackers, Tejanos could equally be proud to have produced some of the finest, and most politically charged, murgas in the country. Over the years, the neighborhoods of La Teja, Paso Molino, and Belvedere (all belonging to district 14) produced a talented assortment of murgas[13] that became known

12. Such was the case with the lyrics produced by a young murga, La Reina de La Teja (The Queen from La Teja), whose debut in 1980 became the revelation of carnival season. Its tribute to the neighborhood started with the following lyrics: "*Murga del pueblo reina, si reina el pueblo que es su esperanza*" (The people's murga rules, when the people, who are also its hope, rule"). Censors approved the lyrics because these separate phrases that toyed with the name of the group had no clear political meaning in the overall context of the song. When La Reina sang the song onstage, however, the words acquired a new meaning, condemning tyranny and calling for democracy, and became an instant national hymn of resistance. See Enríquez 2004, 176.

13. Including Araca la Cana and Diablos Verdes (founded in the 1930s), La Soberana (1969), Momolandia (1976), and La Reina de La Teja (1980).

as *murgas compañeras,* to distinguish them from the less politicized carnival groups in other neighborhoods. Tejano murgas produced lyrics and plays linking references to proletarian wretchedness with positive affirmations of working-class labor and solidarity.[14]

Two murgas that epitomize the militant traditions of La Teja are Diablos Verdes[15] (the Green Devils) and La Reina de La Teja (the Queen of La Teja). Diablos Verdes has ties with the Glass Workers Union—the militant trade union rooted in La Teja—and appropriately describes itself as "La Consecuente" (the unswerving) for its ongoing support of worker's struggles over the years. During the general strike against the military coup in 1973, for example, it brought its music to occupied factories to support striking workers. Today Diablos Verdes still perform at May Day celebrations, political rallies, trade union halls, housing cooperatives, and solidarity recitals. La Reina de la Teja, the other murga from the neighborhood, won instant national and international recognition for its artistic creativity and its openly political lyrics when it first appeared in carnival in 1980.[16] Unlike the other murgas, the brave performances of La Reina expressed overt political condemnations of the dictatorship, inspiring citizens to overcome the culture of fear that prevailed during the military era. Not surprisingly, both murgas were persecuted during the dictatorship and became targets of censorship, and many of their members were imprisoned.[17] Thus,

14. Many of these murgas found a welcoming home among local trade unions or in the neighborhood clubs, like Arbolito or Progreso, where they rehearsed and met their loyal fans. Arbolito had a policy, which it maintained through pressing economic times, of not charging admission to murga events, fund-raising only through sales of beverages and snacks at the canteen. Every season, the club would draft more than one hundred fifty community volunteers to run the tablado and raise funds. The money went to the club, which would then return it to the community through solidarity activities such as the comedor and the health clinic.

15. The Diablos' golden era was in the 1960s, when it ruled carnival official competitions, winning first place in 1961 and 1965, second place in 1960 and 1964, and third place in 1963 and 1968. Diablos Verdes gained national recognition for its artistic performances, fetching the prestigious first prize six times in the city's murga competition (in 1959, 1961, 1965, 1981, 1999, and 2001). See Enríquez 2004, 39.

16. La Reina de la Teja was often among the finalists in the annual carnival competition, winning first prize in 1994. In its short history, it performed more than five thousand times, recorded sixteen albums, and took murga beyond the borders of Uruguay, performing in the United States, Canada, Australia, Argentina, Venezuela, and the Dominican Republic. Even today, La Reina's music and sharp lyrics resonate strongly among the Uruguayan diaspora.

17. The dictatorship could not even control the subversive energy and humor of carnival within its own prisons. When it jailed two legendary murguistas—"Pepe Veneno" (founder and lyricist of La Soberana) and Juan Antonio Iglesias (founder and artistic director of Diablos Verdes)—they founded La Compañera, a murga made up of political prisoners. Inside Punta Carretas prison, they also set up a theater and a musical group, and organized recitals based on texts by Spanish poets like Federico García Lorca and Miguel Hernández. Ironically, following

at a crucial moment in Uruguayan political history, La Teja's gutsy murgas compañeras, drawing from the militant traditions of the community and the infrastructure of its social and sports clubs, catapulted themselves into the forefront of a powerful movement of artistic creation and political resistance against military rule.

The distinctive mix of radical left-wing politics, carnival music, and networks of social and sports clubs gave Tejanos a unique sense of identity difficult to find in other neighborhoods of Montevideo:

> JOSE: When La Reina de la Teja performs at the Progreso Soccer Club everyone goes crazy; people are left outside, it's unbelievable! And during the city carnival contest, when La Reina de la Teja parades at the Summer Theater all you can see are the flags of Progreso and Arbolito. What I'm getting at is there is a special culture here in all this, you see?

It is precisely this local culture—articulated through local clubs—that distinguishes Tejanos from Cerrenses on the other side of the Pantanoso River. In La Teja identity revolves around the sporting clubs, since so much neighborly interaction stems from these clubs; in Cerro this identity was generated through union-based relationships. But the fundamental sentiment is the same: it is the feeling of belonging and of pride.

The blending of powerful traditions of radical proletarian militancy, local soccer clubs, and murga groups provided the cultural matrix used by Tejanos to construct their experiences with decentralization. Not surprisingly, in assessing how decentralization played out in the particular setting of La Teja, I found the experience of local government very different in this neighborhood when compared to the other two covered in this study. Most notably, the community's unique traditions came to decentralization through a prominent Tejano who embodied the pride and aspirations of this remarkable neighborhood. Indeed, Tabaré Vázquez—the first socialist mayor of Montevideo, the man who introduced decentralization in the early 1990s—is himself a Tejano. Born and raised in La Teja, Vázquez, the son of a union leader, rose above his family's humble origins to become a renowned oncologist and national political leader. As a true Tejano, he helped

---

the return to democracy in the mid-1980s, the prison was turned into an upscale shopping mall, and the only part remaining is the front gate arch, which serves as the entrance to the mall for thousands of shoppers.

build some of the key local institutions. He was one of the founders of Club Arbolito in the late 1950s, and later as a young medical student he helped set up the health clinics of Club Progreso and Arbolito. He also was president of Progreso Soccer Club for ten years (1979–89), leading the club to capture the first division championship in 1989.

Amid the celebrations of Progreso's crowning as national champion that year, Vázquez made a surprise announcement to the crowd that had gathered in Plaza Lafone: he would seek the candidacy of the Broad Front in the mayoralty race scheduled for later that year. Vázquez was easily confirmed as the candidate of the left-wing coalition and captured the city government in the historic November 1989 election. In February 1990, a week after Vázquez assumed power, thousands of Tejanos descended on the plaza on a warm summer evening to honor the newly elected *vecino* (neighbor) from La Teja. In true Tejano style, murga performances blended with political speeches to celebrate this remarkable achievement for their barrio. When Tabaré, as he is popularly known in La Teja and throughout Uruguay, came to the podium to speak, he made the official announcement in the very heart of La Teja that he was going to make good on his campaign promise to decentralize the municipal system and to build a truly participatory system of urban governance in Montevideo. The crowd went crazy, as they never would have imagined that a son of their militant community would be the one to change the course of city politics in such a profound manner. At last, the grassroot militant traditions of La Teja had arrived at the center of power in city politics via a leader who enjoyed the admiration of the entire community. As I walk around the same Plaza Lafone nearly fourteen years later, I can still decipher a washed-out graffiti inscription on the school walls across the street; blending soccer, politics, and community pride, it proclaims, "*Se Puede. Progreso Campeón y Tabaré Presidente!*" ("It Is Achievable. Progreso Crowned Champion, Tabaré to the Presidency!"). It was a prophetic statement, as Vázquez continued his political rise to become the country's president in 2004 with the overwhelming support of more than 50 percent of the electorate.

The Evolution of the Neighborhood Council

While the majority of Tejanos remain loyal supporters of Vázquez, their honeymoon with decentralization did not last long, and it had certainly ended when I attended the inauguration of the newly elected council in

2004. The council met at the assembly hall of the popular Belvedere Bowling Club on Carlos María Ramírez, an improvement over the decrepit building where the council used to meet in the late 1990s when I first visited the community. Arriving early, I discover that the club is nearly empty and that nobody is bowling, and wonder whether this could be a metaphor for the decline of associational and civic life in Uruguay, as was suggested by Robert Putnam in the United States in his famous article "Bowling Alone." At the back of the building I find a half dozen men standing at the bar quietly sipping their drinks, and behind the bar I notice a display of trophies sitting beside some bottles of liquor. "We won them in citywide competitions," a proud man tells me, to start conversation. To my disappointment, however, I quickly realize that these men are totally unaware that the newly elected councilors are coming to the club to have their first meeting of the term.

I go back to the assembly hall and see many councilors who have already taken their seats. The atmosphere appears relaxed and welcoming, and the room slowly fills with more than fifty people who look eager to get started. The meeting is called to order by the secretary of the local junta, who will act as chair for the remainder of the meeting. The air of formality reminds me of the meeting in El Cerro: a group of officials take their place at the front of the hall, including the secretary and the president of the local junta, the district's administrative director, and the director of services for the western region representing city hall. Near the front, I also see the district's two social workers and the two university interns.

The first part of the meeting aims to set the tone for the period and to educate the incoming councilors, 80 percent of whom are new in their roles. The representative from city hall tells councilors that the western section of Montevideo, to which their district belongs, is one of the high-priority areas for the city government because of its disproportionate share of social and economic problems. The president of the local junta follows with a brief message that is mainly a peace offering, stressing that the local junta wishes to develop a constructive working relationship with the incoming council and to put past conflicts aside. Following the speeches, social workers and interns hand out binders to each councilor containing very useful information—maps of the district, graphs with basic demographic data, relevant municipal decrees, local election figures, and the council's current bylaws. The mood of the meeting is not nearly so high-spirited as the one I attended in Peñarol, but it certainly feels less tense than the one in El Cerro. Incoming councilors, eager to learn about the expectations and obligations of their roles, freely ask questions of those with more experience, appearing to be less concerned about setting themselves apart from past traditions than did the councilors in El Cerro.

When a returning councilor from La Teja asks about the status of the council's bylaws, however, the mood suddenly changes. Visibly anxious, some councilors propose to postpone discussion of the bylaws to a future meeting, but tension builds as the councilor refuses to back down. As I look around the meeting, councilors look at each other nervously, painfully aware that that this is a sensitive issue that could spoil their first meeting. They finally agree to refer the issue to the council's steering committee, which is asked to bring a recommendation to the next council meeting. The assembly moves to the final order of business, the selection of the steering committee, which proceeds in orderly fashion and without conflict, although it takes over an hour.[18]

The next plenary of the council followed two weeks later, and though a marathon meeting, it was surprisingly free of tension. The newly installed steering committee did an excellent job in preparing a solid agenda and running the meeting in an orderly fashion. Following a local tradition, the plenary session started with an unstructured period, called *previos,* when councilors announce upcoming events and activities and share information about relevant political and social activities not necessarily confined to municipal affairs.[19] The previos were followed by the steering committee report, which proposed a set of operating rules for plenary sessions: councilors' interventions would be limited to three minutes with a possible

18. The steering committee is made up of two representatives from each subzone, who rotate every six months. Since subzones may encompass more than one neighborhood, the issue of who should sit on the committee is a delicate one, requiring negotiation and compromise. In many districts, like district 13, the accepted criteria is to start with the two most voted councilors, who are then replaced six months later with the second most voted, and so on until all councilors sit on the steering committee. Seven of the district's eight subzones had agreed in advance to adhere to this criteria and easily nominated their representatives, but one subzone asked the council to give them one week to discuss the nomination of their representatives.

19. The previos extended for over an hour as many councilors took the floor to make announcements; these covered, among other topics, an upcoming meeting to get local input to map social exclusion in the district, a march by a local network to highlight hunger affecting people in their communities, and a series of cultural events. One councilor proposed to invite a representative from the National Commission in Defense of Water to talk to the council about the current national struggles against privatization of water resources, while another councilor reported an ongoing protest organized by the national housing cooperative federation and asked for council support. Councilors voted unanimously to support the idea that water should remain a public good and to issue a solidarity message regarding the protest organized by the housing cooperatives. They also agreed to invite someone from the network addressing the problem of hunger in the district to give the council a report.

two-minute extension, previos would last no longer than thirty minutes and be reserved for "information-only" items, and a card system would be used to identify those eligible to vote at plenary meetings. The steering committee also proposed to set up a commission to review the current bylaws that was to draft a package of proposed amendments within fifteen days, to be presented at the next council meeting.

It only was after the floor was opened for discussion that I was struck by the poor communication and decision-making skills in the council. Minor issues turned into major stumbling blocks and the chair's futile attempts to keep the discussion on track did not stop the meeting from quickly descending into chaos: some agitated councilors loudly demanded respect for each others' opinions while others complained equally loudly that there was too much bureaucracy in the running of the meeting. In the end, the chaos reflected inadequate communication skills but not necessarily substantive differences among councilors. Still, they managed to make two key decisions—to set up a bylaws commission and to postpone voting on the steering committee's procedural proposal until the bylaw commission brought back its report—thereby averting the outcome I had witnessed in El Cerro.[20] At this point, someone made a timely announcement: everyone was invited to a capacity building workshop organized by city hall. The meeting ended almost two hours behind schedule, leaving councilors worn out and with mixed feelings: they felt baffled by their incapacity to communicate with one another but at the same time they felt encouraged by the fact that they had made some important decisions.

In spite of the problems in the first plenary, most people I talked to remained optimistic about the future prospects of this neighborhood council:

> NESTOR: I believe that it is going to be a good council. I know quite a few councilors who, although new to the council, are recognized as longtime community activists who, in their time, were involved in a neighborhood association or a sporting committee, and I believe that they bring with them a whole other level of knowledge and of working ability.

20. The first topic to come up was the issue of whether voting should be reserved exclusively for elected councilors and under what conditions alternate councilors could vote, a discussion I had personally witnessed back in the 1998 council. After a lengthy discussion it was decided that alternates should be called to replace a missing councilor, starting with the alternate who had received the most votes, rather than matching alternates and councilors from the same neighborhoods. The point was to stress that once elected, councilors and their alternates became representatives of the entire district rather than just their own subzone.

Given the history of decentralization in the district—which was marked by infighting within the council and endless conflicts between the council, the local junta, and city authorities—it was not difficult to understand why the first plenary meeting was seen as a success.[21] Even members of the local junta felt very encouraged by the meeting that had just ended:

> JULIO: The neighborhood council is eighty percent new. This renewal inspires enthusiasm and generates expectations. Considering our friendship with the majority of the councilors, we anticipate a whole other kind of relationship with this council.

The History of Decentralization in District 14

In the early stages, the project of participatory decentralization generated a great deal of interest among Tejanos, who responded enthusiastically to Mayor Vázquez's call to participate in a new chapter in city politics:[22]

> JULIO: When the process started, the social organizations exploded; hope bloomed and the people rushed to join in decentralization, which promised a different form of governance based on participation, and a new relationship between people and state institutions.

Before the institutional design of local government was even decided—as Vázquez negotiated the project with conservative political parties to secure legislative approval—hundreds of people gathered in large plenary sessions in anticipation of the changes to come. By 1990, three years before the inauguration of the first neighborhood council, a rainbow coalition of local organizations set up a steering committee to represent the district vis-à-vis municipal authorities and to prepare for the impending arrival of local government. The committee, made up of delegates designated by social organizations from each of the neighborhoods in the district, was responsible for convening a district-wide assembly every two

21. I had a taste of these bitter struggles when I had first attended meetings of the district's neighborhood council in 1998. Such was the level of mistrust that one councilor used to bring a tape recorder to the meetings and would defiantly record every intervention: "For insurance purposes," he told me, "in case they renege on what they say!"

22. The first councils attracted many social and political activists, but many formal members of leftist parties chose not to join because they did not appreciate this local space as an important site for political action.

months and for coordinating the work of several commissions working on housing, sanitation, carnival, culture, and public works. Many of these commissions would later become thematic commissions of the neighborhood council. By the end of 1991, more than one hundred twenty local organizations, including neighborhood associations, housing cooperatives, social and sports clubs, and religious institutions, had participated in these activities.[23]

Local state officials, such as the district's coordinator and the social workers assigned to the area to set up local government in late 1990s, played a key role facilitating this process. Susana was one of eighteen district coordinators personally picked by Vázquez to get decentralization started in each district, a position that was the precursor of the role of secretary of the local junta. When she assumed her position in the mid-1990s she certainly had the right credentials for the role. A recognized popular educator and community advocate who had lived all her life in La Teja, she brought a wealth of experience in community development. I met this welcoming and warmhearted woman when I first visited the district in 1998, and I have returned to see her every time I have a chance. She always offers rich and insightful analysis of the district and of decentralization more generally.

As I explained in the introductory chapter, the reforms advocated by Vázquez initially envisioned empowering neighborhood councils with decision-making powers, but his plan soon succumbed to pressure from the political establishment and councils were downgraded to the status of consultative bodies, a far cry from the aspirations of most Tejanos. Martín, the current president of the local junta, recounts the disappointment he felt when the municipal assembly approved the final model:

> We had fought to develop a model, but decentralization was started with many shortcomings. We spent three years negotiating in the municipal assembly, and then agreements reached with the traditional political parties changed the rules of the game, because decentralization was supposed to be built on the basis of decision-making assemblies, not on local juntas and neighborhood councils. That's why I say the whole project was wounded from that point onward.

23. Early on, however, conflicts already emerged within the district that foretold some of the difficulties that lay ahead. In 1990, for example, representatives from La Teja withdrew from the assemblies and from the steering committee for one full year due to frictions within the community and conflicts involving Tejanos and activists from other neighborhoods.

Bitterly disappointed by the compromise, Tejanos vowed to resist the shabby model that, in their view, had clipped the wings of local democracy before it had even started to fly. Remaining loyal to Vázquez's original vision—even though he may have moved on, accepting the political realities at city hall—Tejanos would awaken their dormant militant traditions to oppose the shameful pact and make district 14 an example of true participatory democracy for the entire city:[24]

> SUSANA: The council ran up against the reality of having not attained the more direct form of democracy that they were aiming for. They were dreaming of being able to make decisions, but this wasn't possible; it was a battle they lost before the fight even began. So then they figured that they would not collaborate on things that city hall might try to do. I think the attitude was more or less, "If we're fighting, it's an all-out battle; we won't do it halfway."

The first attempt to subvert the model came in 1993 when local activists were called to have some bearing on the configuration of the new organs of local government. Unlike the neighborhood council, which was an elected body of civil society, the mayor appointed the all-powerful political junta based on recommendations from local chapters of political parties. Three longtime community activists received local support to become the Broad Front representatives in the junta and were confirmed in their posts by Vázquez, becoming the majority block in the five-member organization. Formal office certainly marked an important victory for these activists, but it also made them feel awkward, as this body was the visible culprit in a political saga of betrayal and backroom deals. Julio Listre, the first president of the local junta, recalls their dilemma:

> When the council's role was reduced to monitoring and consultation, a group of us thought the junta was a dangerous place to be because local power would end up concentrated there. It was in this frame of mind that we joined the local junta; we had inherited from our culture of opposition a distrust for centralized power. In truth, we were a little ashamed of the positions we were taking on.[25]

24. A 1992 opinion poll conducted in district 14 showed that 86 percent of neighborhood associations in the district believed that the role of local government was to co-govern with local residents, and 43 percent demanded more participation. Regent 2004.

25. Listre 1999, 92.

The new organs of local government were launched on December 1993, and in the inaugural ceremonies the local junta made a remarkable pledge:

> The local junta solemnly swore it would support all the initiatives that came to it from the neighborhood council, proposing a permanent form of joint action that would mock, in some way, the intention of the party system to disempower the neighborhood councils.[26]

This decision de facto transferred decision-making powers from the junta to the council and made the former subordinate to the later. It was the district's defiant response to the backroom deals of the political establishment!

Testing the Limits of Local Government: Squatters and Hunger Strikes

The first test of the junta's oath came only a few days after the opening ceremonies when a group of homeless families seized a vacant municipal lot in La Teja, demanding that city authorities allow them to build their homes on the site. The ten families had been squatting for a number of years in the crumbling building of a former textile factory in the area and were supported in their actions by several community organizations, including a handful of councilors who participated in the occupation. When the neighborhood council met for the first time in early January 1994, the first order of business was a motion to give the squatters full council support, a motion that passed after a lengthy and emotional debate. Without ever consulting local representatives, however, city officials initiated legal proceedings to evict the squatters and announced that they would not negotiate with them until they had ended the occupation. The squatters and their supporters in the council were outraged, declaring they were ready to resist police eviction and from that moment on they would negotiate only with Mayor Vázquez.

As tension mounted, junta members hesitated to live up to their pledge to unconditionally support every decision made by the council. The newly inaugurated junta faced the following dilemma: while they empathized with the squatters' plight as community activists, in their capacity as officials of local government they felt obliged not to give in to pressure before they

26. Ibid., 65.

had a chance to develop a district-wide housing plan that took into account the needs of all families in the district and the resources made available to local government. Since other families had already petitioned them to explore solutions to their housing problems, they felt that allowing a group of families to jump to the front of the line would send the wrong message. They were also opposed to the squatters' stance of refusing any piece of land other than the one they had occupied, a position they feared would compromise future development plans in the district. The space in question was one of the few remaining municipal lots in the district, so giving it to the squatters would effectively deprive local government officials of a resource that could be used for wider community needs. Members of the local junta felt strongly that the ten families had to be accommodated somewhere else.

The junta's reasoning did little to appease the squatters, and within a few weeks the council became deeply divided between those who advocated more radical measures to press for the squatters' demands, and those who wanted to seek a negotiated solution. Outraged by what they perceived as a betrayal of the commitment to social justice by leftist city officials, and frustrated by the junta's refusal to uphold their decision, a small group of activists, including one councilor, decided to step up the pressure:

> RAFAEL: We wanted to ensure justice for the dispossessed. So we said: if there are people without land, and if there is land without people on it, we need to support the occupation of that land by the landless. The council was divided on the matter, but three of us held a hunger strike in support of the occupation.

More than ten years later, Rafael still gets irritated when he talks to me about the junta's refusal to support their hunger strike, a position that seemed to confirm his deep resentment of the irreversible corrupting effects of institutional party politics, a point I will return to below.

The stalemate was broken when Mayor Vázquez announced that the solution had to come from within the district, pushing squatters to negotiate with local government officials. In fact, up until his announcement the main protagonists in this conflict—squatters, local activists, and municipal officials—had in effect bypassed local levels of government: the squatters addressed their demands to central municipal officials who, in turn, responded without consulting local government in the district. Vázquez used his influence to persuade the squatters to consider settling in other lots and to ask the junta and the council to come up with an alternative site. The strategy worked, and following a joint tour of the district, local officials, squatters, and their supporters agreed on a new site for the squatters. Although the occupation was eventually resolved, the wounds opened during the conflict would not heal easily, affecting the functioning of local government for many years. The council remained internally divided, deep mistrust marked the relation between subsequent neighborhood councils and local juntas, and feelings of antagonism toward city officials intensified, making it nearly impossible to foster constructive relations among the various levels of local government.

Learning to Work Together: The Challenge of Building Trust

The squatters' occupation came as a rude awakening for activists in district 14 as they came face-to-face with the harsh realities of local governance and the challenges of building participatory democratic practices. The new politics of space were proving far more complex than the simpler processes of building class solidarity out of more easily identifiable working-class demands and a straightforward definition of class adversaries. Activists would need to learn to negotiate among themselves the multiple, and often contradictory, sets of interests arising in the district and to juggle the scarce resources at their disposal to meet the overwhelming needs of all residents:

> SUSANA: The concept of "territory" as a shared space, a basis of solidarity, is much more complex and rich than that of a belonging to a "sector" [i.e., class]. Everything is encompassed in the idea of "territory": not just your ideological outlook, but also the way you live your everyday life, if you are in solidarity with others. For this reason the relationship is so much richer when you organize on the basis of territory, rather than in the context of a union where you only share one thing with your fellows: work.

The new context required activists to acknowledge that theirs was a community of communities, whose unity was contingent on articulating a common vision based on a balanced respect for the plurality of interests found within the district. Learning to negotiate these different interests that could not easily be framed in class terms was the key to charting a common course to capitalize on the opportunities offered by participatory decentralization. Unfortunately, following the initial experience of the squatters' occupation and the hunger strike, the members of local government remained bitterly divided. For some activists, especially those belonging to the local junta, the affair demonstrated the imperative necessity of shifting from a politics of contention to a politics of proposition, and of building new capacities to work effectively within the new institutional makeup created by participatory decentralization. For others, the outcome of this conflict, confirmed the aptness of the radical traditions of La Teja as the best strategy to keep in check untrustworthy municipal officials and their local allies and to wrestle resources away from a reluctant city government. This last position was advocated by a relatively small but vociferous group of councilors, mostly Tejanos, who would become very influential within the council. Julio Listre explains:

> Confronted with this highly critical outlook toward the city government and the local junta, which held that "the council must organize the people so as to extract resources from city hall," most of the council was paralyzed, fell silent, and later became swept up by urgent demands. So the council became a sound box for explosive topics: organizing demonstrations and protests, taking issues to the media. . . . The entire council dances to the rhythm of specters: you have to struggle against something very threatening and at the same time unite, bond . . . the councilors can show the neighborhood that, by going to the media, they continue the struggle, and that if things don't get done it is because the local junta blocks initiatives, or because the directors have forgotten about the promises they made.[27]

Closing ranks against municipal authorities and their local footman, the local junta, councilors adopted a confrontational stance that became a permanent feature of neighborhood councils in the district, making it nearly impossible to foster more constructive working relations between these two organs of local government. Martín recalls the problems he inherited when he became president of the local junta in 2000:

> In the beginning the relationship with the local junta was difficult because they had set out with the idea that the junta was "the enemy."

27. Ibid., 66.

They got to the point in previous council meetings where they would not even let the local junta members speak. What's more, they weren't wanted at the council table, even though they were supposed to be there to convey information and to carry information back to the junta and its commissions.

The councilors' stance was rooted in the conviction that institutional politics were intrinsically corrupt regardless of political ideology. This mistrust of institutions may have resonated with the community's radical political traditions, but it originated among the more radical wing of the country's political Left, to which only a small but relentless minority of councilors belonged. Although their influence in the council appears to be declining, the mistrust of official politics is still visible today among councilors.

A longtime resident of La Teja, Felipe is an occasional murguista, a community activist, and an unemployed dockworker. He got involved in the soup kitchen at Club Progreso in the 1980s when Vázquez was president of the club, and he currently supports a *merendero*—a locally run initiative that provides free hot snacks to poor children—in one of the asentamientos of La Teja. He is also a member of the Commission in Defense of Water, a national coalition that organized a historic referendum to declare water a public good—and thus off-limits to private companies—that was overwhelmingly supported by Uruguayan citizens in 2004. A former member of several far-left political groups and currently an independent activist, he has been a councilor for La Teja since 2001. Felipe is deeply disillusioned with the Broad Front and with party politics more generally, and is not afraid to say it:

> The political system always comes first. And politics are dirty, false; and I'm referring here not just to the two main parties, but also to all political sectors. Everyone just defends his own little space, each has his own goal.

Drawing on this position, he articulates a particular view of what makes an ideal councilor:

> The best councilor is the lowly one. Not the intellectual who talks nicely; he has vocabulary and education but he sees things from above. Nonetheless, when you hear someone from a squatter settlement who doesn't use big words but is passionate, you can tell he speaks from the heart. Those who live this reality are the most enlightened!

This contrast between an idealized politics from below and a false politics from above framed the attitude of a cohort of councilors like Felipe, feeding mistrust toward the entire system of participatory decentralization. Their suspicions appeared to be confirmed when Mayor Arana appointed Beatriz Silva to the powerful post of secretary of the local junta for the 1995–2000 period. The decision was vehemently opposed by councilors on the grounds that it did not serve the needs or preferences of the district, only serving the pervasive logic of distributing political appointments within the governing coalition. They were right. The appointment of a Communist Party official with little community-based experience to a district dominated by the radical Left was not only politically insensitive but also proved to be a recipe for disaster. To make matters worse, the secretary came to the position with no disposition to work things out with the disgruntled council and with little patience to understand the complexities of participatory grassroot politics in the district. As a party cadre, she seemed more comfortable working through the structures of local political parties, often bypassing a council that grew increasingly more dissatisfied. Indeed, Beatriz epitomized the distant and insensitive politician so despised by activists like Felipe, and her personal approach quickly alienated even the most moderate councilors, exacerbating animosity toward the local junta.[28]

The secretary also clashed with the district's social worker, a seasoned Tejana with more than twenty-four years of professional experience who had been on staff since decentralization came to the district in the early 1990s. María was well respected by community activists and had become one of the most trusted individuals in local government. When I first met her in 1998 I was immediately struck by her understanding of local dynamics, her determination to promote local participation and to build capacities, and her professional honesty as she struggled to negotiate her own position within the complex web of power relations created by decentralization. Caught between her role as a municipal employee and her empathy toward the grass roots, María remained firmly committed as an advocate

---

28. Interestingly, Beatriz Silva belonged to the same political party as Luis in Peñarol, but they differed radically in terms of their orientation toward building local government and working with community organizations. Luis came with a tradition of community activism while Silva came from the party apparatus. Such radical differences among members of the same party leads me to believe that conflicts within the councils could not easily be explained by reference to people's party affiliation. When Gustavo was appointed secretary in district 17, for example, he found a council dominated by members of his political party who supported him wholeheartedly, but soon thereafter he alienated his supporters with his poor work habits and orientation toward community work. I will return to this point in the concluding chapter.

and facilitator of community participation. This approach, congruent with the stated objectives of decentralization, was at odds with the party-centered view of the incoming secretary and would eventually cost María her job. Eventually Beatriz ordered that María be transferred to another district with the approval of Mayor Arana, a decision that produced further animosity and mistrust toward city officials:[29]

> TERESA: The decision was condemned by everyone in the area; we collected over seven hundred signatures demanding that María return. But there was no way to make it happen. When she was displaced from the social workers' team, the new team that took her place had no roots in the area. This era of Beatriz Silva ended in 2000 and by that point everything was fragmented. It was a nefarious time for the area.

María's removal was the latest setback for the district, as the participatory project lost an experienced advocate precisely at a time when her knowledge and legitimacy were badly needed to salvage the rapidly deteriorating reality of local government. Mayor Arana's backing of his secretary signaled rather bluntly that the central political logic flowing from the corridors of power in city hall would take precedence over local preferences. It also sealed the fate of local government in district 14 as a stage for ideological clashes between the moderate and the radical Left.

Local Government's Second Test: Privatization of Municipal Buildings

These conflicts came to the fore in 1998 over the future use of the historic Hotel del Prado, an impressive early-twentieth-century building located at the heart of Parque del Prado. The building, which had served as the Air Force Officers' Club after it was arbitrarily seized during the period of military rule, had recently been handed back to the municipality. When the more radical councilors learned that city officials were considering a bid from a private company to turn it into a banquet hall, they were outraged and decided to block the deal. This was a surprising decision given that

---

29. Ironically, she was transferred to district 13, which gave me an excellent opportunity to draw on her experience in both districts for invaluable comparative analysis.

residents had never made claims over the use of the building, accepting it as a bourgeois enclave within the district. The councilors' reaction was connected to broader political debates within the city legislative assembly over a plan to contract out certain services to private companies. Surprisingly, the proposal did not stir up much controversy within the governing coalition, but it was loudly opposed by a minority faction led by a former Tupamaro leader who resigned his post in the assembly in protest of what he believed was a betrayal of the coalition's long-standing opposition to privatization.

Sympathetic to these views, councilors went on the offensive, hoping this time to make their mark on city politics. They argued that decisions about public buildings in the district could not be made without the approval of local authorities.[30] Claiming that the facilities belonged to the communities in the area and that the proposed banquet hall would only cater to upper-middle-class people from other districts, the council made a counterproposal: place the building under local control and turn it into a cultural center for the benefit of all residents of district 14. Councilors argued that the differences separating their proposal from that of the city government involved two radically opposing visions of the city. The banquet hall project, they pointed out, would effectively hand over a public resource to private hands, something that was utterly unacceptable. The councilors' case was outlined in a document that was submitted to city planners and widely distributed across the city. Quoting the progressive urban planner Salvador Schellotto, the document laid out the two options facing leftist municipal government officials:

> The battle for public space knows no limits in our city. It is a struggle for recognition of the principle that the city, produced by the collective effort of us all, should be there to serve us all. This is a very important part of the battle for a better quality of life. In this struggle, the municipal government cannot be neutral. It will side with the residents, or with the enemy. This is the crossroads that we face so dramatically today.[31]

The council's bid was unsuccessful. Arguing that residents lacked the capacity to manage a community center of such size and that the

30. Their claim was based on a municipal decree encouraging councils to advise the city government on decisions affecting municipal properties in their district. See Junta Departamental de Montevideo, decree no. 26019, article 10.

31. Quoted in Rebellato and Ubilla 1999, 154.

municipality did not have the resources to upgrade and run the building, city hall officials declared the council's proposal unsustainable and offered a twenty-year lease to a private company to upgrade the facility and to turn it into an upscale teahouse and banquet hall. City officials, councilors argued, had effectively sided with the "enemy camp."

I had a chance to visit the newly renovated facilities when my wife and I attended my cousin's wedding party in 2004. As the middle-class guests sat down to dinner and pleasant music played in the background, I looked around to admire the impressive high ceilings, the intricate plaster moldings, and the imposing French doors adorned with elaborately embroidered drapery; for a moment I was transported back in time to the period when the building served the city's upper class residing in El Prado. This pleasant moment, in the company of my relatives and their high-spirited guests, was interrupted when I was struck with an awkward sense of remorse as I started to visualize the faces of the activists I had recently interviewed. The magnificent place, faithful to its former aristocratic days, was certainly a far cry from the cultural center envisioned by community activists a few years earlier. Many councilors are still fuming about the decision of city planners to turn down their proposal, and they still have harsh words for the leftist administration:

> FELIPE: The Hotel del Prado was all about business. When political interests emerge, the public good gets left by the wayside. Even the Broad Front is guilty of this.

> JOAQUIN: If city hall is bad, we have to acknowledge this. If city hall escaped the grip of the Broad Front, this has to be acknowledged; if city hall privatized, we have to say so. Otherwise, we are like the priests who say, "Do as I say and not as I do."

Following the city's decision, the council gave municipal authorities an ultimatum: 20 percent of the profits from the Hotel del Prado were to be transferred to the district to fund existing comedores and merenderos. The city government turned down the proposal, leaving the district empty-handed, an outcome that María believes could have been avoided:

> In La Teja, they were much more critical of the relationship between city hall and the council. The reaction was violent, crude, and confrontational. It is a reaction in tune with the way the people of the

area live: when they have an opportunity to express themselves, they do so violently. The problem was that they lost a lot by always assuming a rejectionist attitude. This manner of rejecting everything without offering a constructive alternative led to our missing out on possible gains in the area, as happened in the case of the Hotel del Prado. We could have asked for other things, but instead took a black-and-white position: either it was a place only for the locals, or it was nothing.

As we talk about the council's intransigence, I start to think how much this stance contrasts with the successful strategy used by community activists in Peñarol to negotiate the railway buildings for the community or to get the army to clean up the tracks. It would appear that the weight of La Teja's legendary radical, oppositional traditions, as in the case of neighboring El Cerro, had become a handicap in the changing context of participatory local government.

From Bad to Worse: Breakdown in Relations Within the Council.

According to some activists, such intransigence could not be explained exclusively by the weight of past traditions or the actions of a small group of radicalized councilors. This stance, they argue, was reinforced by the entry into the council of representatives from the recent asentamientos. Ana, a longtime social activist and Frente Amplio militant, explains:

> They came from the north [of the district], from the most marginalized area, the area most recently marginalized. Before, in La Teja the poor were integrated into the neighborhood; the poor people lived in the squatter settlements, but they were laborers who worked in the factory. However, in the last twenty years, these people have been left without work and a culture of poverty has developed, and it has worsened in the last twelve years as drugs have entered the scene.

The "new poor" were proportionally smaller compared to those living in the asentamientos in El Cerro on the other side of the Pantanoso River. They entered the council thanks to changes to regulations permitting candidates to run with the support of ten signatures, which effectively facilitated access to non-organized sectors. Many community activists in the district passionately opposed these changes to the electoral system on the grounds that they would undermine collective organization. Thanks to these developments, many newcomers were elected to the neighborhood council with the support of some leftist councilors who saw the squatters as the carriers of a new politics of emancipation:

> ANA: The Left has gained much ground in the poorer sectors, as these people have become involved in territorial organizations. They have even made it into the councils, because the more politicized and partisan people want to capture this population: the poorest of the poor, those who we must "save." And this messianic, paternalistic and almost demagogic attitude has led party organizations in the area to channel votes in support of these people, to ensure them a place on the council.

As happened in El Cerro, the councilors from the newer asentamientos quickly grew frustrated by the lack of response to their problems. Lacking traditions of collective organizing and with fewer skills to operate within local government structures, they often ended up resorting to physical and verbal violence, personalizing differences, and disrupting the operation of the council:

> ANA: These people have no patience for discussion. Their attitude is "I want it, I want it now, I will not negotiate," and this led to a serious division within the council. The women felt it most intensely, but the men felt it too. There were only seven or eight who acted like this, but they managed to exert a lot of pressure.

The convergence of two different oppositional groupings—La Teja's traditional militant stance embraced by groups of disgruntled councilors and the squatters' less ideological but still highly confrontational approach—not only magnified problems with the local junta but also exacerbated bickering within the council:

> MARIA: In the neighborhood councils, there was a lot of conflict. Everything prompted a violent reaction. You really noticed this attitude of intransigence, of an unwillingness to negotiate or exchange. It was very hard to achieve a climate of dialogue in La Teja, where places designed to reach accord could easily be turned into places of disagreement.

These clashes and misunderstandings left district 14 ill equipped to negotiate the multiple voices and interests inevitably found within territorially based communities. Creating an atmosphere conducive for dialogue and participation became a challenge of monumental proportions, as an increasingly frustrated group of councilors turned on one another:

> CRISTINA: It has been a history of constant confrontation, of much fighting, of much hurt, from a history that predates the dictatorship, a history from below, of the exploited. When I worked there as a social worker I would tell them, "My job here is to set up the discussion table and your role is to sit and listen to one another, to see what each of you has to offer." This was the hardest part, to try and facilitate a real exchange. Because if there was even the slightest hint that you thought differently from them, they became defensive and conflictive; the smallest of differences would get blown up into something huge!

Incessant infighting eroded the remaining trust in the council and prevented councilors from reaching consensus to draft district-wide development plans. Council meetings became extremely lengthy, inefficient, and inhospitable, especially for women:

> ANA: This culture of relating with verbal aggression that often turned into physical violence led women to pull out of the councils. They couldn't stand having others shout in their faces. And we are talking about working women who get angry at home and shout at their kids—but they are not used to this kind of interaction in public.

Most of the men accused of attacking female councilors were associated with the group of "radical" councilors, like Joaquín, the far-left Tejano who served on the council for two periods and is a close ally of Felipe. When I raise the issue of gender discrimination, he quickly dismisses the charges:

> JOAQUIN: There was never discrimination against women. On the contrary, I was the first to say, in 1998: If I want an economist today, I want her to be a woman, a woman at home, a woman from below, who has to fight everyday for a penny to get bread and milk for her kids. If I teach her a little about the economy, she'll be the best economist around. But neither should you give her too much power, or

she will crush us! Yet I still have not met a combative woman councilor, I have not met a woman who has jumped in and got her feet dirty in mud, or gone, as we do, to the squatter areas where the dogs have scabies.

Joaquín's position, exalting the virtues of women's domestic roles and criticizing female councilors for not engaging with the "real" poor from the asentamientos, offers a lame defense that reveals little understanding of the pervasive dynamics of gender discrimination. Felipe acknowledged that there were communication problems and a breakdown of respect within the council, but as often happens with some leftist militants, he turns the tables on his detractors, appealing to class arguments:

We didn't know how to understand each other, how to respect each other. But we are not going to let the women play victim. Our compañeras formed a group, an elite. There were a bunch of guys who had their reasonable, healthy concerns, but the women made fun of them because they didn't have the vocabulary or education to express them well.

Teresa disagrees, as do most of the men and women with whom I talked. To her, the conflicts responded to unmistakable gendered differences in modes of participation among councilors:

The fellows who go to the council go to make them heard, while the women go to get things done and they are more involved in the thematic commissions. This creates a dynamic with little chance of collaboration taking place between the sexes.

Indeed, as in most other districts, women came to local government determined to "get things done" and had little patience for all the infighting instigated by men in the councils. The escalation of verbal aggression eventually drove most women away from the council, but they remain active in their communities and in other bodies of local government. Women continued to participate in less visible but strategically important spaces, such as the council's thematic commissions. It was precisely in these commissions where women managed to get things done to address the concrete, day-to-day problems affecting their communities. The effectiveness of these commissions resulted in part from the fact that some of the men did not perceive them as important political spaces, leaving them to women.

Yet, by underestimating the value of the thematic commissions, the council failed to acknowledge some of the most important community development experiences in the district:

> TERESA: The thematic commissions kept functioning, leading to action and results, but they have not come out with a discourse to reflect their accomplishments that is sufficiently appealing to be heard in the council. They are part of the council; they are included in the annual reports, but they are not part of the daily functioning of the council. So, the council has these appendages that work, but the heart does not recognize them as truly belonging to the body.

As their contribution went largely unacknowledged by an increasingly introspective council, women felt increasingly more alienated from the council. Many of these women moved on to more "hands-on" community development projects that worked independently from the council. In the end, most of the key community development initiatives wound up in the hands of these women, working in collaboration with male activists who understood the importance of these projects.

The Rupture Between the Council and Community-based Networks

The council's dismissal of the work of women councilors and its repeated attempts to control their activities cost decentralization dearly, causing many of the most engaged councilors to leave:

> MAGDALENA: In the last election, I received more votes than anyone else in the council. I left the council but not my work; I quit going to the council because I would not sit there arguing for hours late into the night. But this doesn't mean I quit doing the work. Each of us kept working in the community.

Magdalena's story illustrates the fate of many local activists. A tireless community activist in her mid-seventies and a member of Vázquez's Socialist Party, she became involved in local government when decentralization was launched. Inspired by the prospect of democratizing city politics and by the possibility of building a truly participatory council, she ran for councilor and was elected in the first elections in 1993. She was then reelected to four consecutive terms—a record held by a handful of activists in the district—but became so frustrated that she quit the council in 2003. Her real passion was always community health development, something she had unselfishly practiced even before decentralization came to the district. When the Broad Front city government set up training courses for activists interested in community health issues, she jumped at the opportunity and became a certified community health educator and advocate. She now administers Policlínica La Teja, the community-run health clinic supported by the murga Diablos Verdes.

District 14 prides itself on having the highest number of health clinics in the city—a total of seven run by the community, three administered by the city, and five run by the Ministry of Health—thanks in part to the effort of countless community activists like Magdalena. In 1992, before decentralization was formally launched, local activists set up the health commission, a coordinating body of all organizations concerned with health issues in the area. Following the inauguration of the first neighborhood council, they decided to become a thematic commission of the neighborhood council, hoping to bring their activities into the heart of local government. Unfortunately, things did not work out as they had expected:

> MAGDALENA: The council was not much interested in health matters. Every now and then we presented a report but the council was not interested. We had no logical place in the council, but even so we keep struggling and working on our own, independently.

Ironically, despite the councilors' indifference to health issues, they unyieldingly insisted on controlling the work of the health commission:

> MAGDALENA: It wasn't easy to get used to the ways of the council, because I always had more freedom to make decisions and to work in the health commission. I felt limited in what I could do, because we always had to consult on everything with people who did not know much about health issues. This was hard.

By the early 2000s, relations between the health commission and the council had become so tense that commission members made a strategic decision: they would break away from the council, becoming once again an autonomous organization. Relations with the council deteriorated to the point that, when the mayor made his annual trip through the district, the council publicly disassociated itself from the health commission's report, alerting the mayor that its recommendations did not have their support even though the council failed to submit an alternative report.

Community activists concerned with widespread hunger in the district had similarly frustrating experiences with the council. For years they worked in merenderos sponsored by local churches, housing cooperatives, soccer clubs, and neighborhood associations. These experiences made up a dense network of several hundred activists engaged in collecting, preparing, and distributing food to thousands of children.

Sonia is a recently elected councilor whom I met at the first council meeting. A single mother in her early fifties, she earns a living selling clothes at street fairs. Although she is new to the council, she is an experienced local activist who has been involved in comedores for years. I visited Sonia's home located in northern La Teja, close to the asentamientos by the Pantanoso River, to talk about a local merendero she set up with a group of women from the neighborhood. Merendero Crecer, she tells me, provides a daily snack to school-age children, and offers a glimpse of hope in a rather depressing situation:

> Most of the people are suffering from extreme poverty; the level of impoverishment, of hunger, of marginalization is alarming. In every corner there are groups of youths who are already smoking pot, drinking wine, and who have no other choices—no chance to work. With the merendero we can at least give them something to eat.

I visited the merendero on an early afternoon to meet the dedicated group of women who patiently were getting ready to serve the snack of the day— a cup of warm milk accompanied by bread and jam—to the three dozen school-age children who show up. The milk is provided free of charge by the municipal government, but all other resources, including the money to pay the rent for the space, are donated by local businesses and community fund-raisers. As a community initiative without the sponsorship of an institution, Merendero Crecer is at high risk of closing down, and every day it stays open constitutes a victory for the organizers. Sonia tells me that they could have solved their funding problems when they started the merendero but the price to pay would have been too high:

> The day that we opened the merendero, the minister of labor, the director of the INDA [Instituto Nacional de Alimentación, National Food Institute], and the media all came. Some sixteen people dressed up in suits arrived and they strung up a ribbon across the doorway

so that the minister and the director could cut it. And this was no INDA merendero they were going to open, it was a neighborhood merendero! It was disgusting. They offered us one hundred kilograms of flour but nobody wanted to accept the offer. This convinced us to start working independently; we went out to find a place and rented it. Then, to punish us, INDA made sure we got no supplies.

The women's political instincts told them that the offer made by INDA, a nonmunicipal agency controlled by one of the country's traditional parties, would have placed them in a highly compromised position that would have affected their autonomy and credibility within the community. Much as I admire their principled stance, I cannot stop speculating about how the more savvy activists in Peñarol would have handled the situation.

Most merenderos, including those supported by religious or social organizations, lacked the resources to cope with the overwhelming reality of hunger in the district. Initially, each organization worked independently, barely covering the needs of children within a few blocks of their base. In 2001 the neighborhood council promoted the creation of a network of merenderos to facilitate the work of each merendero and to better manage the resources provided by the municipal government. The network boosted the activities of the merenderos, giving them greater legitimacy vis-à-vis the municipal government and allowing them to speak with one voice in the district and even in city politics. Participants also promoted discussions about the politics of hunger, including its causes and possible solutions, an initiative that allowed them to contextualize what often felt like a patchwork of limited charitable initiatives. But other, less altruistic factors motivated the council's initiative:

> SONIA: The council wanted the network to become a thematic commission of the council, so that they could access city hall funds and control the finances of the network of merenderos, but the network wanted to remain completely autonomous. Thus we set up regulations that stated we were completely autonomous—that we were not a commission of the council. The relationship between the network of merenderos and the council has now turned bad.

As the network continued to grow, the council stepped up its efforts to control its activities, infringing on the autonomy of a sizeable group of community organizations that were independently doing some outstanding community work. Just as in the case of health activists, relations between the merendero network and the council quickly deteriorated. In the end, the council's stance alienated an important core of engaged grassroot activists, driving them away from the council, convinced that this body had become an obstacle to their work. Sadly, the institution that was created to represent and to reactivate local civil society had isolated itself from some of the most exciting participatory initiatives in the district.

Interestingly, councilors were always willing to support broader popular struggles—such as labor conflicts, the traditional May Day march, or the plebiscite against the privatization of ANCAP—but their support tended to be limited to issuing public solidarity statements, leaving direct participation to individual members. Paradoxically, the council seemed to reduce its sphere of competence to municipal affairs, uncertain of how it should deal with broader issues that escaped the sphere of city politics and hesitant to seek relations with nonmunicipal institutional actors. This tendency to municipalize the work of the council was painfully illustrated by the experience of the Children and Youth Network.

A group of local women had united a wide array of organizations dealing with the problems affecting children and young people in district 14, creating one of the strongest and most vibrant grassroot networks in the city. They had secured funding to conduct a study of the area using the expertise of several local professionals and, working in collaboration with the school board and the National Institute of Child Welfare (Instituto Nacional de Atención al Menor, INAME), they had made some recommendations to address key problems. This partnership represented an important breakthrough for these activists: it was the first time that national institutions and NGOs had selected a territorially based community network to design and implement focused policies for children and youth. Excited by this accomplishment, they approached the council for support:

> TERESA: We went to the council; they met with us and listened to us, but they felt that our work had nothing to do with them. "This is a matter for you to take up with the INAME; if you want a statement of support from us we will provide it," but they were unwilling to take on the project.

Building Synergy with Local Government . . . Without the Council.

The networks that had emerged in district 14 continued to grow independently in spite of the council, but they never gave up on decentralization altogether. A case in point is the network of merenderos, which became a solid, autonomously coordinating body consisting of twenty-three member organizations that provide food to some 3,500 people in the district. As the network distanced itself from the council, however, it cultivated close ties with other branches of local government and benefited from the support of the district's social workers and the secretary of the local junta. Unlike the council, which was crippled by fruitless internal disputes, the network successfully built solid links and bonds of trust among member organizations, developing consensus over operating norms, organizational structures, and the criteria by which to allocate food donations among member organizations:

> JOHNNY: In the beginning the organization lacked experience and it was difficult for a lot of us. Now it is working well and the meetings go pretty smoothly. Our regulations allow us to manage ourselves. There is an internal regulation that regulates revenue intake, how the donations are distributed, the duties of the plenary, of the financial committee, and the treasury that fund-raises. All these people are reelected to their posts every six months.

Johnny has been active in numerous community projects since he moved to neighboring Belvedere about ten years ago. Together with more than thirty members of his religious organization, he operates both a local merendero that feeds seventy children weekly and a modest children's dental clinic, with donated equipment from abroad and the voluntary labor of recent dentistry school graduates. What drew me to Johnny was the fact that he was not like any other community activist I met in district 14. Johnny is the spiritual leader of the local Ogún das Matas temple, one of an estimated four hundred Umbandista temples of the rapidly growing Afro-native religion in the city. Johnny worked hard to build his temple at the back of his home, where he lives with his wife and children, while working full-time in a downtown office. Contrary to my expectations, the gentle man in his early forties is not of Afro-Uruguayan descent. As he shows me the facilities, I am also struck by the near absence of religious symbols in the building. Johnny explains that since many neighbors participate in the temple's community outreach activities without belonging to the Umbanda group, they are careful to keep religious activities separate from their lay community work.

When we enter the ceremony hall, I come face-to-face with the temple's impressive religious emblem. Carved from a large piece of wood, the figure of an indigenous warrior on horseback proudly wearing a feathered head-band, pointing his spear at a jaguar who lies dying beneath the horse's legs. Johnny explains to me that the logo borrows the Catholic symbol of Saint George and the African deity Ogún, adapting them to the Latin American context:

> Saint George, a Catholic saint who fought to defend the Church when it was being persecuted, is a warrior. For the indigenous people, Ogún is their main divinity, the god of war and of struggle. When the blacks came to America, from whom did they seek protection? From Ogún! The Indian also took the image of Saint George and adapted it to his reality. Saint George rides on horseback killing a dragon, but since dragons don't exist, the Indians represent him killing a jaguar, a native animal. The Indians brought him down to the level of their reality, but the symbolism is the same: of a warrior.

I am puzzled by the appeal of this religion in a country with the demographic and cultural makeup of Uruguay. With less than 1 percent of the population formally recognized as black, and with nearly no visible indigenous traces left following the nineteenth-century massacre of the few natives who once populated the region, most Uruguayans are descendants of European immigrants, and most are not avid churchgoers as in other parts of Latin America:

> JOHNNY: It was not easy for our neighbors to accept us. "The witch doctors of the neighborhood," they called us here. Umbanda is a religion that has suffered a fair amount of discrimination, because it is a religion created by indigenous and black people and also because women play a large role in it. It was not easy for our neighbors to accept it, but these days our neighbors are with us and support us because they have seen that what we do here is for the good of the community and not just the religion.

It is remarkable that in less than ten years, the Umbandistas won acceptance in the community, in part because their dedication to community work resonates with the traditions of the district:[32]

32. The success may also be explained by the fact that Ogún das Matas offers direct and immediate access to the supernatural through dancing ceremonies, in contrast with Catholicism, the religion formally endorsed by most Uruguayans, where contact is mediated through the priesthood.

JOHNNY: One of the foundations of the Umbanda religion is solidarity through social work, work that also allows for personal growth and that develops a bunch of values in everyone who participates. The great potential of Ogún das Matas lies in the focused channeling of human resources toward specific social ends.

Evidence of local support was the overwhelming victory of the Umbandista candidate in the 2003 elections for neighborhood council. Although Johnny is a supporter of the Broad Front, Ogún das Matas had never before presented candidates. I learned that, like many others in the district anticipating a victory of the Broad Front in the upcoming national elections, Johnny had rushed to secure positions in the structures of local government to support the new administration.

Although Johnny's Umbandistas are strong supporters of participatory decentralization, they were reluctant to work with the neighborhood council, for understandable reasons:

JOHNNY: The council has been totally removed from real decentralization and local problems. Here, no councilor ever came around to see what problems we faced; at least this hasn't happened yet. And since we had heard that the council didn't work well, we never approached them either.

As people like Johnny lost faith in the council—or worse, as they realized that it had become an obstacle to their own community work—they decided to work directly with the local junta and with the more sympathetic staff in the offices of local government:

JOHNNY: We maintain two connections that always serve as direct communication channels: with the social worker and with the secretary of the junta. We phone them before we present anything formally, to ask them about the process and our chances to get the project approved. Personal ties strengthen the connection. This connection has facilitated a lot in our work with a public office that is so depersonalized.

Such direct personal access to local government officials suggests that decentralization succeeded in generating some space for developing certain levels of synergy between community organizations and the local state.

The Neighborhood Council: Deepening Isolation

As a growing number of social organizations established direct working relations with the junta and social workers, an increasingly divided and isolated council lashed out against those who dared to bypass it. Facing a serious crisis of legitimacy in the community, and unwilling to critically examine why so many organizations were turning their backs on them, the councilors responded by stubbornly asserting that they were the only source of legitimate representation of civil society in the district, a claim that was very much at odds with reality. Some councilors even insisted that the local junta could establish relations only with community organizations that had previously received the formal blessing of the neighborhood council, claiming for them the exclusive role of screening, approving, and legitimizing community initiatives:

> FELIPE: The council is the voice of the people. So, the local junta can only hear what is brought to the council. Nothing more. If we really want to work in this way, I think that we can accomplish a lot.

The councilors' refusal to acknowledge and respect the autonomy of local community initiatives continued to push away the most engaged community activists in the district, and in the end it sealed the fate of the neighborhood council:

> JULIO: The connection with social organizations, with residents, has been cut. From a theoretical point of view, it should work like this: the people, the social organizations, the neighborhood council, organizing and communicating with their organizations, meeting together, exchanging all the necessary information, training, and understandings. But in practice this has not happened.

> JOSE: The council should represent the expression of all the organized bodies in the area. But not all of organized civil society is included in the neighborhood council. There are many neighborhood and union organizations that do not participate in the council. They have links with the district communal center, the local junta, but they do not go to the council as a neighborhood body.

By 2003, six months before the elections for neighborhood council, for all practical purposes the council had ceased to exist, as had happened in

El Cerro. In contrast to El Cerro, however, councilors in La Teja simply stopped meeting, without even making a public declaration condemning some decision of the city government. In reality, many activists had reached a distressing but realistic conclusion: the council had exhausted its potential to promote local participation in district 14, at least for the time being.

Local Evaluation of Decentralization

It came as no surprise to find Tejanos less upbeat than people in Peñarol in their attitudes toward decentralization and more critical of local government than activists in El Cerro. They raised all kinds of criticisms of local government, pointing to the shortcomings of institutional design and the interference of party politics, especially the undemocratic appointment of the junta secretary, the council's lack of decision-making power, and the lack of concrete gains.

Joaquín, one of the most radical councilors, insists that the lack of decision-making power and the local junta's systematic refusal to endorse decisions made by the council placed councilors in an impossible situation:

> In the council of 1998, we ended up having only ten or twelve councilors, though forty were elected, plus the alternates, because they gave the council no power. Residents ask for things and the council could not help them because the local junta would not accept the proposals of the residents. It is easy to say, "I belong to the local junta," but it's the councilor who has to face the residents.

Remarkably, the demand to give greater powers to neighborhood councils is shared by most activists in La Teja, including the most pragmatic ones, who are extremely critical of the council's history of intransigence. These calls to empower the council seem to ignore the poor record of neighborhood councils since participatory decentralization came to the district.

I also discovered that people mean different things when they call to democratize the system of local government. For people like Joaquín, it means a complete and direct transfer of power to create a situation of "dual power," as emerged with the Soviets during the Russian Revolution, where an empowered working class could effectively challenge state power. For people like Johnny, empowering the council is a way to address the lack of efficiency that has plagued this body from the beginning:

The council had little executive power, so there was little it could do. By allowing people to raise issues, you create expectations; but when two years go by before an issue is addressed, people get tired. This leads to a loss of faith, which comes on top of people's general disillusionment with politics.

For Johnny, the challenge that lies ahead centers on bringing all levels of local government together—political, social, and administrative—into a solid partnership to produce synergy across the state-society divide, rather than advocating antagonism between civil society and the state.

The most radical councilors explain the failure of neighborhood councils in reference to the disruption created by political parties being involved in what were supposed to be organs of civil society:

> RAFAEL: The big disaster is that they have inserted political parties into the councils. Water and vinegar don't mix!

They also complain that primary loyalties to the political parties of the governing coalition, rather than to the process of decentralization itself, distorted the workings of the council:

> JOAQUIN: The conflict was between those councilors who worked from a partisan political perspective, and those of us working independently for the good of the people. What happened? You couldn't criticize a certain municipal director who belongs to some party in the Broad Front because everyone would jump at that. They would say, "We're going to defend this director because otherwise they will retaliate by criticizing a director from our party," and so they defended each other. There's the problem with partisan politics.

Such loyalties blinded the council from its main task—namely, to act as a watchdog of the city government and to serve as an autonomous voice of local civil society:

> FELIPE: Certain political sectors that are involved in the government of Montevideo say that we cannot do battle with city hall because it is allied with the Broad Front. Some say we have to keep it all very friendly with Mayor Arana. No, no! Arana is a human being; he defends the political system and if he is mistaken we need to confront him. We are not going to applaud him and bury our heads just

because he is in city hall. This would be dishonest on our part and would lead to total disaster—not only for the decentralization process but also for the whole neighborhood political system.

This account of a council dominated by political parties and unwilling to stand up against the city government does not fully match perceptions of the history of decentralization that were shared with me by other activists. Most people acknowledge that the overwhelming majority of councilors either sympathize with or belong to some political group from the Broad Front, which does not surprise me, given the political history of the district. But I was somewhat surprised to learn that many in the core Broad Front cadre were reluctant to join local government when it was first launched, leaving this unfamiliar space to activists with less organic ties to the parties of the Left. Among these activists, there were individuals who may have been former members of the organized political Left but had subsequently severed formal ties with these parties. Some are even called *los silvestres* (the wild ones) because they tend to operate as "loose cannons" (as did some of the more radical members of council), or as local *caudillos* who use the council as a space to increase their personal positioning vis-à-vis the organized Left. It is in fact only recently that party cadres are running for council seeking to occupy strategic positions in local government in anticipation of a victory of the Broad Front in the national elections

The president of the local junta readily acknowledges that political parties of the Left interfered with the work of the councils:

> JULIO: The Left made a mistake when shifting political party issues to the arena of civil society discussion and participation. In previous councils in the zone there were comrades that brought with them a political party discourse. They confused their party chapter with the council. I don't know; democratization does not always mean more participation.

Julio's final conclusion—that democracy does not always require more participation—echoes the comments made to me by Gustavo, the member of the junta in the more successful case of Peñarol. Interestingly, these similar assessments about the limits of participation were drawn from two radically different lived experiences of trying to build participatory institutions. Both offer important food for thought for advocates of direct democracy, as they point to some of the real difficulties of building democratic practices on the ground.

In contrast to the positive responses from people in Peñarol, when I asked about the gains of decentralization Tejanos struggled hard to come up with a list, as also happened with Cerrenses. Unlike the people of El Cerro, however, who failed to acknowledge significant infrastructural improvements in their district, Tejanos appeared to have little to show in terms of material gains.

Some activists readily acknowledge that decentralization did not produce many material results, but they point out that there were less tangible benefits:

> TERESA: The material achievements are few, but in terms of defining public works priorities in the zone there has been a nice process of negotiation within the neighborhoods, involving those residents who are most active in their local social organizations. Decentralization led to the articulation of different groups and interests, to the laying out of the issues on the table, to the defining of issues, all of which is still underway. If it were not for this decentralization process, we would probably not have accomplished as much.

Certainly these gains are much more modest than those identified in district 13. Still, the seemingly simple fact of bringing people together to identify needs, to negotiate different interests, and to develop strategies—plus the successful creation of effective grassroot networks, as in the cases of the community health and merendero networks—constitute significant achievements for a community with the history of La Teja.

Progress in these areas occurred thanks to the efforts of countless dedicated local activists and to the constructive partnership that emerged between grassroot organizations and some local government officials—especially after the year 2000, following the appointment of Jorge and Martín as secretary and president, respectively, of the local junta. To Johnny, this greater openness and access to municipal authorities are the main advantages of decentralization:

> There have been some significant gains, like having more immediate and meaningful access to certain authorities. One talks with the local junta, with the local secretary or the social worker, and this connection is much more direct than it would be with a centralized social service, there's no doubt about it.

Local government officials effectively mediated between grassroot organizations and central municipal authorities, and facilitated access to municipal resources. In some cases, they legitimated local initiatives originating from community organizations that would have little chance of getting support in city hall without the endorsement of the local junta, as was the case with a project presented by Ogún das Matas:

> JOHNNY: We asked city hall for some land to cultivate in order for the merendero, and some of its members, to become self-sustaining. Cecilia [the social worker] read the proposal and loved it. Jorge [the secretary of the junta] saw it, liked it, and told me that their report is going to be positive. It is important to get the support of the junta, those who know us, because next thing you know the proposal goes to the land commission of city hall, and there they say, "Ogún das Matas, who are these crazy people, witch doctors?" It's for this reason that it is so important that they provide an objective, concrete report or assessment of what our organization is all about.

Thus it would appear as if more embedded and sympathetic local officials who assumed their positions after 2000 successfully facilitated community participation, adopting a similar approach to the one used by María before she was dismissed as the district's social worker. Activists in various grassroot networks benefited from the constructive rapport established with municipal officials, who provided valuable resources and advice on a whole range of issues—from how to run a meeting to how to build a complex, networked organization—facilitated access to municipal and nonmunicipal resources, and made activists aware of opportunities. Some of the most successful experiences in community development came about thanks to the positive synergy established between activists and local government officials, showing a successful side of participatory decentralization in district 14, which came about despite the problems within the neighborhood council.

Conclusions

The deeply conflictive story analyzed in this chapter illustrates the difficulties of fostering participatory processes in communities with the profile of La Teja. Tejanos definitely lacked the kind of inclusive, pragmatic traditions of territorially based collective action nurtured by community activists in Peñarol, which had been so useful to enable them to take advantage of participatory decentralization. Instead, Tejanos came to participatory institutions with powerful traditions of contentious politics that clashed with the provisions of participatory decentralization, producing constant conflict and misunderstanding, thereby undermining any chance to build effective democratic participatory processes. While Cerrenses had also brought to local institutions remarkably similar traditions, they had the good fortune of meeting more pragmatic leaders from the older asentamientos who helped moderate, with relative success, some of the more confrontational tendencies found in the district. Tejanos had no such luck. Belonging to a district with comparatively fewer and newer squatters, they missed out on the possible benefits of the leadership abilities provided by community activists like Pablo and Alicia in district 17.

With fewer asentamientos in their district, Tejanos never experienced the class-based mistrust that had so deeply divided activists in district 17. Nevertheless, activists in their district had a hard time fostering trust and solidarity. They also suffered all kinds of division and conflict that eroded their chances to build effective democratic practices in the institutional spaces offered by decentralization, although these divisions, in contrast to El Cerro, were rooted in political and ideological differences rather than socioeconomic distinctions. La Teja's oppositional political traditions weighed heavily in framing councilors' orientations, exposing the district's neighborhood council to the influence of a small but determined group of radical councilors whose politics may have resonated with the history of the community. Indeed, these councilors drew from the radicalism of La Teja but their political views were linked to their personal disillusionment with leftist parties, views that were not necessarily widely shared by activists in the council. The sway of the most intransigent councilors was boosted by the arrival of representatives from the recent asentamientos, who joined the council with little experience in collective organizing and with no disposition to work things out through a system that seemed too slow to respond to their urgent needs. The two strands of radicalism—that of the small core of left-wing militants and that of the less politicized squatters—came from different ideological origins, but they agreed in their harsh opposition to institutional politics and in their exasperation when required to build consensus and compromise rather than demanding immediate solutions. They also converged in their discursive exaltation of poverty as the privileged source of knowledge and legitimacy.

The district's neighborhood council failed to become an effective facilitator of civil society participation due to all the internal bickering, the confrontational stances toward city authorities, and the high levels of verbal and physical violence that marked the workings of council meetings. These developments—coupled with the council's staunch refusal to respect the autonomy of successful grassroot organizations and to even acknowledge the valuable contributions of so many community activists (mostly female)—ended up isolating the very body that had been created to represent civil society and to facilitate broad-based democratic participation in the area. As a result, the neighborhood council became increasingly detached from vital experiences of community participation in its own district, including those taking place within its own thematic commissions. The gulf separating the council from these experiences widened with its recalcitrant insistence that it was the only legitimate body to sanction grassroot initiatives. In the end, leaders of the inclusive networks that had emerged in the district concluded that the council had become an obstacle to their work and started to seek out the support of other local government officials. In response, the council lashed out and stepped up its attacks on the local junta, accusing it of ignoring what had become de facto an irrelevant and ineffective council, and relations between the two deteriorated even further.

To make matters worse, the appointment of Beatriz as local junta secretary against the express wishes of local activists—someone who had no community work experience and little disposition to negotiate with the council—further exacerbated conflicts between the council and the local junta, and deepened clashes between moderate and radical factions within the council. The top-down appointment appeared to confirm the charges of party politicking made by radical councilors, and to prove how much the logic of party politics had been imposed on the dynamics of participation. The secretary's intransigent stance and her unjustified dismissal of the widely respected social worker assigned to the district provided further ammunition to the arsenal of the disenchanted councilors, whose antipolitics discourse steered the council in a course of permanent confrontation with local institutions.

It became nearly impossible to build synergistic relations among the different levels of local government under these conditions. Nevertheless, participatory decentralization in the district was not a complete fiasco. Many encouraging grassroot experiences sprouted without the auspices of the neighborhood council—especially after the ending of Beatriz's term as secretary of the local junta—and local activists and sympathetic local government officials nurtured constructive relations. Thus, while the council pushed itself over the abyss of irrelevance, many community activists capitalized on the opportunities offered by participatory decentralization through synergistic relations with local junta representatives or with the district's social workers.

The factors that explain the failure of the neighborhood council to become a legitimate articulator of local initiatives, as had happened in Peñarol, are too complex to be explained solely by the shortcomings of the model of participation adopted by the city government, even if the disempowering of neighborhood councils exacerbated conflict between councilors and city officials. Had the councils been granted greater decision-making powers, however, it is doubtful that the outcomes would have been different or that the oppositional course adopted by successive neighborhood councils would have changed. Ultimately, the failure to foster bonds of trust and solidarity within the community of La Teja and across the district, and between neighborhood councils and local junta officials, are explained by the unique interplay of the community's associational traditions, local conditions that amplified the political influence of more confrontational councilors, and the less-than-desirable orientation of the secretary of the local junta between 1995 and 2000.

Conclusions

The experiences of the communities of Peñarol, El Cerro, and La Teja illustrate both the opportunities offered by participatory decentralization and the formidable challenges of making participatory democracy work at the barrio level. Despite the many problems discussed throughout this book, participatory decentralization marked a departure from the paternalistic and clientelistic top-down styles of the old system of city politics. The Broad Front opened the city government to societal demands and demonstrated that it had the political will to introduce participatory mechanisms to help process popular initiatives. It also improved service delivery, redistributed urban resources, and brought the city administration closer to people, encouraging thousands of Montevideanos to work together with their neighbors and city officials to build a more democratic mode of urban governance. These changes are indicative of a fundamental change in city politics and the early blossoming of a new kind of "state–civil society regime" in the city.[1] The project of decentralization, however, produced less tangible results in fomenting participation and enabling residents to transform more fundamental power relations. For this reason, I refrain from characterizing the emerging model as "empowering," as does Baiocchi when he refers to participatory budgeting in Porto Alegre. Although some communities made important gains, as occurred in Peñarol and district 13, their experiences were not generalized across the city, as evidenced in the other case studies covered in this book.

The Broad Front offered an alternative, however imperfect, to more regressive neoliberal projects of decentralization that sought to transfer responsibilities to communities without the corresponding resources, all as a way of pushing market-based policies. Participatory decentralization in Montevideo implemented effective redistributive policies and social programs that ameliorated the effects of the economic and social crisis that

---

1. Baiocchi 2005.

hit the capital city. It also provided citizens with participatory spaces to learn the ABCs of local democracy, to foster democratic deliberative practices, to comanage community development projects, and to build district-wide networks to address their needs. In bringing people from different neighborhoods together in the councils, decentralization also pushed barrio activists to negotiate among themselves the priorities for the entire district, taking into account the conditions of the most needy—a process that was not always successful. These learning experiences provided essential stepping-stones for the future emergence of more democratic values and practices.

The stories in the communities of Peñarol, El Cerro, and La Teja also show that the processes of building democratic participation in the barrios are complex and full of challenges, and that if they are to succeed, the opening of participatory spaces is an important but not sufficient precondition. If the experience in Peñarol illustrates the possibilities of civil society to produce relatively harmonious relations through democratic participation and deliberation, the evidence from El Cerro and La Teja tempers some of the more optimistic forecasts, showing that civil society is also a conflictual site where groups with different agendas, traditions, and levels of power try to work together, not always successfully. It is precisely in the day-to-day workings of participation in the barrios where both democratic and authoritarian practices emerge, side by side and in tension with each other, reminding us of the opportunities and the difficulties offered by participatory projects.[2]

The experiences in the barrios of Montevideo also show that community activists were not equally successful in taking advantage of the opportunities offered by participatory decentralization. Local participatory democracy was experienced quite differently in each community, flourishing in some districts while failing in others, as efforts to build democratic institutions varied widely across the city. Notwithstanding the limitations of the institutional reforms introduced by the Broad Front, the stories narrated in this book show how the outcomes of citywide initiatives were shaped by local conditions, something often glossed over by macro-institutional studies. In each district, community activists and municipal officials brought to decentralized institutions their own capacities, traditions, predispositions,

---

2. Thus the experience illustrates how much conflicts and struggles for democracy and the common good occur as much within civil society as they do between a supposedly virtuous civil society on the one hand and authoritarian state agents on the other. See Carothers 1999–2000.

and personal styles, producing synergies or clashes that either boosted or undermined democratic practices within the various bodies of local government. The contrasting experiences in each of the three districts, I argue, are accounted for by the unique local context in which participation unfolded. I now turn to explaining the differences in outcome among the three case studies in light of their particular local associational cultures, the political predispositions of local officials, and the socioeconomic conditions impinging on each community.

Local Associational Cultures, Mobilization Resources, and Social Capital

Prior to the introduction of decentralization in the early 1990s, all three neighborhoods had produced powerful traditions of collective mobilization and a relatively strong infrastructure of local organizations. The capacities and dispositions generated by local associational cultures, however, varied widely, shaping the different ways in which activists engaged with participatory decentralization. The contrast in experience in each community demonstrates that ownership of solid stocks of social capital is not a sufficient guarantee to ensure success in the kind of institutional spaces created by decentralization. Indeed, while all three communities had strong traditions of collective mobilization and organization, only some possessed the kind of capacities that could be effectively transferred to the institutional framework of participatory local government.

The evidence presented in this book, therefore, qualifies the sweeping generalizations about the value of social capital that are currently in vogue, suggesting instead that its value is context-specific, as different socioeconomic, political, cultural, and institutional conditions may render some capacities more useful than others. El Cerro's class-based, oppositional mobilization capacities, for example, may have been effective to achieve collective goals during the era of the meatpacking plants, but they proved less useful in the context of participatory decentralization. It is hard to imagine a set of universal norms and capacities—trust, cooperation, or networks—that would prove equally useful across different settings to enable communities to pursue their common interests. In other words, social capital—the "capital of the poor"—does not travel with the same ease across boundaries as does the financial capital of the rich in the current era of globalization.

Nevertheless, I still found the concept of social capital useful as a heuristic device to guide aspects of my research.[3] The distinction between bonding, bridging, and linking social capital, for instance, directed me to dig deep into the features of each neighborhood, to investigate relations among communities in each district, and to examine the degree to which local activists cooperated with local government officials. I found that only Peñarol succeeded in fostering all three kinds of social capital; the other two neighborhoods were especially less successful in fostering the bridging and linking forms of social capital, even though they also possessed strong bonds of community solidarity. This finding suggests that the connection between the three kinds of social capital is neither straightforward nor one directional. Bonding social capital is not necessarily a precondition for a neighborhood to develop positive relations with other communities or with government officials; in fact, the case of El Cerro shows how a community may close ranks to oppose others they choose to reject, using bonding social capital as a mechanism of exclusion rather than as an asset to build stocks of bridging social capital.

The associational traditions produced by activists in Peñarol were more easily adaptable to the new institutional makeup of the city. Leaders in this neighborhood, as we saw in chapter 1, were more versed in pragmatic negotiation, conflict resolution, and resource management, and had successfully built numerous community organizations based on democratic and inclusive politics. The community also had stronger traditions of place-based mobilization that had taught activists to operate within the clientelistic networks set up by local caudillos, to use them to their advantage, and to cherish broad-based collective action. Community capacities were further expanded with the infusion of new resource management capacities brought by people from the housing cooperatives who came to the neighborhood in the 1970s. The impressive accomplishments of MIRPA—the umbrella organization founded in the late 1980s—illustrate the degree to which activists in Peñarol had succeeded in building a unique tradition of community activism that predated participatory decentralization, which proved quite useful after 1990. Their capacities were easily adaptable to

3. Foley and Edwards (1999) make the argument for the heuristic value of social capital concept. I am fully aware that the concept has significant limitations and is based on questionable normative assumptions. It has been aptly criticized for its circular logic (Portes and Landolt 1996), weak historical foundations (Tarrow 1996), and poor methodology (Harriss 2001). Harriss argues that the World Bank's use of the concept has turned it into the "Trojan horse" of the antipolitics machine.

the requirements of participatory decentralization, enabling them to nurture democratic practices within the council, build trusting relations within other communities, and establish constructive partnerships with sympathetic officials.

In contrast, activists in El Cerro and La Teja soon discovered that the associational cultures and capacities generated by radical labor politics were less adaptable to the rules of participatory decentralization; consequently, they encountered the greatest difficulties in responding to the shifting context of urban politics in the city. Cerrenses had fostered powerful traditions of class struggle through decades of engagement in contentious class-based politics. For them, the key organizations for the collective well-being were the powerful meatpacking unions, and the preferred method of struggle was the factory strike. Such deeply rooted labor practices developed in a context of weak territorial traditions of collective action (in part because El Cerro had received urban services early in the twentieth century, so most of these traditions were long gone from the community's collective memory), which narrowed the space for the kind of community activism I encountered in Peñarol.

The capacities of squatters like Pablo and Alicia, representing older squatter settlements, were somewhat similar to those nurtured in Peñarol, but the council could not take full advantage of their leadership skills because of the deep divisions and mistrust that existed within the district. Ultimately, the overwhelming socioeconomic problems in this district prevented the rise of more pragmatic voices in the council, ones that could have built bridges among different neighborhoods and established links with local government officials. As a result, the neighborhood council succumbed to internal infighting and ideological (at best) or personalized (at worst) conflicts, failing to become a body to articulate and facilitate resident participation.

La Teja's associational traditions also displayed a strong preference for oppositional, class-based politics. Like El Cerro, it lacked traditions of inclusive local politics or territorially based collective action. La Teja's militant trade unions, however, never gained the centrality of their counterparts in neighboring El Cerro, instead coexisting with other community organizations like sports clubs and murga associations. The factories had long closed when decentralization came to La Teja and neither the remaining trade unionists nor the social and sports clubs joined the council. With fewer leaders with experience in mobilization for urban services, like those I found in Peñarol and among the more established squatters in El Cerro,[4] the council was more likely to turn to confrontational tactics and be influenced by a relatively small group whose radical politics resonated with the communities' former days of working-class militancy. These militants, allied with more recent squatters, imprinted the council with more confrontational politics and, as a result, encountered the greatest difficulties adjusting to the new politics of decentralization. From day one, participation was disrupted by endless internal bickering and clashes between activists and local government officials, thereby alienating the most promising leaders of the district's grassroot initiatives. As the neighborhood council insisted in deauthorizing these leaders and their experiences, it made itself increasingly more irrelevant, losing legitimacy as an organ for the participation of civil society. La Teja painfully illustrates the difficulties of fostering local democracy in the absence of well-established traditions of inclusive, territorially based, democratic politics.

Socioeconomic Conditions

The workings of participatory decentralization were also affected by the social and economic crisis in the city. This situation had a crushing impact on some of the barrios covered in this book, leading to rising poverty, widespread unemployment, and social fragmentation, and contributing to the spread of squatter settlements, especially in the areas around El Cerro. The increased demand for social programs and urban services generated by the crisis came precisely at a time when city resources were shrinking, making it difficult for city authorities to respond to the overwhelming needs of these communities. Local governments were flooded with demands because residents felt that the city administration was more receptive to their needs than were the national government agencies. Thus the urban poor directed all their demands—for services, jobs, health care, housing, and so forth—to the municipal authorities, even when these fell outside the orbit of municipal politics. The crushing realization that city authorities and participatory decentralization could not meet their expectations demoralized many residents, who stopped seeing the value of participation.

4. La Teja, like El Cerro, had developed an urban infrastructure early in the twentieth century and did not possess a strong tradition of space-based collective action when decentralization was introduced in the 1990s.

In every neighborhood residents complained about the social ills produced by the crisis—rising crime, increased violence, growing alcoholism, the spread of drug abuse and drug trafficking—and how these problems were weakening the social fabric of their communities and undermining local traditions of social engagement, sociability, and solidarity. Individuals' perceptions of their neighbors and communities shifted gradually as feelings of mutual recognition, friendliness, security, and trust were replaced by indifference, insecurity, and mistrust. These shifts lessened individuals' dispositions to work collectively with their neighbors to change their immediate environment. This tendency toward growing atomization and individualization was somewhat offset in communities where legitimate broad-based organizations could help keep collective traditions alive and enforce community norms. On this, Peñarol had another advantage in sustaining social engagement compared to El Cerro and La Teja, where such organizations did not exist.[5]

People's abilities to participate were also constrained by more practical factors, such as the time and energy required to generate income or to cover child-care costs, the amount of time and money associated with transport to and from work, and the cost of attending meetings and activities (based on the price of public transportation and the risk of falling victim to crime). All these expenses went up after the economic crisis of 1999, increasing the cost of participation for ordinary citizens. Residents had to work longer hours to make ends meet, and as jobs disappeared from their immediate neighborhood they had to travel longer distances to get to work. Often people who wanted to participate even under such conditions stayed home out of fear of what would happen if they left their houses unguarded to attend meetings at night, and complained that neighbors no longer kept an eye on one another's properties. In this context of rising costs and weakening reciprocity, residents' willingness and capacity to participate in civic activities understandably declined, a point often missed by other accounts of democratic participation.[6]

By the late 1990s, the project of participatory decentralization that city officials had introduced, hoping to reactivate civil society, came to a virtual

5. I draw from similar arguments made by Kaztman and Retamoso (2005, 136–38) in their discussion of the factors that made it difficult for people to participate in Montevideo's labor market.

6. Participation in social organizations—such as sports clubs, neighborhood associations, religious groups, parent associations, or local political parties—declined dramatically during the 1990s primarily due to the impact of these factors.

standstill. It was remarkable to me that under such conditions there were still so many ordinary citizens fighting to sustain solidarity ties and traditions, a challenge of monumental proportions in those districts that had been hardest hit by the economic debacle. The communities in district 17 (including El Cerro) became the most impoverished in the city and turned significantly poorer than the other two districts covered in this book, as shown in map 2 in chapter 1.[7] Their problems were exacerbated by the unprecedented flood of squatters, which left them with 43 percent of all the city's squatters and high numbers of people living in overcrowded conditions, as shown in map 3 in chapter 1. The other two districts, in contrast, lost population and had significantly fewer squatters. They also experienced lower unemployment rates, as shown in map 4.[8]

Not surprisingly, other problems piled up in district 17; for example, young children in some areas were dying at twice the rate as the country's average, and the district came to have the highest suicide rate in the entire city.[9]

The spread of poverty militated against the prospects of sustaining participation and of building solidarity among communities in the district. Facing such crises, Cerrenses fought desperately to pull together against the forces that unraveled community ties, digging deep into their history to maintain an identity sustained by earlier traditions of radical trade unionism. They were also drawn together by their antagonism toward the squatters who had invaded their turf, whom they encountered daily on the streets and in the bodies of local government. They strongly resented the fact that local government resources were disproportionately directed toward meeting the flood of demands for services and social assistance coming from the asentamientos while their own needs went unattended. Frustration mounted with the crushing realization that they could not lead the council not only because they were outnumbered at council meetings but also

7. According to census data, the district's overall poverty rate in 2004 was 47.1 percent, compared to 30.5 percent in district 13 (Peñarol) and 33.2 percent in district 14 (La Teja). See Instituto Nacional de Estadística 2004.

8. Between 1996 and 2004, population increased by 8.1 percent in district 17 (El Cerro) while it declined in the other two districts (3.9 percent in district 13 [Peñarol] and 4.6 percent in district 14 [La Teja]). During the same period, the population in Montevideo declined 1.5 percent, following earlier periods of growth (2.4 percent between 1963 and 1975, and 5.6 percent between 1975 and 1985). See ibid., 1–2.

9. While in 2003 infant mortality in the country was fourteen per thousand population, the neighborhoods of El Cerro, Casabó, and Casavalle in district 17 had infant mortality rates in excess of thirty per thousand. In contrast, most communities in the other two districts had much lower infant mortality rates (Faral 2005).

MAP 4. Unemployment in Montevideo (2004, percentages). Courtesy of Alicia Abayian, National Institute of Statistics, Uruguay.

because their militant traditions were out of sync with the requirements of decentralization.

The case of El Cerro illustrates the degree to which material conditions shape the ability of communities to work together toward common goals. As we saw in the introductory chapter, Evans argues that for communities to cash in their social capital and to develop trusting relations with other communities and state officials requires conditions of relative equality, an argument my findings support. But I would add that it is not so much absolute deprivation per se that prevents communities from acting together—after all, the residents of Peñarol were poor but still mobilized effectively with other communities in their district—but rather the antagonisms produced by cleavages among the poor, such as those pulling apart Cerrenses and squatters.

The economic crisis also struck people in Peñarol and La Teja, but less harshly than in El Cerro. Not only did Peñarol and La Teja have less poverty and significantly fewer squatters, but they also had two additional comparative advantages. The first was that the poor were more evenly distributed across their respective districts (especially in the case of district 13) and had fewer pockets of extreme poverty. Being more evenly poor meant that they stood a better chance of avoiding the deep resentments that divided district 17. The second advantage was that the net loss of population experienced in Peñarol and La Teja effectively helped cushion some of the effects of the crisis, acting as a safety valve for the release of social tensions.[10] Thus, with *comparatively* fewer pressures for scarce resources, people in Peñarol and La Teja had a better shot at building cross-neighborhood solidarity than did their Cerrense counterparts. The leadership capacities of activists in Peñarol allowed their district to capitalize on more favorable conditions. But these chances were missed in La Teja, where activists were divided around political ideology and lacked key community-mobilization skills. In their case, the local government agenda was set by a small group of councilors who steered the council toward a confrontational path that alienated local officials and community activists alike.

Political Variables: The Institutional Model and Predispositions of Local Officials

The experiences in all three communities also highlight how much resident participation is conditioned by institutional imperatives and the predispositions of local officials. The new mode of governance advanced by participatory decentralization installed an institutional framework that set the parameters for legitimate collective action, encouraging certain attitudes while marginalizing others. The invitation to participate in charting a new course in city politics came with some strings attached: to become partners with sympathetic city officials, activists were asked to put aside contentious politics and to cooperate around common projects within the framework of the newly created institutional spaces. The politics of decentralization, therefore, rewarded less radical neighborhoods, which were more likely to accept the new rules of participatory democracy and be less disruptive in their relations with city officials. In this sense, Peñarol's success story is also a story of rewarding restrained community activism. By encouraging such community activity, the system of decentralization effectively delegitimized the more militant traditions found among Cerrense and Tejano activists.

Much as institutional frameworks, associational cultures, and socioeconomic conditions shaped community participation, I also found that the

---

10. Population in these districts fell at twice and three times the rate of population decline in the city of Montevideo, respectively. See Instituto Nacional de Estadística 2004.

particular disposition of individual government officials, such as the local junta secretaries, was key for setting the tone for the dynamics of participation in each district, creating hospitable or hostile environments for resident participation. The impact of these officials was blown up by an institutional model that gave them a great deal of discretionary power to interpret norms, grant resources, and encourage (or discourage) community participation. Still, even though the method to appoint them was far from democratic and they concentrated too much power, these officials were often capable of fostering synergy, especially when they came to the position with the necessary skills and dispositions to work with community organizations. In other cases, they exacerbated discord and antagonism, making local activists angry and demoralized.

In cases where secretaries came to their posts with experience in community organizing, they were more likely to engage constructively with local activists and to even overcome initial resistance to their appointment. This was the case in district 13 (Peñarol), where Washington was appointed against the wishes of community activists but proved himself worthy of the position and quickly became a respected figure. In contrast, where the secretaries came to their positions with a top-down approach and with little disposition to work out differences with community organizations, they failed miserably and ended up alienating community organizations, exacerbating tensions, and ultimately undermining local participation. This happened in the case of Beatriz, the top-down official appointed to district 14 who clashed constantly with counselors from La Teja and other neighborhoods. It also occurred in district 17 in the case of the former school principal who came to the position with widespread support but ended up alienating even comrades from the same party. These examples illustrate that neither the community's history nor the structural conditions in each barrio mechanically determined outcomes, as the experience of participation was also mediated by political intervention and the actions of local government officials.

Back to Macro-institutional Explanations

In the introductory chapter I suggested that I would take a different route to explain the outcomes of participatory decentralization. Most researchers of the experience in Montevideo, I argued, focus primarily on macro-institutional variables to explain the modest results in participation, arguing that given the country's party-centered political culture, local participation had little hope to flourish.[11] The early downgrading in status of neighborhood councils to consultative bodies, produced by pressures from the political establishment, is commonly used as evidence in favor of this view.[12] Researchers also point out that overarching political party identities effectively subverted the dynamics of local participation, as councilors were often guided by party loyalties when they operated in the councils, failing to act as effective voices of their communities.[13] Further evidence of the impact of political party preference on participation draws on electoral data showing that districts that overwhelmingly supported the Broad Front in national elections also had the highest turnout rates in local elections for neighborhood council, a correlation that is said to demonstrate how much preference for the leftist coalition directly determined levels of support and success for decentralization in each community.[14]

The stories of the communities covered in this book tell us that explanations of this kind are only partially persuasive because they exaggerate the actual strength of party loyalties at the local level and play down both the diversity of experiences in each barrio and the role of local associational cultures. Party loyalties are indeed important, but macro-institutional approaches often fail to explain how political identities play themselves out in the particular dynamics of participation that emerge in each neighborhood. In their efforts to provide general explanations, proponents of these approaches tend to brush aside crucial differences in the lived experience of participation and fail to account for the diverse civic practices that emerge

11. Veneziano 2005; Chávez 2004; and Goldfrank 2007.

12. Goldfrank's (2007) multi-country study of participatory local experiments in the cities of Montevideo, Caracas, and Porto Alegre concluded that differences in the relative strength of opposition parties in each city were key to determining differences in outcomes. The three left-wing governments that pushed the reforms had similar goals—revitalizing citizen participation, making local administration more accountable and transparent, and improving service provision—but only in Porto Alegre, he argues, were all three objectives accomplished. Success in this city resulted from the decision of the city government to make available enough resources to make participation meaningful to residents, and from the fact that opposition parties were not strong enough to block the reforms. In contrast, while service delivery and transparency improved in Montevideo, progress in participation was much slower. In Caracas transparency improved but the other two goals were never achieved. In these two last cases, city officials faced fierce opposition from highly entrenched parties that used their power to tame the more radical aspects of the reforms.

13. Veneziano 2005, 119.

14. The three districts covered in this book show higher-than-average support for the Broad Front. While the leftist coalition captured 63 percent of the votes in Montevideo in the national elections in 2004, it received 76 percent of the votes in district 17 (El Cerro), 74 percent in district 14 (La Teja), and 70 percent in district 13 (Peñarol). See Moreira 2005.

at the community level. Explaining these differences calls for the kind of ethnographic, micro-level studies offered in this book.

Zooming in on each barrio revealed that political parties were less prominent and that local traditions were central in shaping participation and local identities. The case studies illustrate that while the country's political culture trickles down to local settings—framing residents' political outlooks and dispositions—the meaning of national political values and traditions is often transformed as it passes through multiple local filters. In other words, when these national political discourses are translated into local realities, the translation is never "literal" because such national political values are necessarily adapted to the values embedded in the communities' associational cultures.[15]

Indeed, the experiences of participation in El Cerro, La Teja, and Peñarol illustrate how much local cultures shape militants' attitudes and political outlooks. These traditions were as important—and sometimes even more significant—than political party affiliation in defining activists' attitudes toward participation. As I struggled to make sense of the political complexity of each district, I found that knowing the party sympathies of individual councilors was of limited value in predicting their views on local issues. In every community I met supporters of the same national political organization who held quite different views on matters of local participation and community activism. The contrasts between Luis, the veteran community activist in Peñarol who became president of the local junta, and Beatriz, the appointed secretary of the local junta in La Teja, is a good case in point; although both were committed militants of the Communist Party, they found themselves on opposite sides in terms of local politics in their respective districts. Such differences among activists of the same political persuasion were far more common than I had originally anticipated, leading me to wonder about the local relevance of the commonly held thesis about the centrality of political identities in Uruguay.

Explaining differences in activists' attitudes toward participation brings us back to the influence of local associational cultures and the activists' own history of community and political engagement. I found that the formative experiences of local activists mattered a great deal in shaping their orientations toward participatory local government. Whether they had been initiated in neighborhood associations, radical trade unions, housing cooperatives, or the apparatus of a political party made a difference, as we have

15. See Hilhorst's (2003) discussion of development discourses and NGOs in the Philippines.

seen. For instance, training in MIRPA's school of participation in Peñarol or in the radical unions of El Cerro equipped people with sharply different capacities and resources. The opportunities to have these formative experiences were obviously conditioned by the unique history of each community and its traditions of collective mobilization. Activist discourses and dispositions often matched their community traditions, regardless of party affiliation. Not surprisingly, the overwhelming preference for pragmatism found among activists in Peñarol and in the older asentamientos near El Cerro was seldom expressed by militants in La Teja or in El Casco del Cerro.[16]

Nevertheless, the argument about the preponderance of party loyalties appears to be supported by the fact that most participants in local government bodies sympathized with parties of the Broad Front coalition.[17] Yet, in observing the attitudes and behaviors of these participants, I soon discovered that councilors' associations with political parties were less structured than I had originally anticipated. Most of them appeared to enjoy relatively high levels of autonomy, and their decisions to join specific grass-root networks or thematic commissions often reflected individual choices rather than strict party directives. The ties that bound activists to political parties tended to be relatively fluid, and counselors often negotiated their relation with parties as they struggled to balance their political loyalties and their commitment to their communities, a point made vividly by Miguel's dilemma in El Cerro. I also met many councilors with leftist sympathies but without formal associations with specific parties. They simply identified themselves as Frentistas. Often, their primary loyalties, when pressed to make a choice, lay squarely with their barrio. Some councilors rejected parties altogether, embracing instead an antipolitics discourse, as in the case of La Teja, which gave city officials and political parties more than one headache with their refusal to accept the logic of party politics.[18]

The Future of Participatory Decentralization

Throughout my research I frequently heard complaints about the "crisis of participation" to refer to the general drop in participation and the high

16. These findings show that local cultures are more important that commonly assumed in shaping the orientation of individuals toward local politics.

17. It must be noted, however, that district 13 (Peñarol) had much greater success in integrating members of other parties.

18. Leftist parties often courted these silvestres to obtain their support for specific issues, but they seldom succeeded in recruiting them into the party structures or bringing them under any kind of party discipline.

desertion rates among councilors. Participatory decentralization had certainly stalled across the city as it failed to sustain the excitement it generated in the early period. Nevertheless, I also encountered many innovative participatory experiences—including vibrant district-wide networks of merenderos and community-run health clinics, ambitious cultural activities, gender awareness and support programs, and so forth. In some districts, these experiences were anchored in the bodies of local government, while in others this did not happen. In the case of district 17 (El Cerro), for example, these initiatives did not even register in the minds of most councilors, while in district 14 (La Teja) they stretched outside the scope of the neighborhood council but in close collaboration with local government officials. In light of this, I would suggest that the crisis of participation may be more precisely defined as a crisis within the system of participatory decentralization, one more acutely felt in the neighborhood councils—the organs set up precisely to facilitate civil society participation in governing the city.

As a solution to the crisis of participation, many activists and researchers have called for greater powers for neighborhood councils. There is no question in my mind that the model of participatory decentralization has to change to provide more incentives for people to participate. I am keenly aware, however, that there is no quick fix to the current impasse in participation and that the way out of this crisis requires a lot more than vesting councils with decision-making powers. In fact, in light of the experiences within some councils, I would guess that the thought of giving these bodies greater powers must make some local officials and grassroot activists very apprehensive. The tremendous obstacles that community activists faced in their efforts to foster participation also tells me that nurturing sustainable barrio democracy requires a clear political will from city hall to infuse significant resources into the decentralized system. New energies and resources are needed to enable local governments to address the pressing needs of their communities, to support innovative local initiatives, and to develop democratic participatory capacities and values among ordinary residents. Renewing participatory democracy in Montevideo will also require a broad-based, participatory evaluation of the experience to identify the strengths and weaknesses and to point out new directions.

The victory of the Broad Front in the national elections that brought former mayor Tabaré Vázquez to the presidency in 2004 opened a potentially more promising context for the project of participatory decentralization. The Broad Front government extended participatory budgeting to those parts of the country where it came to power, and the incoming mayor of Montevideo, Ricardo Ehrlich, introduced his own version in Montevideo, allowing residents to vote directly on specific projects in their district during elections to neighborhood councils. These are encouraging signs, but it remains to be seen whether the Broad Front has the political resolve to further deepen democracy in Montevideo and in the rest of the country. A starting point in this direction would be to resist the temptation of adopting a "one-model-fits-all" approach and to avoid transplanting the participatory model from Montevideo to other cities in the country without carefully considering differences in local associational cultures and socioeconomic conditions.

REFERENCES

Aguiar, Cesar. 1985. Perspectivas de democratización en el Uruguay actual. In *Apertura y concertación*, ed. D. Sarachaga, J. P. Terra, I. Wosewer, and C. Aguiar, 7–58. Montevideo: Ediciones de la Banda Oriental.

Aguirre, Rosario, Gerónimo de Sierra, and Inés Iens. 1993. Descentralización, participación, y los centros comunales zonales vistos por los vecinos. In *Participación ciudadana y relaciones de gobierno*, 113–42. Montevideo: Trilce.

Avritzer, Leonardo. 2002. *Democracy and the public space in Latin America*. Princeton: Princeton University Press.

———. 2006. Civil society in Latin America in the twenty-first century: Between democratic deepening, social fragmentation, and state crisis. In *Civil society and democracy in Latin America*, ed. Richard Feinberg, Carlos Waisman, and Leon Zamosc, 35–57. New York: Palgrave.

Baiocchi, Gianpaolo. 2002. Synergizing civil society: State–civil society regimes in Porto Alegre, Brazil. *Political Power and Social Theory* 15:3–52.

———, ed. 2003. *Radicals in power: The Workers' Party (PT) and experiments in urban democracy in Brazil*. New York: Zed Books.

———. 2005. *Militants and citizens: The politics of participatory democracy in Porto Alegre*. Stanford: Stanford University Press.

Barrán, José, and Benjamin Nahum. 1982. *Batlle, los estancieros, y el imperio británico*. Montevideo: Ediciones de la Banda Oriental.

Barrios Pintos, Aníbal, and Washington Reyes Abadie. 1994. *El Cerro, Pueblo Victoria, y barrios aledaños*. Vol. 6 of *Los barrios de Montevideo*. Montevideo: Intendencia Municipal de Montevideo.

———. 1994. *Antiguos pueblos y nuevos barrios*. Vol. 8 of *Los barrios de Montevideo*. Montevideo: Intendencia Municipal de Montevideo.

Beisso, Rosario, and José Luis Castagnola. 1987. Identidades sociales y cultura política en Uruguay. *Cuadernos del CLAEH* 44 (4): 9–18.

Bergamino, Ariel, Arles Caruso, and Alvaro Portillo. 2001. *10 años de descentralización: Un debate necesario*. Montevideo: Departamento de Descentralización, Intendencia Municipal de Montevideo.

Bernhard, Guillermo. 1970. *Los monopolios y la industria frigorífica*. Montevideo: Ediciones de la Banda Oriental.

Bertola, Luis, and Gustavo Bittencourt. 2005. Veinte años de democracia sin desarrollo económico. In *Veinte años de democracia: Uruguay, 1985–2005: Miradas múltiples*, ed. Gerardo Caetano, 305–29. Montevideo: Ediciones Santillana.

Caetano, Gerardo. 2005. Marco histórico y cambio político en dos décadas de democracia: De la transición democrática al gobierno de izquierda (1985–2005). In

Veinte años de democracia: Uruguay, 1985–2005: Miradas múltiples, ed. Gerardo Caetano, 15–74. Montevideo: Ediciones Santillana.

Caetano, Gerardo, Jose Rilla, and Romeo Perez. 1987. La partidocracia uruguaya. *Cuadernos del CLAEH* 44 (4): 42–43.

Calvo, Juan Carlos, and Adela Pellegrino. 2005. Veinte años no es nada. *Veinte años de democracia: Uruguay, 1985–2005: Miradas múltiples*, ed. Gerardo Caetano, 251–67. Montevideo: Ediciones Santillana.

Canel, Eduardo. 1992. Democratization and the decline of urban social movements in Uruguay: A political-institutional account. In *New social movements in Latin America: Identity, strategy, and democracy*, ed. Arturo Escobar and Sonia Alvarez, 276–90. Boulder, Colo.: Westview Press.

———. 1993. The rise and fall of urban social movements in Uruguay: Redemocratization and the return of traditional political actors, 1981–1988. Ph.D. diss., York University.

———. 2001a. Dos modelos de descentralización y participación en América Latina: Una discusión conceptual. In *Mercados globales y gobernabilidad local: Retos para la descentralización en América Latina y el Caribe*, ed. Hans-Jürgen Burchardt and Haroldo Dilla, 113–25. Caracas: Nueva Sociedad.

———. 2001b. Municipal decentralization and participatory democracy: Building a new mode of urban politics in Montevideo city? *European Review of Latin American and Caribbean Studies* 71 (October): 25–46.

Canzani, Agustín. 1989. La sociedad montevideana: Problemas y desafíos. *Uruguay Hoy* 5, CIEDUR, Montevideo.

———. 2005. Como llegar a buen puerto: Un análisis desde la opinión pública de la trayectoria electoral del EP-FA. In *Las claves del cambio: Ciclo electoral y nuevo gobierno, 2004/2005*, ed. Daniel Bouquet, 63–86. Montevideo: Ediciones de la Banda Oriental/Instituto de Ciencias Políticas.

Carothers, Thomas. 1999–2000. Think again: Civil society. *Foreign Policy* 17 (Winter): 18–29.

Cassina, Ruben. n.d. El APEX cuenta su historia: 1973–1993, Programa APEX-Cerro. http://www.apexcerro.edu.uy/sitio/institucional/historia/index.htm.

Cavarozzi, Marcelo. 1993. Beyond transitions to democracy in Latin America. *Journal of Latin American Studies* 24 (3): 665–84.

Chávez, Daniel. 2004. Polis and demos: The Left in municipal governance in Montevideo and Porto Alegre. Ph.D. diss., Institute of Social Studies, Netherlands.

Chávez, Daniel, and Susana Carballal. 1997. *La ciudad solidaria: El cooperativismo de vivienda por ayuda mutua*. Montevideo: Facultad de Arquitectura/Editorial Nordan-Comunidad.

Chávez, Daniel, and Benjamin Goldfrank, eds. 2004. *The Left in the city: Participatory local governments in Latin America*. London: Latin America Bureau.

Costa, Roberto. 2003. PTI, cuatro años de camino. Unpublished manuscript, Montevideo.

Couriel, Alberto. 2008. El desarrollo humano y la cultura política. *La República*, December 31.

Dagnino, Evelina. 2003. Citizenship in Latin America: An introduction. *Latin American Perspectives* 30 (2): 211–25.

de Armas, Gustavo. 2005. De la sociedad hiperintegrada al país fragmentado: Crónica del ultimo tramo de un largo recorrido. In *Veinte años de democracia:*

Uruguay, 1985–2005: Miradas múltiples, ed. Gerardo Caetano, 269–303. Montevideo: Ediciones Santillana.

de Enríquez, Xosé. 2004. *Momo encadenado: Crónica del carnaval en los años de la dictadura (1972–1985)*. Montevideo: Ediciones Cruz del Sur.

Edwards, Bob, and Michael Foley. 1998. Civil society and social capital beyond Putnam. *American Behavioral Scientist* 42 (1): 124–39.

Elliot, Jennifer. 2008. Development as improving human welfare and human rights. In *The companion to development studies*, ed. Vandana Desai and Robert Potter, 45–48. London: Hodder Education.

Evans, Peter. 1996a. Development strategies across the public-private divide. *World Development* 24 (6): 1033–37.

———. 1996b. Government action, social capital, and development: Reviewing the evidence on synergy. *World Development* 24 (6): 1119–32.

———. 2002. Introduction: Looking for Agents of Urban Livability in a Globalized Political Economy. In *Livable cities? Urban struggles for livelihood and sustainability*, ed. Peter Evans, 1–30. Berkeley and Los Angeles: University of California Press.

Faral, Luis. 2005. Los clásicos de la salud. In *Veinte años de democracia: Uruguay, 1985–2005: Miradas múltiples*, ed. Gerardo Caetano, 193–220. Montevideo: Ediciones Santillana.

Filgueira, Fernando, Herman Kamil, Fernando Lorenzo, Juan Andrés Moraes, and Andrés Ruiz. 1999. Decentralization and fiscal discipline in subnational governments: The bailout problem in Uruguay. RES Working Paper 3152, Inter-American Development Bank, Montevideo.

Foley, Michael, and Bob Edwards. 1999. Is it time to disinvest in social capital? *Journal of Public Policy* 19 (2): 141–73.

Foweraker, Joe. 2003. New political actors. In *Governing Latin America*, ed. Joe Foweraker, Todd Landman, and Neil Harvey, 147–65. Cambridge: Polity Press.

Frente Amplio. 1989. Documento 6. *Bases programáticas para el gobierno departamental*. Comisión Nacional de Propaganda.

Fung, Archon, and Erik Olin Wright. 2001. Deepening democracy: Innovations in empowered participatory governance. *Politics and Society* 29 (1): 5–41.

———, eds. 2003. *Deepening democracy: Institutional innovations in empowered participatory governance*. New York: Verso.

Gillespie, Charles. 1985. Desentrañando la crisis de la democracia Uruguaya. In *Uruguay y la democracia*, ed. C. Gillespie, L. Goodman, J. Rial, and P. Winn, 1:109–40. Montevideo: Ediciones de la Banda Oriental.

Goldfrank, Benjamin. 2002. The fragile flower of local democracy: A case study of decentralization/participation in Montevideo. *Politics and Society* 30 (1): 51–83.

———. 2003. Making participation work in Porto Alegre. In *Radicals in power: The Worker's Party (PT) and experiments in urban democracy in Brazil*, ed. Gianpaolo Baiocchi, 27–52. New York: Zed Books.

———. 2007. The politics of deepening democracy: Decentralization, party institutionalization, and participation. *Comparative Politics* 39 (2): 147–68.

González, Luis. 1985. Transición y restauración democrática. In *Uruguay y la democracia*, C. Gillespie, L. Goodman, J. Rial, and P. Winn, 3:101–20. Montevideo: Ediciones de la Banda Oriental.

Gwynne, Robert, and Cristobal Kay. 1999. Latin America transformed: Changing paradigms, debates, and alternatives. In *Latin America transformed: Globalization and modernity*, ed. Robert Gwynne and Cristobal Kay, 2–30. New York: Oxford University Press, 1999.

Habitat. 2000. Descentralización en Montevideo: Intendencia municipal de Montevideo (Uruguay). Ciudades para un Futuro más Sostenible, Madrid. http://habitat.aq.upm.es/bpal/onu00/bp096.html.

Harriss, John. 2001. *Depoliticizing development: The World Bank and social capital.* New Delhi: Left Word Books.

Hilhorst, Dorothea. 2003. *The real world of NGOs: Discourses, diversity, and development.* London: Zed Books.

Howell, Jude, and Jenny Pearce. 2001. *Civil society and development: A critical exploration.* Boulder, Colo.: Lynne Rienner Publishers.

Ibarra, Luis. 2001. La competencia en un campo hegemónico: La campaña electoral en Montevideo. In *La geografía de un cambio: Política, gobierno, y gestión municipal en Uruguay*, ed. Maria Elena Laurnaga, 49–62. Montevideo: Ediciones de la Banda Oriental/Instituto de Ciencia Política.

IMM (Intendencia Municipal de Montevideo). 1985a. Proyecto promoción social y asistencia comunitaria (promotores sociales). Documentos de Trabajo, Unidad Asesora de Proyectos Especiales, Montevideo.

———. 1985b. Informe anual de actividades de la UAPE. Documentos de Trabajo, Unidad Asesora de Proyectos Especiales, Montevideo.

———. 1998a. Aquí va el dinero de los vecinos: Presupuesto, 1998. Mimeo.

———. 1998b. *Montevideo, capital.* Montevideo: IMM.

———. 2002. *Montevideo en Cifras, 2000.* Montevideo: IMM.

———. 2004a. Devolución de compromisos de gestión por la comisión especial de atención al programa de integración a asentamientos irregulares. Unidad de Participación y Coordinación, Departamento de Descentralización. Mimeo.

———. 2004b. Elección de concejales vecinales año 2004: Datos básicos. Unidad de Participación y Coordinación, Departamento de Descentralización. Mimeo.

———. 2004c. Plan estratégico de desarrollo zonal (PLAEDES), districts 13, 14, 17. Mimeo.

Instituto Nacional de Estadística. 2004. *Censo 2004, fase 1.* Montevideo: Departamento de Montevideo, Síntesis de Resultados.

Kaztman, Ruben, Soledad Avila, Ximena Baraibar, and Fernando Errandonea. 2004. Modalidades de participación popular urbana en los 90: Los asentamientos irregulares en el area metropolitana de Montevideo. Working Paper Series, Center for the Study of Urbanization and Internal Migration in Developing Countries, University of Texas, Austin.

Kaztman, Ruben, and Alejandro Retamoso. 2005. Spatial segregation, employment, and poverty in Montevideo. *CEPAL Review* 85:125–41.

Lindahl, Göran. 1962. *Uruguay's new path: A study in politics during the first colegiado, 1919–33.* Stockholm: Library and Institute of Ibero-American Studies.

Listre, Julio. 1999. Descentralización participativa: Aprendiendo desde los conflictos. In *Democracia, ciudadanía, poder: Desde el proceso de descentralización y participación popular*, ed. Jose Luis Rebellato and Pilar Ubilla, 85–97. Montevideo: Editorial Nordan-Comunidad.

Litvack, Jennie, Junaid Ahmad, and Richard Bird. 1998. *Rethinking decentralization in developing countries.* Washington, D.C.: World Bank.

Lustemberg, Hugo. 1974. *Uruguay: Imperialismo y estrategia de liberación: Las enseñanzas de la huelga general.* Buenos Aires: Achaval Solo.

Mainwaring, Scott. 1988. Political parties and democratization in Brazil and the Southern Cone. *Comparative Political Studies* 20 (2): 91–120.

Martorelli, Horacio. 1978. *Urbanización y desruralización en el Uruguay.* Montevideo: Fondo de Cultura Universitaria/Centro Latinoamericano de Económica Humana.

———. 1986. Políticas sociales, participación ciudadana, y acción municipal. Documento de Trabajo 34, CIEDUR, Montevideo.

Masdeu, Willan. 2003. *Descentralización participativa y presupuesto municipal: El proceso de definición de los compromisos de gestión en Montevideo.* Mimeo. Montevideo: Intendencia Municipal de Montevideo.

Mercer Human Resource Consulting. 2005. Quality of life survey. http://www.city mayors.com/environment/eiu_bestcities.html.

Moreira, Constanza. 1993. Cohabitación y lógica de gobierno: Un análisis de la experiencia municipal de Montevideo (1990–1992) de cara a sus relaciones con el gobierno nacional. In *Participación ciudadana y relaciones de gobierno,* 161–91. Montevideo: Trilce.

———. 2005. El voto moderno y el voto clasista revisado: Explicando el desempeño electoral de la izquierda en las elecciones de 2004 en Uruguay. In *Las claves del cambio: Ciclo electoral y nuevo gobierno, 2004/2005,* ed. Daniel Bouquet, 27–42. Montevideo: Ediciones de la Banda Oriental/Instituto de Ciencia Política.

Nylen, William. 2003. *Participatory democracy versus elitist democracy: Lessons from Brazil.* New York: Palgrave Macmillan.

O'Rourke, Dara. 2002. Community-driven regulation: Toward an improved model of environmental regulation in Vietnam. In *Livable cities? Urban struggles for livelihood and sustainability,* ed. Peter Evans, 95–131. Berkeley and Los Angeles: University of California Press.

Oxhorn, Philip. 2006. Conceptualizing civil society from the bottom up: A political economy perspective. In *Civil society and democracy in Latin America,* ed. Richard Feinberg, Carlos Waisman, and Leon Zamosc, 59–86. New York: Palgrave.

Pearce, Jenny. 1997. Between co-option and irrelevance? Latin American NGOs in the 1990s. In *Too close for comfort? NGOs, states, and donors,* ed. David Hulme and Michael Edwards, 257–74. London: Macmillan.

Pereira, Javier. 2003. Spatial dimensions of social policies in Santiago and Montevideo. Summer Field Research Report, Department of Sociology, University of Texas, Austin.

Perelli, Cristina, and Juan Rial. 1983. El discreto encanto de la social democracia en el Uruguay. Working Paper 86, CIESU, Montevideo.

Pi Hugarte, Renzo, and Daniel Vidart. 1969. *El legado de los imigrantes.* Vol. 1. Montevideo: Nuestra Tierra.

Portes, Alejandro, and Patricia Landolt. 1996. The downside of social capital. *American Prospect* 26:18–21.

Portillo, Alvaro. 1996. *La ciudad de la gente.* Montevideo: Facultad de Arquitectura/ Nordan-Comunidad.

Putnam, Robert D. 1995. Bowling alone: America's declining social capital. *Journal of Democracy* 6 (1): 65–78.

Rama, Carlos. 1972. *Historia social del pueblo uruguayo*. Montevideo: Editorial del Sur.

Rama, Germán W. 1987. *La democracia en Uruguay: Una perspectiva de interpretación*. Montevideo: Grupo Editor Latinoamericano.

Rebellato, Jose Luis, and Pilar Ubilla. 1999. Un recorrido por el proceso. In *Democracia, ciudadanía, poder: Desde el proceso de descentralización y participación popular*, ed. Rebellato and Ubilla, 123–62. Montevideo: Editorial Nordan-Comunidad.

Regent, Susana. 2004. Recopilación histórica de orígenes y desarrollo del barrio La Teja/Pueblo Victoria. *Periódico El Tejano*, September.

Rial, Juan. 1989. Continuidad y cambio en las organizaciones partidarias en el Uruguay: 1973–1984. In *Muerte y resurrección: Los partidos políticos en el autoritarismo y las transiciones del Cono Sur*, ed. Marcelo Cavarozzi and Manuel Antonio Garretón, 243–96. Santiago: FLACSO.

Rodríguez, Héctor. 1965. *Nuestros sindicatos (1865–1965)*. Montevideo: Ediciones Uruguay.

Rubino, Silvana. 1991. Los habitantes de Montevideo: Visión de la intendencia en una coyuntura de cambio. In *Gobierno y política en Montevideo*, ed. Carina Perelli, Fernando Filgueira, and Silvana Rubino, 69–108. Montevideo: PEITHO.

Santos, Boaventura de Sousa. 1998. Participatory budgeting in Porto Alegre: Toward a redistributive democracy. *Politics and Society* 26 (4).

Sen, Amartya. 1999. *Development as freedom*. Oxford: Oxford University Press.

Silva, Marcelo Kunrath. 2003. Participation by design: The experiences of Alvorada and Gravatai, Rio Grande do Sul, Brazil. In *Radicals in power: The Worker's Party (PT) and experiments in urban democracy in Brazil*, ed. Gianpaolo Baiocchi, 113–30. New York: Zed Books.

Solari, Aldo, and Ronaldo Franco. 1983. *Las empresas públicas en Uruguay: Ideología y política*. Montevideo: Fundación de Cultura Universitaria.

Tarrow, Sidney. 1996. Making social science work across time and space: A critical reflection on Putnam's *Making Democracy Work*. *American Political Science Review* 90 (2): 389–97.

Thompson, E. P. 1968. *The making of the English working class*. London: Penguin Books.

Universidad de la República. 2002. Proyecto de investigación sobre la población que habita en las zonas en situación crítica sanitaria de Casabó y Cerro Oeste. Mimeo. Programa APEX-Cerro.

Valia, Luís. 1998. Al oeste: El Cerro . . . *Vientos del sur*. Montevideo: Intendencia Municipal de Montevideo, Departamento de Cultura.

Van Roy, Alison. 1998. Civil society as idea: An analytical hatstand? In *Civil society and the aid industry: The politics and promise*, ed. Van Roy, 6–30. London: Earthscan.

Veiga, Danilo. 1989. Segregación socioeconómica y crisis urbana en Montevideo. In *Las ciudades en conflicto: Una perspectiva latinoamericana*, ed. Mario Lombardi and Danilo Veiga. Montevideo: Ediciones de la Banda Oriental/CIESU.

Veiga, Danilo, and Ana Laura Rivoir. 2005. *Sociedad y territorio: Montevideo y el área metropolitana*. Montevideo: Departamento de Sociología, Universidad de la República.

Vellinga, Menno. 1998. The changing role of the state in Latin America. In *The changing role of the state in Latin America*, ed. Menno Vellinga, 1–26. Boulder, Colo.: Westview Press.

Veneziano, Alicia. 2005. *Reflexiones sobre una reforma orientada al ciudadano: La descentralización participativa de Montevideo*. Madrid: Instituto Nacional de Administración Publica.

Vidart, Daniel, and Renzo Pi Hugarte. 1969. *El legado de los imigrantes*. Vol. 2. Montevideo: Nuestra Tierra.

Wampler, Brian. 2007. *Participatory budgeting in Brazil: Contestation, cooperation, and accountability*. University Park: Penn State Press.

Winn, Peter, and Lilia Ferro-Clerico. 1997. Can a leftist government make a difference? The Frente Amplio administration of Montevideo, 1990–1994. In *The new politics of inequality in Latin America*, ed. Douglas Chalmers, 447–68. Oxford: Oxford University Press.

Woolcock, Michael, and Deepa Narayan. 2000. Social capital: Implications for development theory, research, and policy. *World Bank Research Observer* 15 (2): 225–49.

Yashar, Deborah. 2005. *Contesting citizenship in Latin America: The rise of indigenous movements and the postliberal challenge*. Cambridge: Cambridge University Press.

Zibechi, Raúl. n.d. Sobre el movimiento obrero y popular. http://www.ecocomunidad.org.uy/ecocom/zibechi.htm.

INDEX

Page numbers in *italics* refer to illustrations.

www.ingramcontent.com/pod-product-compliance
Lightning Source LLC
Chambersburg PA
CBHW021858020426
42334CB00013B/382